CYBERSEDUCTION

CYBERSEDUCTION

REALITY IN THE
AGE OF
PSYCHOTECHNOLOGY

DR. JERI FINK

Prometheus Books

59 John Glenn Drive
Amherst, New York 14228-2197

Published 1999 by Prometheus Books

Inquiries should be addressed to
Prometheus Books, 59 John Glenn Drive, Amherst, New York 14228–2197.
VOICE: 716–691–0133, ext. 207
FAX: 716–564–2711
WWW.PROMETHEUSBOOKS.COM

03 02 01 00 99   5 4 3 2 1

Library of Congress Cataloging-in-Publication Data

Fink, Jeri.
    Cyberseduction : reality in the age of psychotechnology / Jeri Fink.
        p.   cm.
    Includes bibliographical references and index.
    ISBN 1–57392–743–0 (hardcover : alk. paper)
        1. Computers—Psychological aspects. 2. Human-computer interaction.
3. Virtual reality. I. Title.
QA76.9.P75F53   1999
004'.01'9—dc21   99–046628
                                                                                     CIP

Printed in the United States of America on acid-free paper

To Ricky,
Thank you for sharing my dreams. What a trip!

CONTENTS

Acknowledgments   9

PART I: FROM CAVES TO CYBERSPACE

Cyberseduction   15
The Body Snatchers   21
Lines in the Sand   33
Genes or Genesis?   39
Monkey Sees, Monkey Does   47
Stone Age Computers   55
From Caves to Cyberspace   77
Bibliography for Part I   89

PART II: TO BE OR NOT TO BE

Your Very Own Self   95

Sticks and Stones	103
The Cyborg Metaphor	113
Media Mayhem	125
Jurassic Jabs	137
Virtual Kin	151
Gender Wars	159
To Be or Not to Be	171
Bibliography for Part II	179

PART III: BACK TO THE FUTURE

Upgrading Stone Age Computers	185
Where in the World Is Cyberspace?	189
"Relatives" in the Age of Psychotechnology	195
Knock, Knock. Who's There?	203
Digital Neighboring	215
Elites, Wannabes, and Guerrillas	229
Virtual Law and Disorder	239
Reach Out and Touch Someone	255
Stranger Than Fiction: A Collection of True Stories from Cyberspace	267
Final Thoughts: Coming Home— An Author's Reconstruction of Self	293
Bibliography for Part III	299
Index	303

ACKNOWLEDGMENTS

*P*SYCHOTECHNOLOGY WAS BORN from two decades of living with computers, virtual realities, and the Internet. Equally as important, it was nurtured through the willing ears and imagination of some very special people. These are minds that took those first tentative steps into a new philosophy, considering some of the exciting and chilling possibilities of a future infused with virtual reality simulations. They encouraged me, they disagreed with me, they fantasized with me, and most of all, they gave me the incentive to pursue ideas that most of us don't often consider.

I would first like to thank the foresight and courage of Steven L. Mitchell and the people at Prometheus who made *Cyberseduction* a real book—not just a virtual thought.

I could not have survived the work without the diligent attention of Bunny (Roberta Chapman) who kept my life organized so my imagination could run wild.

My Internet "buddies" have, and will continue to be, very much a part of my electronic life. Thank you for joining me in cyberspace—Sheila Peck, Ron Rubin, Storm King, Rob Bischoff, and all the voices that fill my screen with ideas, laughter, insight, and camaraderie.

A special thanks goes to the entire staff of the United States Steel Carnegie Pension Fund who answered questions, supplied trivia, and with humor and enthusiasm gave me ongoing insights into popular culture.

I also want to thank my tireless friends who were always there when I needed them:

Ellen Davidoff, for happily listening to me over sushi and green tea.

Shelley Frank, for helping me climb to the top of the mountain.

Mary Ann Hannon, for sharing "Dairy Barn," Nordstrom's, and a very special friendship.

Donna Paltrowitz, for sharing our crazy ideas and believing that there was no deadline I couldn't meet.

Barbara Saks, for being my "sister."

…and Ken, Burt, Pat, Stu, and Carl who put up with their wives' unpredictable friend.

This story would not be complete without three people whose friendship, respect, and company I love. Jerry (a.k.a. "Rock") and Jill Lash have gone the distance with my family and me, always ready to support, encourage, and party. Craig Oldfather has leaped into the fantasy of my work as only an artist, philosopher, and cowboy could.

I want to thank my ever-increasing family, who have become a personal support group, smiling at my oddities, putting up with my distractions, and complimenting me on my actual as well as virtual productions. The Finks, Beckers, Michelsons, Ryans, and Woolleys are always in my heart as I journey through the wilds of cyberspace. Of particular note are Edna and Harvey Fink, a.k.a. Grandma and Grandpa, who read my books, chuckle at my words, and show me over and over again that age has nothing to do with youth; "Auntie" Dora Eisenstein who, with humor, charm, and love has always encouraged me to pursue my dreams; my wonderful, funny, newsworthy and always entertaining e-mail companion, Barbara Woolley; and my surrogate brother Kevin, his wife, Savida, and their two delightful kids, Samantha and Jason. When I look into Kevin's eyes I feel as if I'm peering into a mirror.

My work would not be complete without acknowledging the role of "Unkka," Herbert Michelson, who has been a father, spiritual guide, and intellectual mentor to me. His words, his presence, his ideas, and his respect mean more to me than perhaps he'll ever realize.

As I have acknowledged in the past, and will continue to acknowledge in all my work, the ongoing presence of those very special people who have passed on and still remain, in spirit, with me: my mother, Ruth Roth; my sister, Judy Becker; and my aunt and buddy, Persis Burlingame.

Last, I want to thank the "men in my life": David, my firstborn, who challenges me both spiritually and intellectually, venturing along with his mom into the brave new world of cyberspace; Russell, my "baby," who understands my work as only a fellow artist can, laughing, analyzing, and accepting nothing but the best; and Ricky, my husband, lover, best friend, and very patient editor, who remembers me when I was seventeen and dreaming about writing books. Once again, we did it!

If the work of the city is the remaking or translating of man into a more suitable form than his nomadic ancestors achieved, then might not our current translation of our entire lives into the spiritual form of information seem to make of the entire globe, and of the human family, a single consciousness?

—Marshall McLuhan, *Understanding Media*, 1964

PART I
FROM CAVES
TO CYBERSPACE

CYBERSEDUCTION

Slowly the fiery orange sun settles in behind the mountains. The world is shrouded in darkness. A frail crescent moon emerges in the starless night. It hangs precariously low in the sky as if, at any given moment, it can be plucked from their view. They gather silently around the glowing embers of the fire, sitting on cool, flat rocks placed strategically in a circle. Their voices are muffled as they begin a deep, onerous chant. Help us. Protect us. Save us. The shaman rises above the fire. All eyes are on him. His glistening body shudders deeply. He raises his arms. He will find a way.

*A*RE THEY CAVEMEN? Cultists? Or game players separated by thousands of miles, peering into their computer screens? They all have one thing in common—they are occupying a virtual reality.

From caves to cyberspace, virtual reality has been an integral part of human life. What is this strange, illusive place that we all recognize and have such difficulty defining? Why is there cyberseduction? In order to understand the nature of a virtual reality we need to first identify *reality*.

Scientists, artists, philosophers, and ordinary people have been trying to figure that out since the dawn of human consciousness. Some say it's everything that is physical and concrete. Others argue that it is the sum total of an individual's perceptions. Many believe that it is what the group agrees on, a *consensus* reality. But then strange questions are raised. Does the tree that falls in the forest make any sounds when there is no one to hear? How many angels can dance on the head of a pin? Can blind people see? What is the difference between brain and mind?

Without neatly packaged answers, we have to rely on the basics. For example, one of the most significant separations between humans and animals is consciousness and the consequent awareness of existence. People know that they are alive. Thinking and feeling are uniquely singular experiences. It is as if there were an entity *within* that accomplishes these feats. This entity is very different from walking, breathing, or eating. Knowing that others have similar inner entities, most people generally assume that these internal processes are made up of something other than the physical body. One might even say that our inner selves exist in essence but not in actual or concrete form, which is, of course, the definition of virtuality.

The psychic division between the virtual internal and the actual physical processes underlies much of philosophy and religion. It was, and continues to be, the struggle to understand the relationship between mind and body.

Early philosophers identified the human condition as falling into two categories: mind and body. The spiritual, or the soul, represented mind, or what we might call *virtuality*. The material, or the physical, represented body or *actuality*. This was consistent with human experience. You can touch body, but not mind. You can eat and digest chocolate, but not pleasure. While cyberspace was not available to the Greek philosophers, they still understood the virtual nature of inner processes. To enter a virtual reality they used different technologies. Modern philosophers suggest that there is no real differentiation between mind and body. The brain is the physical location of the mind; the mind is what the brain does.

In this context, virtual reality is not a revolution but an evolution, a space humans have occupied since the first awareness of a qualitative difference between mind and body. One of the goals of technology throughout history was to enhance virtual reality by making it increasingly accessible. To develop the body, one had to nurture the mind. Myths were as crucial as guns; metaphors as influential as facts. The social, intellectual, and psychological development of humans incorporates both virtual and actual histories. History is marked by great technological discoveries that enhance virtual realities: petroglyph stories painted on rocks; the development of writing and the subsequent virtual experience of fiction, poetry, and drama; musical instruments that create sounds designed to carry listeners to "another place"—the list is endless.

Consider a very ordinary "virtual" experience: the telephone. The telephone is a basic communications tool that plunges speakers into virtual conversation. When involved in conversation, speakers "forget" that it is plastic, wires, and electronic relays that connect them. We behave as if the "other" were actually there. This is particularly apparent in the now common occurrence of people who are walking on a street, driving a car, or sitting in a restaurant using a cellular telephone. They often appear totally removed from their surroundings, immersed in the virtual voice broadcast through the telephone. This is even more apparent in the virtual realities created by the media. Does your heart race as a celluloid serial killer stalks his human prey in a horror movie? Do you cry when the miniseries heroine "dies"? Are you angry when your favorite cop leaves *NYPD Blue*?

No place, however, is more virtual than cyberspace. It is here, in this disembodied environment, that the psychological structures designed to mediate virtuality begin to flourish. We do not have to struggle with conflicts in reality. We do not have to depend on fantasies interrupted by commercials. We are not passive observers. In cyberspace, we are willingly and actively seduced by a virtual reality.

Clearly, a new psychology is emerging from our increasing involvement in virtual, electronic environments. New behavior is evolving from social concepts possible only in a virtual reality. The illusion of electronic anonymity and the absence of social constraints free people to readily experiment with different "life" styles. Old relationships are redefined: love means shared fantasies and virtual caresses; friendship is an exchange of words on a screen; collaborators are links on a home page or in a chat room. Simply put, when reality is replaced by virtuality in cyberspace, anything can happen. Cyberseduction grabs us, tantalizes us, and irretrievably snares us.

Before we can fully understand our latest postmodern immersion into virtuality, we need to explore where it has come from. We need to understand the nature of virtuality and the role it has played in our past and our present to empower our future. What is happening? Why? How does this affect the way we see ourselves? Where are we going with it?

Evolutionary psychology provides a framework for understanding human thought, emotions, and behavior. It applies the principles in evolutionary biology to study the human psychological structures that fuel adaptation. These structures are so basic that we often overlook them when considering normal psychosocial behavior. But they are extremely powerful—functioning as catalysts in much of everyday life.

Most popular psychological theories are based on the belief that each individual is born with a set of potential abilities such as being able to learn, to rationalize, or to participate in a social environment. Psychoanalysts often argue that each individual has basic, instinctual drives that are mediated by an environmentally sensitive ego. They assume that content comes from the environment—through things such as people, places, and experiences. Another way to understand that frame is to compare it to a computer. A computer has the potential to complete many tasks, but it can't do anything unless there is input from the environment in the form of software that utilizes the potential. Evolutionary psychology takes these ideas one step further. It maintains that the mind is not that discrete from the body. Instead, the mind is designed to utilize *neural* networks that solve problems in adaptation to assure survival of the species. Using a computational frame, the mind consists of "chips" or modules that preprogram our hardware to work with the software of experience. Simply put, our mind is constructed in a way that prepares us to adapt to environments that span time, space, and geography.

What does this have to do with virtual reality? Charles Darwin repeatedly illustrated how changing conditions can produce significant effects on animals. For example, animals that live in cold climates develop thicker, shaggier fur than those in more temperate zones. Bats who live in dark environments have a highly developed "echolocation" system that enables them to pick up tiny insect footsteps, minute changes in air currents from vibrating insect wings, or the ripple on the surface of the pond from a minnow's fin.

Human adaptation, in comparison to the rest of the animal kingdom, forces adaptation into a more complex, circuitous process. People utilize synthetic as well as natural change that involves both mind and body. Heinz Hartmann, author of the seminal book *Ego Psychology and the Problem of Adaptation*, clearly stated that "human action adapts the environment to human functions, and then the human being adapts (secondarily) to the environment which he has helped to create" (pp. 26–27).

How does that play out in daily life? Individual and external environments, *as well as* species-wide origin and development, influence the process of human adaptation. Humans have to adapt not only to the conditions and communities they have helped create, but also to those that have been designed by people who come before and during their lifetimes. In other words, people create, adapt, and eventually create-to-adapt in both reality and virtual reality. This book is about the *mind* that guides us through the adaptation and evolution of human virtual reality. Why is it so seductive? How has it developed? Where is it taking us?

Reality in the age of psychotechnology is not a beginning or an end, but a factor that is part of ongoing human history. Psychotechnology links the old and the new and is a force that will be pervasive in the third millennium. Psychotechnology represents a new approach to psychology, where patterns of human interaction emerge from virtual realities. Human experiences in self, community, and identity take on new meaning in virtual environments. Our roles shift dramatically. What happens in cyberspace looks, feels, and sounds very different from what happens in the streets in front of our homes.

Why do we mix psychology and technology? History has shown that dramatic developments in technology have altered human adaptation. Just as the onset of the ice age changed how life behaved on the planet, so technology has changed the way we behave in our homes, cultures, and societies. No one can argue the impact of human technology on human behavior. Consider how the discovery of fire or the first "tool" affected human life, or later technological innovations such as inventing writing in 3000 B.C.E., using blocks of stone to construct buildings, industrialization in the eighteenth century, and the automobile. What would life be like without that technology? Where would we be without today's computers? Psychology and technology have become natural partners, plunging us into a future where their complicity will have an even greater effect on how we perceive ourselves and our world. Reality in the age of psycho-technology is a merger of yesterday, today, and tomorrow.

Let's surf those realities in the mind where disembodied space, metaphor, fantasy, and simulation live—where cyberseduction courts your imagination.

THE BODY
SNATCHERS

A MERICA WAS IN an uproar. It was March 1997, and the First Amendment was being challenged in cyberspace. Some of the greatest minds in the country had gathered to hear arguments on the Communications Decency Act. The United States Supreme Court had to decide whether the Internet could be censored. It was not an easy job. How does one regulate a medium that gleefully ignores all national, ethnic, and cultural boundaries? If online indecency is banned in New York, it invariably shows up in New Mexico. Try outlawing it in the United States and the pornographers simply set up shop in Thailand. Some futurists were suggesting that cyberspace could be the beginning of the end for the nation-state as a political entity. If one could readily swing beyond the legal, social, and cultural definitions of a centralized government, then maybe the world would end up as a single global village.

The Supreme Court did not find any simple solutions. It was apparent that cyberspace had yet to be defined. The justices searched for a metaphor, a way to conceptualize the definition of a technologically created virtual space. Is the Internet the same as broadcast media—radio or television? If so, the government has a legal right to ban obscenity. But there are very troubling differences. No one talks *with* a television. Online, people converse in chat rooms, newsgroups, and Web forums. In that context, cyberspace is more like a telephone, an interactive medium. Telephone communications are clearly protected—the government can't ban free speech. Yet the Internet is more than telephones, radios, and televisions—there are groups, organizations, and sprawling virtual communities. The metaphor could lie in the concept of public space—the Internet as a street corner, park, or town—where freedom of speech is unquestionably protected by the Constitution. Ultimately, the Court concluded that the Internet is unique, a completely new means of global communication. In that context, it's protected by the First Amendment.

The Supreme Court was on the right track. The Internet *is* a unique medium. But it's not new. As the justices discovered, the metaphor is far more complex than a simple analogy. Technology has brought us to a place that humans have visited since the dawn of consciousness. Traditional parameters of time, space, and location have no meaning online. With the exception of sight and sound, physical senses tell us nothing about this electronic environment. Is it a dream, a fantasy, or a very vivid imagination? Humankind has been there before, using many different technologies. It's all of the above and none of the above—a very strange and fanciful space called virtual reality.

WHAT IS A VIRTUAL REALITY?

Virtual is generally defined as something that exists in the mind without actual physical fact, form, or features. Virtual images are the product of human creativity, ingenuity, and imagination. They emerge from conscious or unconscious processes that work to construct mental images. The process is similar to perception, which results from the utilization of sensory input in an actual or physical environment. The difference is that virtual realities occur in inner mental space, reflecting *internal* environments.

Virtual reality has a far narrower focus. It is used to describe the technology that enables users to move around in computer-simulated environments. Virtual-reality worlds have no form or substance, existing only on a computer screen or through special interface devices that continuously feed visual and aural information to sustain the illusion of an actual reality.

Neither says anything about the process, experience, or effects of being in a virtual place. By definition, virtual space is intangible, measured primarily by psychological constructs. Time, distance, and place are determined by content, not physics. It is a space where people are *disembodied*—where mental rather than physical presence dominates. The laws of actual reality apply only when the virtual visitor chooses to use them—they are flexible, adaptive, and contextual.

Consequently, an accurate definition of a virtual reality must go beyond technological simulation. It's similar to looking at two mirrors reflecting one another—you see an endless series of like images disappearing into infinite space. Logic tells you that it's a flat, rigid piece of glass. It doesn't *look* flat. It doesn't *feel* flat. But if you touch it you'll find a cool, hard surface without depth, color, or philosophy. Which is more real? The glass or the image?

Artists, philosophers, and scientists have all struggled with these concepts. In 1872 Lewis Carroll suggested a particularly compelling scenario. When Alice fell through the looking glass she entered a land where "it takes all the running *you* can do, to keep in the same place. If you want to get somewhere else, you must run at least twice as fast as that!" (p. 193). It was a checkerboard world peopled by characters that mingled reality and fantasy. A cranky Humpty Dumpty, sparring Tweedledee and Tweedledum, and a field of gossiping flowers spoke to both children and adults. Was it fairy tale or parody? Truth or heresy? When readers ventured through Alice's looking glass into virtual space, it didn't quite matter. It was simply a good story. Only the vivid colors and sounds of Disney animation could make it better.

Carroll's message suggests that actual reality and virtuality are essentially relative, not opposing, terms. Like the ends of a seesaw, reality and virtuality balance one another out in the human experience.

How can that be possible? Much of Western science has taught us that there is a Cartesian distinction between mind and body. Nothing is true until you can establish proof. *Cogito, ergo sum:* I think, therefore I am. Modern research methodology is usually based on the immutable scientific method where "knowledge" is discerned from empirical observation and measurement. We have been raised to grasp for proof—numbers and infallible logic that treat reality as a phenomenon with distinct, concrete, and ubiquitous parameters. At the same time we hunger for soul, celebrating the fanciful, spiritual, and dreamlike spaces that give our "reality" pleasure, meaning, and substance. Our imaginations tell us there is more to the human experience than physical parameters. Our language often provides physical metaphors for virtual concepts: *he's got heart; it's all in her head; he's my lifeblood;* and *she's got guts;* yet we insist on defining ourselves as living primarily in actual reality.

It's a conundrum. As Lewis Carroll wrote in *Through the Looking-Glass and What Alice Found There,*

> "How *can* you go on talking so quietly, head downwards?" Alice asked, as she dragged him out by the feet, and laid him in a heap on the bank.
>
> The Knight looked surprised at the question. "What does it matter where my body happens to be?" he said. "My mind goes on working all the same. In fact, the more head downwards I am, the more I keep inventing new things." (Carroll, p. 266)

How do we account for a virtual reality as active as actual reality? The most compelling resolution is to expand our concept of virtuality, examining it as an integral part of human cognitive abilities. As such, virtual phenomena grow, adapt, and change alongside history, culture, and human development. The definitions shift to more closely reflect human experience. In this broadened context, a virtual reality encompasses the entire mental environment where virtual events take place. Virtual visions, emotions, metaphors, symbols, and images align themselves in both conscious and unconscious thought. They are loosely arranged in several primary and overlapping styles: stories, archetypes, and simulations. These styles are not static; they are constantly changing and evolving so that what we experience today can be "organized" quite differently tomorrow. In addition, virtual-reality styles are a function of psychological evolution. Our virtual realities adapt to our mental environment. Twenty-second-century virtual realities will *look* very different from those in the twenty-first century. In concept, however, they have remained the same from caves to cyberspace. Let's look at the primary virtual-reality styles used by humans.

VIRTUAL-REALITY STORIES

We all have and create our own spontaneous virtual-reality stories. These vary widely: a vivid sexual fantasy; a daydream; a mental scheme to clamber up the corporate ladder—the list is as diverse as the human imagination. Utilizing our own individual powers of creativity, fantasy, and visualization, we traverse different mental planes, experimenting, acting out, and designing inner pleasures. We do it both consciously and unconsciously. The stuff of our dreams is unconscious images that symbolize struggles, pleasures, fears, and other intense emotions that are expressed and acted out in the safety of our own personal virtual reality. The stuff of our daydreams, conscious fantasies and imagery, carries us through each of our days, replete with intensity and ennui, the mediocre and the extraordinary.

Many seek to enhance virtual spaces through the infinite variety of tools available, such as meditation, creative imagery, spiritual visualization, hypnotic trance, mysticism—the possibilities are constantly evolving. Others try quick means that are potentially damaging to the body—drugs, alcohol, and naturally occurring hallucinogens. However, the most readily available means to enhance our virtual reality stories *outside* of our own repertoire are through the "storytellers" that take us there via their own chosen medium.

Virtual-reality storytellers are perhaps the most beloved, envied, and maligned people in human society. These are the artists, writers, and technicians who forgo much actual reality in order create and produce virtual realities. They draw pictures and sounds that are so vivid we become partners in their highly seductive mental imagery. As with self-created virtual realities, their tools are limited only by imagination and, in certain spaces, technology. The variety of storytellers is as colorful as their productions:

- Warriors who tell stories of their exploits.
- Actors on a stage.
- Writers relating tales of pleasure, horror, and amusement.

- Artists capturing visual dramas.
- Musicians creating sound paintings.
- Clerics drawing spiritual pictures.
- Filmmakers introducing us to vivid locales and intriguing people.
- Computers thrusting us into interactive simulated environments.

The common element is that through a storyteller's invention we enter a virtual reality where we become both participant and observer. Thus a young man shares the story of his sexual exploit, and before long both buddies are shuddering with pleasure. An eighteenth-century writer describes poverty-stricken London in his novel, and we are suddenly transported to a Dickensian horror. An actress dramatizes her "pain" on stage, and almost four hundred years later we empathize with Shakespeare's Lady Macbeth. A wealthy, popular film star metamorphoses into *The Terminator*, and we feel his awesome powers. A computer programmer sits at his console and creates a world where we plunge into *Doom*, blowing away the enemy with firepower we would be terrified to touch in actual reality.

The cyberseduction of virtual-reality stories is irresistible.

VIRTUAL-REALITY ARCHETYPES

Carl Gustav Jung maintained that we each inherit a "preconscious" psychological program that enables us to react as humans. Each person is born with a communal, species-wide memory called the *collective unconscious*. It's essentially an armory of compositions based on several archetypes or patterns. The archetypes exist at the unconscious level and are actualized in consciousness as mental images. While there are only a few basic archetypes, an infinite number of images can be traced back to these species-wide patterns. Jung maintained that we are born with archetypes that structure our imagination and link mental or virtual spaces closely to our bodies. He believed that the same universal themes and symbols appear in all cultures. They give us a blueprint to respond to critical aspects in the real world—a means to integrate our actual realities. Jung argued that even the very fate of "great nations" is essentially the sum of all the psychic changes in individuals. Jung's ideas are consistent with the theories in evolutionary psychology, as discussed later in Part I.

Some of the archetypes identified by Jung include the shadow, the anima or animus, the child, and the self. Understanding Jungian theory explains virtual realities that emerge from collective experience rather than individual creations. To illustrate, think about one of the most basic archetypes, the shadow. The shadow is both a part of who we are and an archetype for negotiating the world. It represents the dark side—the primitive animal and sexual instincts that Freud earlier identified as the psychic content of the id. We like to deny that part of ourselves. Consequently, we tend to project the dark side onto others—we interpret them as enemies, evil spirits, demons, or exotic, dark personas. In our culture the shadow is constructed as a serial murderer, evil despot, the beast in a warrior's tale, the satanic worshippers, and the heinous neighbor who wants to cut down your prized old sycamore.

In like manner, virtual-reality archetypes follow mental patterns consistent with cultural imagery. They are experiences gleaned from collective, preprogrammed information rather than individual creations. Their images are both familiar and compelling:

- Dr. Jekyll and Mr. Hyde.
- The political adversary as archenemy.
- Angels watching over you.
- The good mother.
- Touching the heart of God.
- The indomitable hero.

These virtual realities are designed by the predetermined archetypes: evil versus good; heavenly protection; heroism. They offer ample material to storytellers, particularly those seeking to initiate collective responses. Many books, movies, computer games, and environments are filled with symbols from mythological archetypes. Religion emerges from the archetypal divine—virtual beings that are identified as "gods." The archetypes in science fiction are particularly intriguing. Captain James T. Kirk of *Star Trek* is a classic archetypal hero. The Borg are classic archetypal shadows—forces of evil. George Lucas, the director of *Star Wars*, is a close personal friend of Joseph Campbell, a leading authority on mythology. Together they filled *Star Wars* with archetypal symbols and Jungian themes such as

Darth Vader (the shadow), Darth Maul, and Luke Skywalker (the hero). Venture into a video arcade or play computer games and the archetypes jump out at you—knights slaying dragons and saving damsels in distress; futuristic warriors saving the world; athletes battling to defeat the "enemy" competitor. In virtual-reality simulations, archetypes are often enhanced by strange names, alien features, and otherworldly dress, bringing them even closer to myths and legends of early human civilization.

Virtual-reality archetypes pervade our lives, bringing pleasure, amusement, and deep, unconscious satisfaction.

VIRTUAL-REALITY SIMULATIONS

The wind ravaged her body, its fingers flattening her breasts and forcing her breath into short, ragged gasps. He stood behind her, holding her tightly, exposing her to the ravishing panorama before them. She shuddered. Gently, defying the power of the wind, he raised her arms to the world, embracing the unruly sea before them and the throbbing ship beneath them. Their passion knew no bounds—it leaped with a dizzying crescendo as the vision dipped and panned to catch the lovers in a world of dreams. The moment dangled breathlessly in time as surround sound pounded at the viewers until they could feel *the wind, share* the lust, *and know, with prophetic wisdom, the agony of what lay before them.*

Millions of people were enthralled by that scene in *Titanic,* the top-grossing movie of all time. Leonardo DiCaprio balanced co-star Kate Winslet on the bow of the great, doomed steamer while viewers watched spellbound by the spectacle. The movie would take in over $600 million domestically, get fourteen Academy Award nominations, and perhaps be the most talked about and purchased (in video) film ever produced. With director James Cameron and his crew's vision and technological savvy, moviegoers were seduced into a compelling virtual reality.

It had all the right ingredients: a good story embedded in a technology with special effects that brought each viewer deeply into the virtual experience of the disaster. It seethed with virtual archetypes: good against evil, everlasting love, the hero and the coward. Perhaps most compelling, it was a skilled execution in a medium that had captivated audiences since its earliest inception.

The twentieth century was the first time technology was able to offer this type of immersion in virtual environments to the masses. The metaphor was simple: create technological simulations of real life.

A virtual-reality simulation uses technology to create copies of actual reality. What the viewer or user experiences is virtual in structure, but in content it is perceived as real. This phenomenon reflects the natural, inborn human ability for telepresence (see Part II). Simply put, if it looks human, if it feels human, and if it sounds human, we instinctively perceive "it" as human. Therefore, when we watch the six o'clock news "live" we observe it as actuality, not as the confluence of electronic signals, cables, and circuitry in a receiver device we call television.

Accordingly, virtual reality simulations are easy places to "go." We don't need to invest in our own imaginative muscle, we don't need to search for archetypes, and we certainly don't need to dig down deep into individual or collective unconscious. All we need is to go with the flow. Let it *happen*.

This makes virtual-reality simulations both compelling and treacherous. We put ourselves at the mercy of those who create the simulations. It is their virtual realities that envelop—and numb—us. To illustrate, visualize a television travelogue of the High Sierras. The camera takes you into the towering mountains, panning across the lofty redwoods, the ancient craggy rocks, and the wild flowers swaying in the wind. Time, money, and other constraints keep you from hopping an airplane and going there in actuality. So you experience the High Sierras in virtual-reality simulation. *And you believe.*

But are you really experiencing it? Do you feel the crisp, cool wind against your face or feel the crunch of pine needles beneath your feet? While the director and producer zoom slowly up the trunk of a giant sequoia tree, do you really feel the awesome power of the largest plant on earth? If you were there you might want to look at the icy brook that runs along the trail or an odd rock formation or any myriad of natural objects. But you can't. You're there through the eyes of the camera.

That's fine. Because at the point in time you're watching the travelogue you really can't *be* in the High Sierras. It makes virtual-reality simulations very compelling. However, the flip side can be like walking on the thin ice that covers the brook you couldn't see. With so much virtual-reality simulation, people tend to substitute it for the real thing. Postmodernists assert that simulation, as a "copy" of actuality, becomes our new reality. In other words, the copy is more "real" than the original. Look around you. Children fantasize about their favorite characters like Barney and Teletubbies while adolescents argue about the behavior of characters on soaps and sitcoms. Television portraits show us the "real" politician, performer, or celebrity, and we believe we know the person—even though all we see is a carefully groomed media persona. Copycat behavior from films and television has become a serious problem—people are getting killed imitating stunts set up by directors. In Japan, young people dress up like video-game characters and attend huge conventions. How many people go to "New York, New York" in Las Vegas and feel like they've been to the Big Apple without ever setting foot in that city?

Actual reality can become disconcerting. Face-to-face communication can be awkward, and intimacy an invasion of privacy. It's much easier to watch hours of nature programming or countless love scenes than hike in the woods or sustain a close relationship. Will it get worse? Will we end up, like so many science-fiction stories, in synthetic worlds where computers induce hallucinations, deceive human senses, and compel us to repeatedly choose the virtual world over the real? Critical boundaries are already blurred between the self and other, men and women, nature and machine (see Part III). Even death loses its meaning when playing a game, a role, or a fantasy adventure where multiple lives are accrued through successful play and death is essentially a loss of credits.

Virtual-reality simulations pervade postmodern life. In Disney World you can stroll through a frontier town complete with singing grizzly bears or plunge into the darkness of a Space Mountain pierced by screams, flickering lights, and horrific "alien" noises. The list grows when you consider "theme" parks such as Universal Studios, Opryland, and Sesame Place. Then there are the arcades, theme restaurants, hotels, and entertainment complexes that invite us to partake in a few moments of virtuality. There is even an entire city that is devoted to this concept: Las Vegas. What is more virtual than a hotel that looks like a Sphinx, a human-made volcano that erupts hourly, and thousands of machines that nurture fantasies of great wins (and riches)? Virtual-reality simulations increasingly define our lives.

Today, most of us have been born into a world filled with virtual-reality simulations. These simulations have defined much of our lives.

Who is to say that a virtual-reality simulation is better or worse than actual reality? Many speculate that our technological virtual realities will eventually bring us to different planes of experience—perhaps a fourth, fifth, or sixth dimension of existence. When we arrive will we bring the parts of us that are indisputably human, or will we have adapted into a new species of cyborg?

LINES
IN THE SAND

WHERE DOES ACTUAL reality end and virtual reality begin?

- We have sex in actual reality and fantasize in virtual reality.
- We read a murder mystery in actual reality and become the detective in virtual reality.
- We pray in actual reality and visualize heaven in virtual reality.
- We watch a horror movie in actual reality and are terrified in virtual reality.
- We hold a plastic telephone in actual reality and have an intimate conversation in virtual reality.
- We press buttons on a keyboard in actual reality and fight cyberspace demons in virtual reality.
- We type e-mail in actual reality and correspond in virtual reality.

We are faced with a paradox—is there a point in time or space where actual reality ends and virtual reality begins? Or are they completely discrete, unconnected parallel spaces? Juxtaposing earlier definitions of reality with present scientific knowledge can help answer these questions.

Western science traditionally defines human knowledge as derived from empirical observation. This was necessary during the eighteenth-century Enlightenment when civilization needed an all-encompassing philosophy to view the world in mechanistic terms. Postmodern science is increasingly finding that the world is not as ordered or simple as the earlier Western empiricists chose to believe. Unexplained (but observed) phenomenon like quarks and black matter tell a far different story. The plausible, but not comforting, ideas set forth in Chaos Theory suppose a very different set of natural forces. We no longer *have* to believe that what's formless or virtual is separate and distinct from actual reality. We have learned that what we *don't* know far exceeds what we *do* know. Sweeping assumptions simply don't work. Even our definitions of actual reality have come under scrutiny. Consider the existence of black holes in outer space. We can't see them. We don't know what they are made of. We don't really even know what they *are*. But because of the gravitational effects on surrounding bodies, we know that they exist. This forces us to question our ability to perceive actual realities. There are so many things on our own planet that we can't see, hear, or feel. Once we acknowledge that many elements of actual reality stretch beyond our reach, virtual realities are far easier to comprehend.

We really don't *need* to substantiate the existence of virtual space. Experience has told us that from the first moment of consciousness. We learn very quickly that what occurs *inside* greatly impacts the *outside*. Think about emotions. We all know the impact of emotions on daily life (actual reality). Anxiety, self-doubt, panic, depression constantly boil over into physical spaces. The old adage that "the eyes are the window to the soul" seems as true now as when the words were first spoken. Confidence, passion, and love have an almost magical way of being projected outward. Have you ever had a dream so "real" that when you wake up you were convinced it really happened? Did you ever employ that "sixth sense" to predict an event or behavior? We all do these things so naturally and effortlessly that we don't even consider what is happening and where it takes place. It just seems to *happen*.

Sigmund Freud, among others, tried to explain this mingling of virtual and actual spaces by designing a model of psychological structures where the id (the repository of inner, primitive drives) and the super ego (the conscience) met the outside world through the mediating powers of the ego. More recently, research increasingly shows that virtual realities really do impact on actual realities. For example, it is widely accepted that highly stressed people are at an increased risk of illness. This is because immune responses are influenced by the central nervous system, which in turn is affected by social and psychological processes. Perhaps less known are studies that have found that religious faith can have a direct impact on human health. Consider the following findings:

- Patients who depend on religious faith and social support are more likely to survive open-heart surgery.
- People who attend weekly religious services have stronger immune systems.
- The stronger a person's religious faith, the faster he or she will recover from depression.

Religion, spirituality, or deep faith in God is essentially a virtual reality. Religions utilize virtual stories, archetypes, and, in some cases, technological simulation to enhance belief systems. What is more virtual than divine intervention? Or an otherworldly heaven reserved for the righteous? The Bible is essentially a collection of stories in which prophets, saints, and angels represent essential archetypes. Even our technology has enhanced religious virtual realities through classic movies like *The Ten Commandments* and *Miracle on 34th Street;* in television shows like *Touched by an Angel;* and in the myriad computer simulations of spiritual people, artifacts, environments, and ideas.

Interestingly, the research found that the specific religion was not significant—only the faith. *Belief* in the existence of a religious virtual reality—a deeply spiritual space without actual physical fact, form, or features—had direct, measurable effects on the physical well-being of the body. While all scientific research needs to be viewed with a highly critical eye, this reinforces a rapidly growing body of literature that connects mind and body, virtuality and reality.

In contrast, many contemporary reductionists are eager to describe virtual phenomena as purely physiological events. This can be as misleading as the enlightened mind-body separatists. Research in everything from dreams, emotions, and behavior has been linked to organic components. Perhaps the most expansive research has been in the Human Genome Project, a fifteen-year global effort to discover the location and exact chemical sequence of over 100,000 human genes. With this information, scientists can develop genetic tests that indicate susceptibility, treatments that reverse or prevent disease, and pharmaceuticals that can alter DNA imperfections. Each day they are discovering more connections between genes and physical or mental traits. While researchers increasingly argue that there are few cause-and-effect relationships between a single gene and a single trait, many people seek to interpret the information as proof of a biological basis for all human experience.

We find ourselves in murky waters. If mind and body are not discrete, how are they related? Are human beings completely predetermined? What about the chicken-and-the-egg question? If there is a physiological component to virtual experience, which came first? For example, science has found that there are anomalies in the brains of schizophrenics. Did the anomalies cause the schizophrenia, or did the schizophrenia cause the anomalies?

How does all of that affect the differentiation between virtual and actual realities? Perhaps the answer lies in the gray area—they exist on a circle where at any point they can oppose or compliment one another:

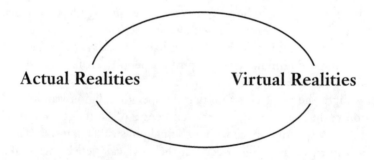

Actual Realities   Virtual Realities

In this context, virtual reality and actual reality are both features in the gestalt of human experience. Depending on where it lies on the continuum, a virtual reality can be perceived as more or less "real," while an actual-reality experience can be readily adapted to virtual. The infant technology of *augmented reality* may further modify the relationship between virtuality and actuality. Augmented reality refers to computer-mediated experiences or environments where the physical world is *enhanced*, not replaced. Unlike virtual reality, the user maintains a clear sense of presence in actuality with virtual images augmenting his or her perception. For example, an obstetrician in the future might use an augmented-reality system to superimpose a virtual picture of the living fetus on the pregnant mother's abdomen. The doctor will be able to "see" inside without any invasive procedure or test. In other words, the future augmented-reality user can plant one foot firmly in actuality and the other in virtuality, hovering in a place that professor and director of the ETC Laboratory at the University of Toronto, Dr. Paul Milgram, refers to as "mixed reality." Milgram has designed a reality-virtuality continuum that acts as a framework for identifying whether one is in a primarily virtual or primarily actual space. When added to our circle, it looks like the following:

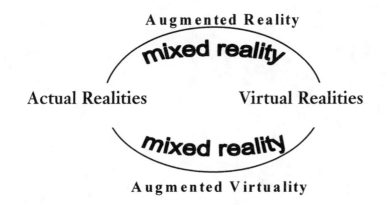

Augmented Reality

mixed reality

Actual Realities   **Virtual Realities**

mixed reality

Augmented Virtuality

The biggest obstacle faced by researchers in augmented reality is that virtual and actual objects must be perfectly registered, or the user will be disoriented, making augmented reality completely useless. Human acuity is so highly tuned that it simply won't accept perceptual distortion in actuality. Technology will undoubtedly overcome many of these problems.

In order to fully understand these relationships we need a more global system—something that can explain things in a larger context. Steven Pinker, MIT professor and author of *How the Mind Works*, suggests that "the mind is a system of organs of computation, designed by natural selection to solve the kinds of problems our ancestors faced in their foraging ways of life, in particular, understanding and outmaneuvering objects, animals, plants, and other people" (p. 21). To fully understand our realities—both actual and virtual—we need to apply the process of "reverse-engineering." In forward engineering you design and build a machine to do something—complete a task. In reverse engineering, according to Pinker, the job is the opposite: you have the machine, and the job is to figure out what it was designed to do. Reverse engineering is what we do when we know we have an arm, we know what that arm is able to do, but we don't know why and how it happens. It is the same concept in psychology. We know we have a mind that experiences both actual and virtual realities. We know what happens. This book proposes to answer why that mind was designed for cyberseduction. The answers lie in a new approach toward understanding human behavior: evolutionary psychology.

GENES OR
GENESIS?

The emperor lived in a big, bustling city. His main passion in life was clothes. He loved to dress in the finest garments, showing off his extensive wardrobe. One day two con men arrived in town. They told the emperor that they could weave the finest, most beautiful cloth imaginable. The clothing sewn from this fabric was magical— it was "invisible to anyone either badly suited for his or her position or unforgivably stupid."

The emperor gave the weavers money, gold, and silk to set up their looms and begin weaving. After some time, he was overcome with curiosity. So the emperor sent his prime minister to see how things were going. The minister saw nothing. Afraid to tell the truth, he reported that the weavers had created lovely patterns and vivid colors in the cloth. After all, he didn't want to lose his job.

Eventually, the emperor decided to see for himself. He brought his entire retinue to the looms. They were empty. "Am I stupid?" he asked himself. "Am I not fit to be emperor? That would be the most appalling thing that could ever befall me." So the emperor and his retinue all agreed that the cloth was really very beautiful.

On the day of the procession, the con men "dressed" the emperor. As he walked down the crowded city streets, the people admired their emperor's beautiful clothes. Suddenly a child cried, "But he has nothing on!" The words rippled through the crowd. The emperor knew the kid was right—but he wouldn't dare admit it.

So the emperor continued proudly down the streets with his servants carrying a train that did not exist.

D I D   T H E   E M P E R O R   really have new clothes? Or did his sub-jects share an illusion created from political, psychological, and societal pressures?

Consider how many illusions like the emperor's new clothes that we share in today's world. We go along with popular definitions with little or no questions, accepting them as "reality." The evening news on television is "real," not digital signals on a plastic tape. A one-hundred-dollar bill has intrinsic value far beyond the cost of its paper and printer. Who will dispute that a telephone conversation is anything but "actual"—a genuine conversa-tion where we speak directly with one or several people in a single call? Crit-ical diplomatic decisions have been made using this modern reality. A case in point is the chilling telephone call between President John F. Kennedy and Secretary of State Christian Herter in 1961. Time was frozen in the days that followed Kennedy's call stating that if the Cubans attacked Guantanamo, they would be kicked out with force. Nuclear holocaust hinged on a virtual com-munication. From heads of state to global financial negotiations to choosing a restaurant for dinner, the telephone defines and guides a critical part of our reality. But is it anything more than the emperor's new clothes?

What really happens on a telephone "call"? You hold a small plastic instrument in your hand. It can have a wire attached, it can send signals to a base unit, or it can be cellular. Either way, the plastic encases electronic components that translate your voice into electronic signals that are invis-ible to the human eye. These signals speed through wires or bounce off complicated human-manufactured devices orbiting the earth. The signals travel through relay stations that magically reassemble them into signals read by another plastic receptacle that spews out something we recognize as a voice formulating words. Is this really *real?*

Howard K. Bloom, author of *The Lucifer Principle: A Scientific Expedition into the Forces of History* suggests that "reality is a shared hallucination. . . .

Pure individual perception does not exist" (Bloom 1997). He maintains that our sense of being *here*, our definition of what is real and not real, is the sum total of a species-wide evolution. The goal of this aspect of evolution is to make sure that we see what other members of our species see, allowing us to formulate a collective definition of the past, the present, and the potential future. In other words, we *are* what we *were*: psychologically evolved creatures designed to adapt to our environment.

WHERE DID IT ALL BEGIN?

He was born privileged, the grandson of wealthy, highly respected men. Josiah Wedgwood, his maternal grandfather, had started the world-famous pottery business that today still bears his name. His paternal grandfather, Erasmus Darwin, was a well-known doctor and friend of Wedgwood, gifted in both science and literature. Erasmus was known as the most distinguished English poet of his time, a man who combined literary and scientific creativity. He designed many new inventions and was credited with giving the idea of the steam engine to his friend James Watt. In modern terms one might say that Charles Darwin carried the genes of great intellect—giving insight into the origins of his own thinking. He grew up in a world that was still shuddering from the birth pangs of the Industrial Revolution. It was a time when the authority of government was being questioned in the marketplace, when there was a need to expand and liberate thought to match the furious pace of industrialization.

As a young child, Charles loved collecting, hoarding, and hunting for pretty things in nature. He was fascinated with birds, insects, and other animals. He loved what was then called natural history, a study that most people around him did not find particularly compelling. As he grew older and his thoughts more focused, Charles Robert Darwin entered higher education, briefly studying medicine at the University of Edinburgh. But the windy cliffs and medieval designs of Scotland were not right for the young man. He left, searching for another way to understand his world. He ended up at Cambridge University, intending to become a clergyman.

His plans changed suddenly when he was twenty-two years old. Darwin was invited to sail aboard the H.M.S. *Beagle* as an unpaid naturalist on a scientific expedition around the world. It was the trip that would last five years and forever change Western thought. Darwin wrote, at the conclusion of his book *The Voyage of the* Beagle (1860):

> Among the scenes which are deeply impressed on my mind, none exceed in sublimity the primeval forests undefaced by the hand of man; whether those of Brazil where the powers of Life are predominant, or those of Tierra del Fuego, where Death and Decay prevail. Both are temples filled with the varied productions of the God of Nature:—no one can stand in these solitudes unmoved, and not feel that there is more in man than the mere breath of his body.

When Darwin climbed on board the *Beagle* there was a general belief that each species was individually created. Life forms did not change. Seventeenth- and eighteenth-century British empiricists postulated that human knowledge and reason emerged from experience. John Locke, the founder of the school of empiricism, argued that the human mind was essentially a *tabula rasa*, or blank slate, upon which experience imprinted knowledge. Later philosophers such as David Hume and John Stuart Mill agreed, stressing human reason as a function of senses. They maintained that each of us enter this world knowing *nothing*. We use our senses (experience) to make associations that are close in space or time, coming up with rational thought. Empirical philosophy influenced subsequent scientific thought— if people are born with a "blank slate" then the content of their minds is derived solely through the environment and their senses.

Darwin refused to buy it.

Darwin spent five years aboard the *Beagle*. Captain Robert FitzRoy of the Royal Navy was given command of the small ship when he was only twenty-three years old. He was an intense, religious man whose job was to survey the coasts of far-off lands. FitzRoy wanted a naturalist onboard—a companion as well as a scientist who would verify his creationist views of the world. Although he and Darwin became close friends, they eventually developed an ideological tension that was never quite resolved. FitzRoy, like so many of his contemporaries, wanted the Bible to be *proven* true. Darwin discovered the opposite.

The *Beagle* was only ninety feet long and about twenty-five feet at her widest. She carried seventy-four people in cramped quarters. Her decks were often cluttered with Darwin's specimens spread out to be preserved, sorted, categorized, or packed to ship back home. As the ship's naturalist, Darwin spent his five years on the *Beagle* doing what he loved best— exploring, collecting, analyzing, and categorizing the vast array of life and inorganic evidence found around the globe. He sailed south from the British Isles, stopping at the Canary Islands and Cape Verde Islands before reaching South America. Everything Darwin saw was fresh and exciting, revealing ancient stories that his keen eyes and sharp intellect could read. He kept meticulous notes filled with endless facts that would eventually become the groundwork for the theory of evolution. He worked furiously and tirelessly, showing no signs of the mysterious illness that would debilitate his adult years after his return home and marriage. Darwin studied geology and botany, taking careful notes on the evolution of environments. He collected and studied insects, small mammals, birds, and every kind of sea creature he could find. He was astounded by the rich diversity of life and environments. In a letter home, Darwin wrote about his experiences: "[It is] like giving to a blind man eyes, he is overwhelmed with what he sees and cannot justly comprehend it" (Gallant, p. 72).

Gradually, Darwin saw clear proof that empiricism didn't quite add up. There were fossils of extinct species that were oddly similar to living species in the same geographical area. Animals tended to *adapt* to where they lived, developing different forms from their biological brethren. There had to be something more—something intrinsic to each life form that guided these adaptations.

We would never be the same.

Simply put, Darwin observed that individuals in any species compete through natural selection. The individuals that survive pass on, through heredity, "desirable" variations that best assure continuation of the species. Through a slow, continuing process, life evolves, adapting to the environment. The key to survival lies in this natural selection of desirable variations through reproduction. Darwin concluded that all "species are the modified descendents of other species," and "man, like every other species, is descended from some pre-existing form" (Darwin 1871).

Darwin wasn't the first. He acknowledged that at least thirty-four highly respectable scientists had maintained that species evolve, or do not have their own separate and distinct creation. These predecessors fueled his work and his thinking. He clearly recognized their contributions, writing in *The Descent of Man* (1871):

> This work contains hardly any original facts in regard to man. . . . It has often and confidentially been asserted that man's origins can never be known; but ignorance more frequently begets confidence than does knowledge: it is those who know little, and not those who know much, who so positively assert that this or that problem will never be solved by science. The conclusion that man is the co-descendant with other species of some ancient, lower, and extinct form is not in any degree new. Lamarck long ago came to this conclusion, which lately has been maintained by several eminent naturalists and philosophers . . .

Fifty years before Darwin published his theory, Jean Baptiste de Lamarck, a French botanist and zoologist, argued that more complex life forms evolved from simpler species. Many other theorists discussed and wrote about this strange concept of evolution. But it wasn't until the 1859 publication of *On the Origin of Species* that the idea was heard around the world. Darwin noted his own intellectual evolution, remarking how his grandfather, Dr. Erasmus Darwin, "anticipated" Lamarck. The scientific and philosophic world braced for a clear, unfaltering voice that presented what many believed to be blasphemous ideas. Erasmus's grandson was that voice.

Darwin's theory of evolution threw the scientific and religious communities into an uproar. Darwin challenged centuries of Western thought, attacking the very soul of religion. Even before *On the Origin of Species* hit the presses, Darwin dreaded its effects. Science and religion would ultimately be divorced, never reunited in the same manner. Theologians firmly believed that God had created each individual species. No species had the power to change by itself. In this ideology, evolution was a direct blow to religion—an unequivocal rejection of God.

The debate was fierce. "Darwinism" was put on trial, argued from churches to laboratories to classrooms. Darwin was accused of claiming that humans had descended from apes and monkeys—a subject he astutely avoided. It took ten years after the publication of *On the Origin of Species* before Darwin conceded to that claim. It all came out in his book *The*

Descent of Man. Battle lines were drawn. Darwin kept himself out of the direct line of fire. He chose to let his work stand on its own merit. But the world around him raged.

It continues today. Creationists still passionately argue the fallacies of biological evolution. The most hardcore maintain that humans were created 10,000 years ago. These biblical fundamentalists interpret Genesis literally—God created the earth and man in six days. One of the most famous clashes between evolutionists and creationists took place in 1925 in Dayton, Tennessee. The infamous "monkey trial" accused high-school biology teacher John Scopes of violating the Butler Act, a Tennessee law that prohibited teaching evolution because it contradicted the biblical definition of creation. Clarence Darrow and William Jennings Bryan battled it out, with Scopes ultimately convicted and fined $100. It wasn't until the middle of the century before the idea was legally reconsidered—with the U.S. Supreme Court declaring that a state could not prohibit teachers from discussing evolution. The fierce debate was far from over. More recently, Don Aguillard, a Louisiana high-school science teacher, raised the legal the issue of *requiring* teachers to present creationist doctrine. In 1987 the U.S. Supreme Court ruled that states could not order teachers to discuss "creation science" along with evolution.

The new millennium has given rise to a fresh breed of creationists. Neo-creationists believe in evolution as a design created by the hand of God. This context offers a compromise between traditional theology and modern biology. The numbers clearly reveal that Darwin's brand of evolution still does not completely dominate modern American thought. A recent survey of 387 Louisiana biology teachers found that 29 percent believed that creationism should be taught in high school biology classes. In Alabama, many teachers use high school biology books with the following disclaimer from the State Board of Education:

> Evolution is a controversial theory some scientists present as scientific explanation for the origin of living things, such as plants, animals and humans. No one was present when life first appeared on earth. Therefore, any statement about life's origins should be considered as theory, not fact. (Christensen 1998)

Laurie Goodstein, in a recent *New York Times* article, reported that in a poll of 1,000 scientists, 55 percent believed that "God had no part in the process of evolution," while 40 percent said that while they believed in evolution, "God guided the process including the creation of man."

Viewing it from a more global perspective, Darwin's ideas have expanded our concepts of the world. Neo-Darwinists describe us as inhabiting constantly changing, continuously evolving bodies. As old ideas crumble under the power of evolutionary thought, new thinkers emerged. The study of biology was revolutionized. New insights were introduced in other fields. There was a powerful effect on child psychology. Human children were no longer seen as miniature adults. Instead, they went through species-wide stages of development that promoted adaptation to their environment. One of the most influential thinkers in this new philosophical environment was the man who was sometimes known as the "Darwin of the mind": Sigmund Freud.

Charles Darwin wrote eight more books after *On the Origin of Species*. When he took his last book to be published, Darwin explained that it had taken him many years to write on a subject that was very important to him but would not really interest the public. Within a year, six editions of the book were printed. It was about earthworms.

On April 19, 1882, Darwin died of a heart attack. Twenty members of Parliament signed a letter requesting that he be buried in Westminster Abbey, the final resting place for Britain's kings, queens, and intellectual leaders. In a nook of the Abbey dubbed "Scientists' Corner" is a simple black slab to mark his grave. Nearby is an imposing memorial to Sir Isaac Newton. *On the Origin of Species* is not sold in the Abbey bookshop.

MONKEY SEES,
MONKEY DOES

*D*ARWIN'S THEORY MADE it clear: evolution, driven by natural
selection, was a continuing process in life. The logic, whether one
believed in creation or in evolution, was hard to argue. If you stuck to the
biblical view, you had to ignore an increasingly mounting collection of
evidence. If you chose Darwinism, it made earth's "highest" species look
a lot more like everyone else. And it caused big problems in Sunday
school.

Obviously, evolution makes sense. In any environment where food and
resources are limited, life must compete to exist. We see this every day in
human culture. Perhaps politics is our best socially constructed metaphor
for that very essential concept. In nature, some life forms survive, others
don't. Choosing who survives, and subsequently, what genes are passed
down, is based on the slow, time-consuming process of natural selection
through sexual reproduction.

Let's take a closer look. What does this unrelenting rule of evolution suggest? Each species must conform and be diverse at the same time. In other words, they must have critical elements that identify them as part of a species, give them the ability to work in harmony with their brethren while at the same time be uniquely singular—have characteristics that may or may not affect adaptation to the environment. For example, all horses have four legs, two eyes, and strikingly similar brains. Yet they vary in many different ways—some horses are broad and heavy, others are swift and lithe. They have different colors, different tails, different manes—in fact, no two horses are exactly alike. In an environment with limited resources, the variations within a species enable them to better adapt to their environment. If there were no diversity, if all animals within a group were exactly (genetically) the same, there would be big trouble. We would quickly see genetic damages proliferate. Diversity gives us the ability to repair nature's mistakes. This is achieved through the slow, often awkward process of sex. By having to mate with another life form, genetic damage can be repaired through the production of diverse offspring. In human terms, this is a very operational way to view one of the most powerful and seductive aspects of life. Perhaps that is why the taboo against incest can be found in most human cultures. Too much in-breeding destroys diversity and threatens the adaptive process of natural selection.

Roy A. Gallant, in *Charles Darwin: The Making of a Scientist,* clearly illustrates this phenomenon in the story of a common, light-colored moth that was found in Manchester, England. Many of the trees in and around Manchester had light-colored bark. When the moths landed on the trees, their wings blended in with the bark, protecting them from birds searching for dinner. Every so often, the light-colored moths produced offspring with dark-colored wings. Some of the dark-colored moths lived long enough to produce offspring, but on the whole they did not survive very long because when they landed on the trees the birds could easily spot them. The variation in wing color made them poorly adapted to the environment, unable to survive and reproduce. It was a variation that simply did not work—until there were changes.

Industry and the subsequent increase in population swelled the city of Manchester. The factories used enormous amounts of fuel. The large numbers of people moving into Manchester had to heat their houses and cook their food, and the choice of fuel was coal. Coal use increased dramatically, resulting in soot released into the air. Coal soot can be relentless in its discoloration of the environment. The once light-colored bark of the trees became stained with soot, shifting to a darker color. The light-colored moths that had adapted to a preindustrialized Manchester were suddenly at a disadvantage. Now the birds could see *them* clearly and easily found their dinner. The environment had changed. The dark-colored moths that had been the oddities were camouflaged by the dark, soot-covered bark of the trees. The birds couldn't see *them*. From an evolutionary standpoint, it was no surprise when the light-colored moths were gobbled up and the dark-colored moths survived and multiplied.

It happens all the time. Bacteria and viruses become resistant to drugs. Species become extinct because they can't adapt to a change in the environment. A breed of bird called cliff swallows that live along the Platte River in Nebraska survives harsh weather because the birds' bodies are larger and symmetrical, while their smaller and asymmetrical kin die. Lizards in the Caribbean adapt to their environment by evolving differences in the length of their limbs and the size of their toepads. In other words, by adapting to their environment, life forms increase their likelihood of survival and reproduction. Life forms with less "desirable" characteristics will have more difficulty adapting and be less likely to reproduce. It's a slow, time-consuming process that works more effectively than the finest machines created by humans. The evidence is all around us.

Humans have utilized the process of selecting desirable characteristics for thousands of years. Hybrids are a cross between species that have led to "improved" varieties of life. Features such as increased kernel size in corn, disease-resistant crops, and combinations of fruits and vegetables are relatively common. Humans have bred female horses with male donkeys to create sterile offspring—mules. A mule has the head, ears, and tail of a donkey and the stature of a horse, but it excels in endurance, surefootedness, and longevity.

Consider animal breeders who have used *artificial* selection to create special characteristics in purebred dogs. For example, to miniaturize a dog, breeders took the smallest animals and bred them. They then selected the smallest animals in the new litters and bred them. By repeating the process, each succeeding generation was, on the average, smaller. Humans "designed" miniature dogs such as poodles, collies and dachshunds. Inevitably, careless breeding led to hundreds of genetic defects in pure-bred dogs. Too many breeders in their zeal to create profitable pets did not provide enough diversity.

Human history is filled with similar examples. Perhaps the most famous is the "royal disease," or hemophilia, caused by an X-linked recessive gene that, until recently, was untreatable. Only a few hemophiliacs survived to reproduce because the smallest cut on the skin or even relatively minor internal bleeding could be fatal. It usually affects males because the gene is carried on the X chromosome. Males carry only one X, and if it is defective, they will suffer from the disease. If a woman carries a defective X, the other normal X chromosome will compensate. Consequently, women usually carried the disease. In the case of royalty, the inbreeding of royal families in Europe led to its spread. Great Britain's Queen Victoria clearly carried the gene for this disease. It first appeared in her family in her eighth child, Prince Leopold. He was one of the "luckier" ones—through constant surveillance he survived until he reached the age of thirty-one, dying from a minor fall. Her other sons were free of the disease, which is why today's royal family, descendents of Edward, are also not hemophiliac. Queen Victoria's daughters, however, spread the gene into other European royal families that eventually included Spain, Germany, and Russia. Their sons were not as fortunate. Many suffered painful deaths at young ages from minor cuts, wounds, or falls.

Improved technology has led to the field of genetic engineering, where scientists change an organism's genetic material to eliminate undesirable characteristics or produce selected new ones. Farmers now talk about biotechnology, asking questions such as which gene is "best." Gene splicing has led to potential cures for many human diseases as well as treatments for genetic defects. It has also lead to cloning mammals and the serious ethical considerations involved in such practice. Human technology has enabled us to create fruits that delay ripening to reduce spoilage, crops immune to plant viruses, cows that produce more milk, and pigs that produce more meat. Applying this technology to human species presents some very troublesome issues.

In contrast, *natural* selection is slow and directed toward more efficient adaptation to the environment. To illustrate, when Darwin studied finches in the Galapagos Islands he found that their beak structure was related to the island they lived on. Overall, the finches looked alike—they had the same bodies, the same kinds of nests, laid the same color and number of eggs. They also resembled finches found on the South American mainland. However, finches with heavy beaks cracked nuts and crushed seed. Finches with long pointed beaks ate soft fruits and flowers. Other finches had beaks designed to catch flying insects or dig into tree bark. The shape of the beak had enabled the finches to adapt to the island they lived on, adjusting their diet to the food available in the environment.

The finches and the moths both illustrate how evolution enables life forms to survive. The same concept applies in evolving *new* life forms. Simply put, one life form can slowly, over hundreds of thousands or millions of years, develop into an entirely new form. This idea dealt a resounding bow to the religious claim of many that humans were created 10,000 years ago. The real human story started up to five *million* years ago.

The study of human evolution is itself still evolving. New discoveries are constantly being made about human prehistory. Old theories are being revised or thrown out completely, and new information is helping us form what we hope are more accurate pictures of our origins. Like our bodies, the picture is constantly shifting, shedding light on our limited knowledge of the past. For example, human DNA has been found to be very similar to chimps and gorillas. What does that tell us? Humans belong to the family of hominids—two-legged, humanlike creatures. Our species name is *Homo sapiens*, or "wise man." We are further classified in the subspecies *Homo sapiens sapiens*. Keep in mind that these classifications in evolution are human designations. In natural selection they are imperceptible—part of a slow, continuing process taking place over long periods of time.

Dr. Robert Ornstein, author of *The Evolution of Consciousness*, estimates the beginning of human history at 5 million years ago, when the forests of east Africa thinned out and tree-dwelling creatures had to adapt to a different environment. There were new challenges: how to live in open country, how to hide from predators, how to protect the young.

This is when "Lucy" enters the picture. Lucy was one of the earliest life forms to mingle human and ape characteristics. Although there are many debates on whether she is a direct ancestor of humans or, as creationists often claim, just an ape, she was called *Australopithecus*. She lived in northeast Africa, in what is today Ethiopia. Lucy stood only three to four feet tall and walked upright. She probably lived in some kind of cooperative group with others like her, maybe sharing child-rearing responsibilities and food. Interestingly, Lucy's discovery suggested that walking upright on two legs came before what would be identified today as human intelligence.

While evidence of other species related to Lucy were found, probably the most significant to modern humans was *Homo habilis*, or "handy human." They were the earliest known human species, living between 1.3 and 2.2 million years ago. *Homo habilis* lived in the open bush and savannah country of East Africa, walking upright, using tools, and cooperating with one another. Their brains had made an evolutionary leap—they were 30 percent larger than their predecessors' brains. *Homo habilis* adapted to their environment by building a communal life. They shared tools and food, hunting and gathering in a cooperative association. Ornstein points out that highly evolved skills were required for hunting, including speed, accuracy, and the ability to plan, communicate, and cooperate. This suggests a "superior intelligence: to think and reason, speak a language, and create a culture" (p. 35). It probably took over 1.25 million years, or 75,000 to 125,000 generations, to get from Lucy to *Homo habilis*.

Homo erectus appeared 400,000 to 2 million years ago with a huge evolutionary change—their brain size was 50 percent larger than that of *Homo habilis*. These were the first humans believed to have migrated out of Africa, moving into Europe and the Far East. They lived during the ice age and had to adapt accordingly—developing skills such as cooking in pots, making advanced tools, clothing, and shelter. *Homo erectus* may have begun the slow evolution into *Homo sapiens*, the earliest form of today's species, about 300,000 to 400,000 years ago.

Perhaps one of the most intriguing mysteries in early human history is the role of the Neanderthals (*Homo sapiens neanderthalensis*). Scientists debate whether they were a closely related subspecies of modern humans or a collateral line of *Homo erectus*. Recent research indicates that Neanderthal DNA is different from modern humans', suggesting that they might have been two species living at the same time, not descendants of one another. It is possible that modern humans were the result of interbreeding between these two species. Many scientists analyzing fossil remains argue that they did not interbreed or, in fact, have very much to do with one another. It remains a mystery. Either way, the Neanderthals had an organized society and lived primarily during the ice age, mostly in Europe and southwest Asia. Researchers from Duke University have speculated that Neanderthals had the ability to make modern human speech sounds. They were a strong, robust species who could endure the harsh climate of the Pleistocene era. An elaborate, 60,000-year-old grave was found by archeologists in Iraq, suggesting the early existence of a spiritual life. Interestingly, as social organization progressed, archeologists have found increasing signs of violence and warfare.

Anatomically modern humans can be directly traced to the earliest *Homo sapiens sapiens* found in East Africa. These first "moderns" lived around 100,000 to 200,000 years ago. They were not adapted to the cold and appeared very different from the Neanderthals. These people probably migrated out of Africa about 100,000 years ago. While we usually refer to their European descendents as Cro-Magnon, named after a rockshelter site in France, it actually applies to all anatomically modern humans. In essence, we are all Cro-Magnon.

Ornstein vividly describes this latest human evolution. "With the outburst of language, the pace of evolution stepped up. Everything Neanderthals did, Cro-Magnon did better" (p. 38). Cro-Magnon, using language, could communicate, plan, organize, and work together in more complex social organizations. Their thinking expanded rapidly—abstract thought, symbols, and deepening intellectual capabilities became more apparent. By 15,000 years ago, the human mind had evolved to what we see today. Considering that it took almost 5 million years to get there, the chances of any major evolutionary change in the human brain occurring since that time period is slim. In other words, all our technology, our science, our modern and postmodern civilization is seated in what is essentially a Stone Age brain.

Consider some of the accomplishments of these Stone Age ancestors. They adapted to a wide variety of climates and learned to utilize their tools to change their environments. The power of language led to abstract thought, enabling them to speak, think, and create a set of common ideas and beliefs that could be passed on to subsequent generations. Most lived by hunting and gathering, creating significant social divisions in gender.

Women gathered berries, nuts, and grains, as well as made utensils, clothing, and baskets. They gave birth to new offspring and raised children—clearly requiring greater shelter and protection. Men hunted, made weapons, formed groups to find and kill food, and developed fighting skills to protect their social groups from dangerous animals and marauding human beings. As tools were refined with inventions such as the spear and later the bow and arrow, hunting became easier. Eventually these hunters and gatherers moved into the Neolithic Revolution, 4,000 to 10,000 years ago, when the concept of food production was discovered. By growing plants and raising food-producing animals, humans were able to exert more control over their environment, organizing themselves in settled, stable communities.

That was when we hit the beginning of what we call civilization.

STONE AGE COMPUTERS

W*HAT KIND OF* brain evolved to enable the human species to develop our incredibly diverse world?

Consider where we have gone. Originating in Africa, anatomically modern humans spread across the globe. We've adapted to tropical jungles, parched deserts, cold mountaintops, frozen tundra, and congested cities. We've survived massive floods, volcanic upheavals, climatic disasters, and political anomie that assaulted our environments. We've built cultures with different languages, different behaviors, and different spiritual belief systems. Our bodies have adapted to diets ranging from meat to vegetables to fast foods. Writing and reading books reflect our insatiable hunger for information and the ability to relentlessly pursue knowledge. More recently, we've invented cyberspace, a new environment that removes us from traditional physical parameters, plunging us into mental worlds of fantastic ideas and imagery. Could all of this be a function of evolution?

Perhaps alien creatures did land on earth and speed up our development. Or was there the hand of a greater, divine power guiding our way? Understanding the psychological transformation of how we evolved from cells to a flawed but diverse species with the potential to leave our planet and explore the universe affords the best clue our science, philosophy, and imagination can offer.

Look at the story of life on our planet. It has been one of natural selection, adaptation, and survival by reproduction. It is also the story of intelligence, the growth of brain size and function, and the continuous increase in the ability to perceive, organize, and process information. Jerome Barkow, Leda Cosmides, and John Tooby, editors of *The Adapted Mind*, suggest that "an account of the evolution of the [human] mind is an account of how and why the information-processing organization of the nervous system came to have the functional properties that it does" (p. 8). Their field of expertise, evolutionary psychology, utilizes Darwinian concepts to understand human behavior. Simply put, it maintains that there is a functional relationship between adaptation and human psychology. To illustrate, an evolutionary psychologist might explain that men seek more sexual partners than women because it is adaptive behavior. A Stone Age man needed to spread his genes and sought a variety of women to guarantee diversity and new offspring. In contrast, a Stone Age woman needed to protect her precious, limited number of eggs. She needed to select the father of her offspring carefully and so be more discriminating in order to optimize reproductive success. Consequently, modern men tend to be more sexually promiscuous, seeking multiple partners, while women are more discerning, drawn toward monogamous relationships.

Gender-related explanations in evolutionary psychology can be further expanded, supporting research showing that women, when introduced to male populations, such as prisoners, tend to calm and settle men, reducing violence and aggression. The best example, of course, was the American West, where violence prevailed until women settlers arrived, made homes, and bore children. Maybe we need more female heads of state to avoid wars! Evolutionary psychologists would say that this behavior is programmed into our neural circuits. To guarantee species survival, men had to go out into the wilds, hunt aggressively, and protect their families and clans from environmental threats. Men had to be tough, violence-prone, and combative, always ready to jump into fierce competition with beasts or other men. To guarantee species survival, women had to establish a stable base camp, a place where the group would be safe, could refuel nutritionally and psychologically, and children would not be harmed. Both roles were essential for the survival of the species. It was only later, in "civilized" society, that different values were assigned to male and female roles. Clearly, from a biological or psychological perspective, one gender role is not more important than the other.

These examples demonstrate the reverse-engineering approach of evolutionary psychologists. They seek to unravel the processes that underlie individual as well as cultural behavior. Evolutionary psychology offers a new perspective on human nature. It carefully acknowledges that the same designs that enlighten us, limit us. Human ideas and classifications are also limited by our evolutionary design—they shed light on understanding who we are, where we came from, and ideally, where we are going. They provide snapshots of what some call reality and others call design.

Utilizing evolutionary psychology offers a more diversified knowledge but not necessarily the complete picture. Perhaps the human mind was engineered to elude total self-awareness, protecting us from the ravages of a truth that organic beings would find intolerable. Ernest Becker addresses this in *Denial of Death* (see next chapter: "From Caves to Cyberspace" and Part II) as he attempts to explain an impossible human paradox: to be aware of ourselves as living creatures is to be aware of our inevitable demise as organic, time-limited machines. In our struggle to understand, to compile workable knowledge, and to ultimately predict our futures, we are drawn deeper into the quicksand: the more we learn the more we discover what we don't know. It is the inevitable Catch-22: we search, we learn, only to find more complexity. When we discovered that Earth was not the center of the universe, we found other planets, then other solar systems. We moved beyond into galaxies and the grand universe. All our experience tells us there is a beginning and end to everything we perceive. Conceivably, parameters exist only within our mental design—a species-wide survival tool to constrict our imaginations to a workable size. Time and space can be seen as a function of context rather than immutable constants. Truth is relative. Evolutionary psychology serves as one of many windows that illuminate a biological and psychological universe we will never be able to fully comprehend. Evolutionary psychology brings together the past and the present, offering us a philosophy that can serve as an entrance to the future. It helps us perceive the timeless nature of cyberseduction and the evolution of reality in an age of psychotechnology.

Cosmides and Tooby, codirectors of the Center for Evolutionary Psychology at the University of California, Santa Barbara, propose five principles of evolutionary psychology to help organize and classify the human mind. These principles help clarify the mind-body relationship, putting it in terms that readers can readily understand. Y3k, or the year 3000, will present an entirely different set of ideas and discoveries, new adaptations that will make today's life painfully archaic. Like the human history described in *Monkey Sees, Monkey Does*, philosophic and intellectual development migrates in multiple directions. Sometimes, like the Neanderthals, "lines" combine or die out completely. Others continue to evolve, adapting to new environments and once again creating new technologies that compel us to adapt to our own creations. Evolutionary psychologists superimpose logic on this process, clearly illustrated in the following principles.

1. The brain is a physical system that functions in a way similar to a computer. It uses neural circuits instead of electronic circuits. The evolutionary purpose of neural circuits is to generate behavior that will enable us to survive in our environment.

The brain is organic, a system of cells (mostly neurons) and electrochemical reactions. The mind is what the brain *does*. In other words, the mind processes information that enables our species to adapt to our environments. Many evolutionary psychologists see the mind as a set of modules "programmed" to solve adaptive problems. Neurons have the same physiological features. Neurons are distinguished from one another by the patterns of activity and connectivity between them. The differences in these patterns and activities enable them to run different "programs." According to S. Pinker, these programs are essentially organic information-processing units, or "tiny circuits that can add, match a pattern, turn on some other circuit, or do other elementary logical and mathematical operations" (p. 26).

The computational theory of mind helps us better understand evolutionary psychology. Pinker explains:

If evolution equipped us not with irresistible urges and rigid reflexes but with a neural computer, everything changes. A program is an intricate recipe of logical and statistical operations directed by comparisons, tests, branches, loops, and subroutines embedded in subroutines. . . . Human thought and behavior, no matter how subtle and flexible, could be the product of a very complicated program, and that program may have been our endowment from natural selection. The typical imperative from biology is not "Thou shalt . . . ," but "If . . . then . . . else." (p. 27)

Neurons, like circuits in a computer, are connected in a highly organized system. The connections determine how information is processed. In a computer, a circuit might determine how information is displayed on the screen—how many colors, the size and shape of the font, the layout of the desktop. Similarly, in the computational theory of mind, neural circuits connect to neurons that run through the body. For example, there are neural circuits that connect to the eye, others to muscles, still others to the ears. In other words, sensory receptors that pick up data from the outside world are connected to neurons that carry information to the brain, process it, and implement the adaptively appropriate response. In this way information from the environment is processed in the brain, utilizing multiple neural circuits that are designed to cooperate in quickly generating a response.

Using evolved, information-processing systems rather than specific behavioral responses enables humans to adapt to a wide variety of environments and environmental problems. For example, if neural networks are programmed to maintain body temperature, humans will take action based on their environment. If it's snowing, you'll put on a coat and seek a warm place, whether it's a cave with a fire or a house with oil heat. If it's hot, you'll seek cooler temperatures, whether it's splashing in the river or turning on the air-conditioning in your car. Think about how many cooperative neural processes must be employed in the brain to translate the cold, white stuff in the air to a bulky garment in your closet, a potentially hazardous flame in your cave, or a house that receives, monthly, two hundred gallons of black, gooey stuff that the world goes to war over in a dry, hot, and distant place called the Middle East.

This cognitive computational model of mind is very different from the "brain as a computer" model. The computers we use have far too few connections, relying on blueprints rather than the self-construction of the human brain. Silicon circuits may be faster, but their patterns are far more limited. Computers don't *think* in human definitions. They can't process the enormous variety of information that a human receives, sort through it, choose the critical pieces, and then process it into consciousness. We have wonderful robot machines that can construct cars, but no machine that can perceive the social hierarchy in a group of three-year-olds. Computers are based on exact, logical definitions and deductions programmed by humans. No one has yet figured out how to program the illogical, the trial-and-error thought that occurs in daily life—the uniquely human ability to integrate consistencies with inconsistencies, continually adapting and readapting to the environment. Pinker concludes that in essence, human psychology is "the analysis of mental software" (p. 26). Built into this system is a vast supply of undifferentiated neural circuits that can be used for new adaptive needs, so-called neurological spare parts. While computers are limited by their design, human limits are yet to be fully tested. "What magical trick makes us intelligent?" asks Marvin Minksy, MIT professor and pioneer in artificial intelligence. "The trick is that there is no trick. The power of intelligence stems from our vast diversity, not from any single, perfect principle."

Many theorists believe that this concept in evolutionary psychology is too limiting. They maintain that there is a gestalt to human intellect: the whole is far greater than the sum of its parts. As much as one might dissect and analyze the components of human psychology—behavior, thought, perception, etc.—it does not add up to the end result. The whole is a system that operates as a unit in a manner that no computer can ever fully reproduce.

Leading proponents of artificial intelligence (AI) strenuously disagree. AI scientists believe that humans will eventually be able to construct an "intelligent" machine. The key will lie in the diversity of approach—the understanding of human thought and psychology—an area in which new millennium science is still greatly limited.

And others still stridently maintain that the sheer complexity of human intellect and physiology is guided by transcendent design—a divine or spiritual force that accounts for our amazing diversity, adaptability, and ingenuity.

2. Neural circuits evolved through natural selection to solve problems faced by our ancestors.

Ever listen to baby babble? It's a world of sounds that have no meaning to your ears—some sweet, some harsh, some funny. Mom and Dad laugh at those sounds, cuddle baby and babble back, talk, tell stories, include their child in their daily lives. And then the day comes when baby says "da-da" or "ma-ma." There is a screech of delight as baby is swept up into mom and dad's arms. Baby has done something very, very right.

Language is perhaps the most intriguing of human cognitive skills, a process that organizes and defines our reality. No other species on earth uses language like *Homo sapiens sapiens*. It is part of who we are, how we communicate, and, unquestionably, how we think. Language has been studied by some of the best minds in human history who attempt to formulate its physiology, psychology, and philosophy. One of the most intriguing aspects of language is its acquisition. It really isn't taught—in fact, most children are fully conversant long before they enter school. Grammar is internalized at a very young age, along with sounds, expressions, and gestures that accompany words. The neurological process is extremely complex; however, the concept behind language acquisition is essentially simple. The baby is, literally, babbling all the sounds in every language known to humankind. The Chinese baby babbles English, French, and Swahili sounds. The English baby babbles Japanese, Hebrew, and Navajo sounds. In other words, human babies produce undifferentiated sounds. Learning language is a process of elimination, a focusing on the sounds in the environment. So the Japanese baby quickly loses the ability to produce English sounds because the brain is adapting to his or her Japanese environment. The English baby loses the ability to produce Japanese sounds because the brain is adapting to his or her English environment. That is why it becomes more difficult, as children grow older, to learn other languages. "Our amazingly redundant brain oversupplies us with possibilities for living all over the earth (or, rather, has made this diversity possible)," writes Ornstein.

It is as if we are given the ability to speak hundreds of thousands of languages, make thousands of gesture and sign organizations, be able to live in thousands of different areas, and that evolution, working to adapt to the world and working to protect our physiology, has provided us with a brain with "a thousand forms of mind." (p. 127)

A thousand forms of mind enable babies to adapt to the language spoken in their environment. Human brains have evolved to contain the neural circuitry that triggers language adaptation. As an information-processing organ, it is critical for the brain to have the wherewithal to adapt to any language. What would happen if the English baby could reproduce only Japanese sounds? Or the Navajo baby could reproduce only Russian sounds? Solving problems of adaptation are essential to the survival of any species. What would have happened to *Homo erectus* if they were not able to adapt to the harsh conditions of ice-age Europe? What would have happened to the English farmers if they were not able to adapt to the harsh conditions of industrialized urban life? What is happening to the people around us who are unable to adapt to computers and cyberspace in the digital age?

Adaptive problems in an evolutionary psychology context have two defining features: they occur repeatedly during the history of a species, and their solution affects the reproduction of individuals (by definition, the process of natural selection). This means that adaptive problems usually involve how we work, eat, mate, communicate, socialize, and learn. *Homo erectus* had to solve the adaptive problem of living in ice-age conditions. They adapted by cooking in pots, designing more advanced tools, clothing, and shelter. Similarly, the farmers who moved to the cities during the Industrial Revolution had to adapt to a very different environment— learning how to find food they didn't grow themselves, shelter they didn't build, and a very different style of labor. The adaptation to cyberspace is just underway. It's a process that has already changed the way we live, love, and play. As long as the neural circuits are intact, we will continue to solve these problems. However, evolutionary psychologists are quick to point out that our brains evolved over millions of years, and the history of human civilization is a just a tiny part in our evolutionary process. So while our brains evolved systems to solve adaptive problems, they sometime go awry in the digital age. Consider the "fight or flight" response, a human reaction to danger.

Imagine a hunter-gatherer wandering through the woods 7,000 years ago. Suddenly he or she confronts a wild animal, ready to pounce. What must be done? The body mobilizes immediately. Action must be taken. There are two choices—flee the scene and run for your life, or stand your ground and fight. Both choices require increased blood flow to the limbs, chemical changes in the body—activation of the sympathetic nervous system, which speeds up the heart and mobilizes the body for action. It serves the hunter-gatherer well. The powerful "fight or flight" response will spur him or her into life-saving action. If there was a pause in the response, if the hunter-gatherer stood before the enemy and rationalized the best course of action, he or she would be dinner long before any conclusion was reached. The fight or flight response was a life-saving mechanism for early humans.

Now take that same brain, the same neural circuits, and a latter-day hunter-gatherer. Instead of coming across an enemy in the woods, you're sitting at a desk in a corporate jungle, struggling to survive by hunting down ideas and customers, gathering dollars, and protecting the condo cave in the suburbs. The enemy arrives: a coworker who wants the same thing. The enemy might be smarter, quicker, or more able to charm the boss. This enemy stands directly in your path, a dangerous obstacle to your survival. The neural circuits are mobilized. Fight or flight? You can't do either. Yet your body is ready—run like the wind or fling the spear. Your body tells you to act, and your dress shoes, work clothes, and corporate culture block the action. If you run, you lose. If you fling that spear, it can end up lodged in your own heart. What you need to do is exactly the opposite of what your body is prepared for: pause and think through your next move. It creates a physical and an emotional conflict. In modern civilization we call it stress. The body is mobilized for an action that is impossible to take. You have to resist what your body tells you, deny the physical response, and take a course that your hunter-gatherer brain was not designed to navigate. The resulting stress keeps the body in a constant state of mobilization. It inevitably results in the long list of stress-related disorders that we know so well today. Our minds might be in cyberspace, but our brains are still distinctly Cro-Magnon.

3. Our neural circuits allow us to experience a small fraction of what actually happens.

We call this consciousness. Consciousness is very misleading. It convinces us that neural circuitry is simple. If we were conscious of every physiological or psychological event in our behavior, humans would never be able to survive.

When was the last time you felt your bile duct? Is your pancreas having a good day? How's your femur hanging in? We simply don't ask ourselves those questions unless there is a specific need to address them. Your bile duct might become very important if you were just diagnosed with gall bladder disease. Thinking about pancreatic function is a daily event for diabetics. Nobody worries about a femur—until it's broken and you're stuck in a leg cast.

Obviously, while we like to believe that we are attuned to everything that goes on inside of us, nothing is further from the truth. Consciousness is only a small part of human experience. Freud revolutionized human thought when he identified the structures of mind, including a huge part that was a morass of unconscious drives, emotions, and needs. If so much of our existence is unconscious, then it is important to distinguish the difference between what we know and what we don't know about ourselves.

Consciousness is generally seen as awareness—knowledge of what is occurring to *you*. So many things go on in our bodies and our minds, that if we were conscious of all of them, we would find ourselves suffocating in awareness. Consider breathing. We inhale and exhale automatically. Our bodies filter out many impurities while delivering air to the lungs. In a complex physiological event, gas is exchanged and oxygen is delivered miraculously throughout our bodies. We never know or feel any biochemical processes taking place. But what if we did? What if we knew each time a speck of dust was filtered out from the air? What if we knew each time our lungs exchanged gases, forcing us to exhale carbon dioxide while holding on to the precious oxygen? What if we felt every cell as it utilized the oxygen? What if we could experience those red blood cells swishing around our bodies? We couldn't *live* with such a constant assault of information.

In order to adapt self-awareness to complex physiology *and* psychology, our minds evolved to shield us from most of what happens. We depend on automatic processes, preprogrammed mental schemas, unconscious emotions, and species-wide behavioral blueprints to guide our lives. "Consciousness," writes Ornstein, "far from being in control all the time, is usually not needed. . . . [It is] a weak force in most of our minds, easily overridden by circumstances, by eloquent people, by lower forces of the mind, by automatic routines" (p. 226).

Why be conscious at all? Our conscious minds are necessary for deliberate, determined decisions, for those times when automatic control simply doesn't suffice. It gives us access to information and information-processing that supercedes automatic response. Consciousness is the soul of self-awareness, knowledge about ourselves and our environments that can equip us to change, grow, expand, exploit, and do the very best and very worst acts known to humankind. Conscious information can be collected, stored, and automated. When you first learned to drive a car you had to memorize the steps: key in ignition, foot on brake, shift into gear, foot on gas . . . How many times do you *consciously* repeat those steps after learning how to drive? We build mental databases based on our conscious experience, using the information to construct both actual and virtual realities.

It's not easy to be conscious. Touch a hot stove and you automatically pull away your hand. Looking at a restaurant menu and trying to figure out which dinner would best satisfy you in a specific time and place, with a specific set of companions, *and* not add too much cholesterol, is a far more arduous process. We have to work at conscious thought. If our bodies depended on that slow, often awkward method, we would never have made in through the last 5 million years. In fact, we wouldn't be able to make it through the day.

All human awareness, however, does not depend on consciousness. We often find ourselves in situations where subconscious information affects us, for instance: putting a cake in the oven when potential buyers come to look at your house; using a subtle perfume or cologne to entice the new man or woman in your life; wearing bright colors on a rainy day; or playing soft music in a doctor's office. Consciousness is a flexible, transient phenomenon that defines who we are.

Consider the complex mingling of conscious, unconscious, and automatic neural circuitry involved in a simple event:

It's a cold, gray day two weeks before Thanksgiving. The wind blows in your face, stinging your skin and reminding you that winter is right around the corner. For a moment, you think about the ice and snow on its way—the frigid, light-starved days that will fill your life. A tiny vision forms in your mind: the swirling waves of the ocean, shimmering in the summer sun, the white sand of the beach cradling you as the warmth seeps into your skin.

You shake the picture from your mind. It only makes you feel worse.

As you continue down the main street in town, a glass door opens. Suddenly the powerful smell of hot apple pie, fresh from the oven, hits you. Hot apple pie—thick with cinnamon and butter, languishing in a crisp, rich crust nestled in a deep glass dish. You remember Mom's apple pie, served in thick slices passed around the table while your eyes grew wide with anticipation. It was always a very special event when Mom baked those pies. You, your dad, and two brothers would wait eagerly when she would serve it, hot and steaming, for dessert. The pie seemed surrounded by laughter in a time long before Mom got sick and your older brother moved to a different state nearly 2,000 miles away. You could almost hear the dog barking in the background and the pine trees outside rubbing against the windows of your snug childhood home.

Suddenly you're hungry. It doesn't matter that you finished lunch only half an hour ago. It doesn't matter that you made a vow to lose those five pounds before the holidays. The smell of the pie makes you ravenous. You have to have it. *Now.*

Within minutes you're opening the glass door, entering the restaurant and ordering a hefty slice of apple pie.

That's the conscious experience. What you *know.* What you don't know—and don't feel—are the neural circuits being triggered by the smell, the connections firing madly, the patterns being drawn from a wide variety of physiological and psychological locations in your brain. You don't know about the sensory receptors in your nose that pick up the smell of the apple pie and send the information through neurons into your brain. You don't know about the neurons in your brain that connect to other circuitry. The smell of the apple pie must be identified, then associated with "apple pie." Then messages are sent out along multiple circuits—signals that tell your stomach to grumble (which is part of another circuit that indicates "hunger"), signals that associate "apple pie" with memories scattered throughout your brain—memories of good tastes, memories of childhood, memories of the dog barking and the pine trees against your house. Those "memories" are also computations of various conceptual events—the past, the experience of eating, the association of Mom and apple pie. *Pleasure.* Some very primitive parts of your brain are activated. It doesn't stop there—mental images are reconstructed, setting into action a whole new set of circuits that must construe the right image, color, and shape, define it in a reasonable and recognizable image, and reproduce it in association with the other neurological and psychological events occurring almost instantaneously. And this is an enormous simplification of what actually happens. The physiological processes would baffle the most sophisticated computer, utilizing biochemical powers that stagger the imagination. How did an odor from a greasy-spoon diner on Main Street, U.S.A., suddenly translate into visions of your childhood, memories of your mother, pictures of a time when your family was together? And what did that have to do with your brother's living 2,000 miles away, the pine trees pummeling the house, and the dog barking? How did smell lead to hunger? How did smell conjure up a slice of memory? Why does it all add up to pleasure?

You simply don't know. You don't have to know, because your mind made instant associations: smell→Mom's apple pie→I want to eat it. Everything else took care of itself. If you were conscious of the entire process you would be lost in the computations, drowning in connections long after the smell had abated and the apple pie was cold and stale.

Consciousness enables us to adapt and solve the problems of our environment. The complex process that supports consciousness is simply beyond our awareness. What seems easy and direct is really the composite of a vast array of neural circuits working to create an illusion of simplicity. I smell apple pie and I'm hungry. I see the ocean and know it is blue. I touch the snow and feel the cold. My stomach rumbles and I'm hungry. I meet someone and fall in love. I hear a joke and laugh. It all works so easily with so little effort. Consciousness affords us the illusion of simplicity— misleads us into believing that our neural circuitry is simple. The most basic behaviors are actually highly complex, involving intricate connections. By being conscious of the illusion—recognizing that awareness itself is deceptive—we can maximize our Stone Age computers.

4. In order to accomplish the diverse functions necessary in humans, neural circuits are specialized.

Specialized groups of neural circuits can be classified as "mental modules." "The mind is a set of modules," writes Pinker, "but the modules are not encapsulated boxes or circumscribed swatches on the surface of the brain." Pinker explains that these modules are organized by our genetics—but it doesn't mean that there is a gene for every trait, every behavior, and every personality aspect in our makeup. Nor does it invalidate the importance of learning. We tend to polarize our thinking. In other words, if we say that our mind has evolved through natural selection, it doesn't mean that everything we do is biologically adaptive. Nor does it mean we have the same minds as apes. "And the ultimate goal of natural selection," notes Pinker, "is to propagate genes, but that does not mean that the ultimate goal of people is to propagate genes" (pp. 23, 24).

Pinker proposes, along with other evolutionary psychologists, that the brain is a physiological organ, and the mind is essentially what the brain *does.* Similarly, the heart is a physiological organ, and pumping blood is what it does. These distinctions are critical in understanding that mind and body are not two distinguishable features of humankind. They are actually descriptions of the same phenomenon.

If the mind is the function of the brain, then what, exactly, is its function? Pinker proposes that the mind is actually a system of organs which "we can think of as psychological faculties or mental modules" (p. 27). These mental modules, composed of neural circuits, are highly specialized to accomplish specific jobs. They interconnect, allowing communication between modules. This follows the essential differentiation of the human body. Our body runs fluidly because stomach tissue works differently than liver tissue, bone cells work differently than blood cells. If they were all alike, we would not be able to live. "A jack-of-all-trades is master of none," writes Pinker, "and that is just as true for our mental organs as for our physical organs."

What does the existence of "mental modules" mean? The brain is not a general problem-solver but works, in concept, like a computer to integrate the parts into a meaningful whole. This means that each part or module has to have a program to accomplish its job. To illustrate, a sound card in a computer is programmed to reproduce specific sounds, whether beep, a voice, or jazz. It has to have the program to produce sounds but will do nothing until it receives instructions for the appropriate sound. A human hand can grip and throw a baseball but will do nothing until it receives instructions from the brain to do so. In the same context, mental modules are equipped with basic programming that enables them to carry out their function. Their basic programming makes certain assumptions that fill in for missing, faulty, or unavailable information. Obviously, these assumptions worked very well for our ancestors. The brain can be conceived of as an information-processing system of interconnected mental modules that work independently or in conjunction with one another to produce environmentally appropriate (and adaptive) behavior.

The concept of mental modules defies the old tabula rasa theory of being born without knowledge. Clearly, we accomplish quite a bit without learning or experience. These accomplishments are species-wide. While our cultures are vastly different, all humans see, talk, and think about objects in the same basic manner. Newborns don't learn to see or cry. They don't learn to hear or think. They suck, they respond to caregivers, they recognize fear—the list is long and diverse. Researchers have shown that human infants go through what are essentially the same basic stages of development that prepare them to live in their social, cultural, and familial environments. While glitches in the program occur—usually through physical disorders such as damage to the optic nerve, preventing vision— there are clear physiological and psychological programs that guide human development. This leads many people to argue that everything is genetically based—we will eventually reduce all behaviors to a sequence of genes. Once again, the human mind seeks to simplify the paradigm. Pinker argues otherwise. "There have been no discoveries of a gene for civility, language, memory, motor control, intelligence, or other complete mental systems, and there probably won't ever be" (p. 34). Mental modules are complicated, with intricate programs that can't be simplified in an intellectually soothing manner. In the same way that one bug can crash an entire computer, a genetic defect can mess up the entire process. It does not mean that the module, or the entire system, for that matter, is simple.

One must keep in mind that *learning* is a key to the entire system. Because it is so complex, with so many programs assisting function, the mind is "freed" to learn, to use the entire system to become an evolved problem-solver, one who can use powers of inference, logic, and reason to generate sophisticated behavior that is highly attuned to its environment. In other words, a creature of this kind would be able to adapt to its environment, create new things in the environment, and then secondarily adapt to its creations. Stone Age minds can—and do—create cyberspace.

5. We're still very Cro-Magnon.

In evolutionary terms, 10,000 years is a micromoment, a tiny speck of time. Cro-Magnon brains are still pretty much the same, with intact mental modules preprogrammed to assure our adaptation. What does that mean?

Simply stated, our minds were not designed to sit in traffic jams on endless highways; work in tight shoes and business suits in crowded skyscrapers; watch television and eat fatty junk food; and live in communities where we might not even know our next-door neighbor. Ornstein describes the modern human paradox:

> We are forever behind ourselves, adapting to keep up with a world that is past. We are like animals rooted in the ground, reaching for the stars. It is no wonder that we are stressed and break in the middle since our rules about how to adapt keep changing. (p. 75)

Who were our evolutionary recent ancestors, and why are we so poorly prepared to reach for the stars?

The hunter-gatherers were a nomadic bunch, doomed to follow the seasons and changes in vegetation, weather, and migratory patterns of animal prey. They wandered, always on the move for better foraging. And they wandered far—it was this behavior alone that led to humans' inhabiting all major continents and island groups on Earth. The human species was well designed for global dispersal. The key was in their unique ability to adapt to a vast array of environments—climate and topography did not deter them. Human innovation in creating technologies that eased adaptation is the same powerful force that today has polluted, decimated, and threatened to destroy the very planet that supports us. It is an intriguing conundrum—what makes us powerful also enables us to destroy ourselves.

Perhaps the greatest technological revolution occurred in those early years of global dispersal when some 5 to 8 million people lived around the world. Unlike the digital age, the Neolithic revolution was slower and more erratic. It began about 8000 B.C.E. The date is far from exact—it is an estimate of when a technological shift occurred in human subsistence. The key was food. People discovered that food could be cultivated and animals domesticated, which enabled them to have greater control of the environment.

In today's eyes, an agricultural revolution seems ordinary, certainly nothing to write home about. Understanding this dramatic shift in human behavior affords enormous insight into our more recent adaptations in virtual reality. Consider the changes. By cultivating food, people became less dependent on the environment and consequently more in control of their destiny. No longer did they have to wander to survive; the efforts of hunting and gathering were shifted to producing. Small nomadic groups could band into towns where people could gather, live together, have greater protection, and specialize their skills. It wasn't an easier way of life, only very different, setting the groundwork for what we now call civilization. What else happened when people began to stay put and live together in larger groups?

More children were born and survived to adulthood. It's been estimated that human population increased tenfold with the introduction of agriculture. People living so closely together were forced to develop new social systems and new tensions in protecting their territories. By remaining in the same place, individuals were able to specialize. For example, if communal efforts were aimed toward cultivation and animal domestication, those people who could make and develop tools were allowed to pursue their skills to further improve technology. New problems had to be solved: how to store and channel water, how to cook and preserve food, how to design different types of shelter, how to utilize the new materials in everything from clothing to containers. Inevitably, villages located in areas rich in certain commodities would produce more materials in demand by villages who did not have such advantages. Exchanges between villages took place, leading to one of the most powerful incentives in human history—trade. Even social roles changed. Men took over the roles of heavy labor, creating new tools and weapons, and taming and breeding large animals. It's been suggested that during this time the social and economic position of women declined, leading to the unequal status of men and women so apparent in ensuing civilization. During this time one of the most famous cities was built—Jericho. Jericho still exists today, with a human population of over 25,000 people. It highlights the fact that human "civilized" history is pitifully brief.

The move from Cro-Magnon to Jericho, from steam engines to computers, suddenly looks very different. How could we change in such a brief period of time? So much has happened, and yet, in fact, very little has changed. We still live in families. We still live in cities. We still war over territories. We still smile and laugh, cry and grieve. Our environments have shifted, but our Cro-Magnon brains were designed to adapt to any environment. Adaptation was hastened by human-designed technology. Whether it was technology that invented igloos or wigwams, pottery or circuit boards, it all served to enhance human adaptability. Humans were designed to develop technology that would enhance adaptation.

We need to understand the nature of human technology. As a construct, it is a neonate in the history of humankind. We tend to think of it only in modern terms—digital technology, computer technology, rocket technology. But those hunters and gatherers used some very sophisticated technology without ever knowing about microchips.

The actual term *technology* evolved in the nineteenth century during a time of enormous mechanical invention, including such things as locomotives, streetcars, transition from iron to steel, and vastly increased mechanized factory production. It initially referred to the practical arts or applications of scientific discoveries. Physicist and philosopher of science Stephen Toulmin proposes that it was the result of "revolutions in natural sciences and history," where Newton's science and Descartes's philosophy created a "world of physical theory and technical practice" (p. 14). The idea of technology gave more status to mechanical invention, applying an abstract concept to a very practical, concrete process.

Obviously the concept existed long before the word, but the word gave people a new way to describe the human condition. Many began to view human development as the story of technological progress. Technological time periods were identified in history: the Stone Age (stone tools), Bronze Age (bronze tools), Industrial Revolution (machines), and Information Age (computers). But technology involves more than titles and inventions—it is an intrinsic evolutionary tool to enhance adaptation. Technology represents human innovation at its very best and very worst, reconfiguring social realities and creating new demands to adapt to technologically created environments. Essentially, technology is the use of organized knowledge, a specific body of information produced to solve problems. Whether we are solving problems in assuring a continuing supply of grain, as was accomplished in the Neolithic revolution, or in how to communicate in disembodied place called cyberspace, the concept of technology is the same.

As history has so clearly demonstrated, dramatic changes in technology lead to dramatic changes in human behavior. Consider the early technological developments when humans discovered how to create fire or build shelter. Imagine the change in lifestyle. Similarly, subsequent technological innovations have had enormous impact on human life. Think about the immediate and long-term effects of the following technologies:

- the invention of writing in Mesopotamia, circa 3000 B.C.E.
- the Greek discovery of using marble columns in architecture, circa 5 B.C.E.
- the development of the printing press between 1445 and 1450
- James Watts's construction of the first steam engine in Scotland during the 1760s
- Alexander Graham Bell's telephone in 1876
- the discovery of penicillin by Sir Alexander Fleming in 1929
- the first personal computer in 1975
- the introduction of the World Wide Web in 1990

What would life be like without that technology? Present technological innovation in the Age of Information has nurtured a human population of "cyborgs," where there is a physiological and psychological merger with machines. Along with each new technological leap there are significant alterations in how we view our loved ones, our worlds, and ourselves.

Is this a new twist in evolution?

Heinz Hartmann, in his seminal book written in the mid-twentieth century, *Ego Psychology and the Problem of Adaptation*, attempts to resolve this dilemma. He suggests that people utilize synthetic as well as natural changes that involve a "psychophysical" system. First, human behavior adapts the environment to human function. For example, the Neolithic people began to cultivate wheat so they no longer had to forage. This created a "new" environment that required a secondary adaptation. The new environment is one that humans have helped to create. The same people who adapted by cultivating wheat now have to adapt to a new set of circumstances. They need to set up a permanent settlement so they can tend and protect their fields. That means new means of shelter and new means of social organization. Hartmann concludes that the process of human adaptation is influenced by the individual and the external environment, as well as species evolution (pp. 26, 27). Individual or social adaptation may compliment—or clash—with species adaptation. And beneath all these changes resides that old Stone Age brain.

Hartmann notes that humans have to adapt not only to the conditions and communities they have helped create, but also to those that have been designed by people who came before and during their lifetimes. In other words, the more technology, the more we must adapt to our invention. While early technologies were slow, giving humans more time to catch on, the very existence of technology accelerates the development of new technology. It took nearly 9,000 years to move from the Neolithic agricultural revolution to the Model T Ford, but it took only forty-one years to move from mass production of the Model T to *Sputnik*. Human technology seems to take on a life of its own, which is apparent in the steady growth of the number and frequency of technological discoveries. In 10,000 years of "modern" human history, more scientists are alive and working today than ever before. The more scientists, the more discoveries, and the more advances in technology. The more technology, the faster the change, the more humans adapt to it and, accordingly, produce the people and the machines adapted to the environment.

Evolution cannot keep up with the pace. Our brains have not, and will not, change at the rate of our technology. Built-in adaptive mechanisms enable us to survive. After all, that is what humans do best—survive in new environments. Yet the inconsistencies are all around us. We're terrified of snakes but will think nothing about cars whizzing by us at seventy miles an hour. In an electronic age where information is our most valuable commodity, we crave youth, the time of life when knowledge is at its minimum. We get jittery in the dark but think nothing about climbing aboard a metal cylinder and flying 35,000 feet above the earth's surface. We're more afraid of the mouse that scurries across our floor than the electronic socket that can zap us with 110 volts.

Welcome to the new millennium.

FROM CAVES
TO CYBERSPACE

He faces his world. The hunter-gatherer is known for his courage, for his willing-
ness to brave uncharted lands, leap across dangerous precipices and wade through
swamps that plunge him into wild, perilous terrain. He takes a deep, cleansing
breath and begins his search. His piercing green eyes turn inward. What am I
looking for? *The answers rumble wordlessly from within. There is a road to follow*
but he can't see it. Just move. *He squares his shoulders and proceeds in the sweet,*
fluid motion of his species. There is somewhere to go. I know it.

    The hunter-gatherer relentlessly seeks the place. And then, on the horizon, it
appears: a community. A village of others like himself, a warm fire to share. I want
to talk. *It comes as a surprise, an idea deeply entrenched within him.* I want to be
with them.

    He enters the gates of the community and is welcomed. "Stranger," *they say,*
"identify yourself." And so the hunter-gatherer gives them his name, his tribe, his
place of birth. It does not take long before he is a part of this place where other
hunter-gatherers meet and laugh and argue and love and protect their homestead
from marauders. He belongs. That's all he ever really wanted.

The hunter-gather sighs with contentment. He logs off from his virtual community and returns, in mind, to the icy, anonymous apartment he calls home. From the hallway, he can hear voices. It doesn't matter. The hunter-gatherer doesn't even know his neighbor's name.

*H*OW DO WE leap from caves to cyberspace? The answer is simple: we don't. Our Cro-Magnon brains still seek the same comforts, fear the same dangers, and use the same mental modules to think, hear, see, and feel. We carry briefcases instead of spears and eat fast food instead of wild berries, but the process essentially remains the same. We adapt because we are designed to learn and invent technology that allows us to shape our environments. But we pollute and build nuclear bombs because our minds and our philosophies have not kept pace with our technology.

It would be easy to attribute everything we say and do to a concrete evolutionary cause-and-effect, but that feeds into our need to simplify and classify our worlds. Yes, we are designed to be able to accomplish all that our species has achieved, but we are also designed to learn, to experience consciousness, to invent, and to utilize virtual realities.

Conceptually, the psychological difference between actual reality and virtual reality is simple. In actual reality the environmental input depends on concrete, physical information that is perceived through sensory receptors and interpreted, stored, and processed in the mind. In virtual reality the environmental input is received through internal experiences such as mental images, memories, ideas, stored perceptions, fantasies, and emotions that have little or no mediation from the physical environment. Even virtual-reality simulations, such as film and television, have limited physical environmental input. After all, a screen is simply a flat, two-dimensional object with patterns of light coordinated to sound. The real action takes place in the mind.

Consider the essence of a virtual reality. It is a disembodied experience that occurs in the mind, a series of mental images strung together to create a nonphysical environment. To understand the adaptive importance of being able to experience a virtual reality, we first must define the nature of a mental image. Pinker describes mental imagery as "the engine that drives our thinking about objects in space" (p. 284). He suggests that it involves intellect and emotions, utilizing memory, visual mental modules, and cortical connectivity to produce what all of us can readily recognize as a mental image. But take a closer look. Mental images are essentially fragments; they are only parts of a complete picture. To illustrate, imagine a wooden rocking chair. You probably see the shape, the color of the wood, even a rocking motion. Can you feel it? Is it old or new, well-constructed or ready for the garbage bin?

Now imagine that same chair with an old woman sitting in it, rocking gently. Her soft, wrinkled hands grip the arms. A frayed red afghan is tossed over her lap. Look closer. Wisps of gray hair lay unattended across her forehead, falling haphazardly to her shoulders. Her skin is deathly pale, her blue eyes glazed as she stares at a point beyond your sight. A single tear slowly makes its way down her face, drifting between the furrows of her wrinkled skin, telling a story of horrific loss, of grief far beyond the chair she sits in and the ancient hands gripping the wood.

What happened in your mind? The same wooden rocking chair took on a persona. The old woman crying, the grief, the frayed red afghan brought you into a virtual moment with the potential to lead you deep into a story filled with sadness, joy, tragedy, pain. The virtual tale was limited only by your imagination and mental involvement. Mental imagery is only one part of the virtual-reality experience. Like grains of sand that create the beach, virtual realities involve an array of mental modules that conjure up intellectual, emotional, and spatial experiences. These experiences are very much a part of human adaptation, facilitating species-wide functions that, in an evolutionary context, enhance survival.

What are some of the critical evolutionary functions of virtual realities?

INFORMATION-PROCESSING

As discussed earlier, the human mind can be seen as an information-processing system. *Homo sapiens sapiens* is a highly complex species with mental modules programmed to respond in specific ways to information from the environment. This information can be processed, stored in memory, and used for learning, enabling humans to control, rather than be controlled by, their environments.

Evolutionary psychologists maintain that form follows function; in other words, the form evolves in response to the need to resolve adaptive problems. In this context, what abilities would best serve a life form more dependent on intellect than on physical prowess?

Think about the pitiful physical odds against human survival. The human newborn, unlike many other species, is totally dependent on adult care. Other life forms have bodies far better equipped for physical survival. Giraffe babies can get up and follow their mothers only a few hours after birth. It usually takes a human baby at least a year to toddle across the floor. Zebras, who live for an average of twenty years, are fully mature by age three. It takes years before a human child can even approach self-sufficiency. In the electronic age almost 25 percent of an average lifespan is devoted to "growing up" and preparing an individual for self-sufficiency. Most animals are also equipped with built-in weapons—claws that defend, teeth that rip, wings that can be used for rapid attack or retreat. Bats hear better than people; eagles see better; lions run faster; seals swim more efficiently. In order to survive, the human species developed information-processing abilities that substituted minds for hopelessly inferior bodies. Information-processing is critical to the species—equivalent to sea gulls flying, dolphins swimming, and horses running. Without information-processing, humans would have been a long-extinct dinner item in the animal kingdom.

Virtual realities play an intriguing role in information-processing. In a virtual reality people can process information independently from environmental input. The advantage is clear: you don't have to be *present* in order to study, assess, or invent adaptive strategies. For example, your environment is cold. Programmed mental modules make it very clear that to survive you need to maintain body temperature. Behaviorally, that means "get warm." Of course, this is a flagrant simplification of the process, for it does not address the vast array of physiological and psychological connections that are made to bring to consciousness "I am cold." But you really don't need all of that information. What you do need is a conscious mind telling you that you need to get warm. You look at your choices. Build a fire from the branches on your neighbor's tree? Borrow a nearby bearskin? Both will work. At least, they will work for the moment. The fire and the coat will make you "warm."

Information-processing takes the problem to the next step. How can I be "warm" all of the time? You sit around the fire in the cave, wrapped in a bearskin, and begin to wonder. Your mind processes virtual information: where will a fire keep me really warm? How can I find such a place? Maybe my neighbor's cave is better situated. Why? Is it better protected from the cold than my cave? You run a playback of the cave in your mind. The walls are thicker, with only one entrance. There are no drafts. Instead of wearing the bearskin, you could put it across the opening. Wouldn't it be interesting if you could build a cave that fit those requirements?

What you did was to place yourself in a mental or virtual environment and process information gleaned from memory, learned knowledge from your environment, and reasoning skills to come to a conclusion: build a better cave. You didn't have to go into the snow, you didn't even have to get cold. All you had to do was to enter your virtual environment and redesign it to suit your needs. It took quite a bit of mind power: numerous mental modules connecting unconsciously, neurons firing, and the activation of those elusive qualities known as human reasoning and ingenuity. But it worked. Theoretically, the adaptive problem of "how not to get cold" was solved in the comfort of your bearskin.

Mental images can be easily conjured and plugged into a virtual-reality scene. Trial-and-error becomes a disembodied process: will a spear make me warm? No. Will a rock make me warm? No. Will better shelter make me warm? Yes. Like the old lady in the rocking chair, the "story" is constructed in a virtual-reality scenario. What kind of shelter? How can I build it? Where can I put it? The information is processed without physical environmental input, vastly increasing range, flexibility, and speed of solution. This aspect of virtual reality is so common that most of us are hardly aware that it actually occurs. Have you ever had a problem at work? Did you solve it by "playing out" in your mind what should be done? Ever plan a special occasion, like a first date or a surprise party, where you visualized the entire story in your mind? How many times have you made decisions, good or bad, based on a mental scenario? Pinker writes that "many creative people claim to 'see' the solution to a problem in an image." He relates Einstein's experience of imagining "what it would be like to ride on a beam of light or drop a penny in a plummeting elevator" (p. 285). Virtual information-processing short-circuits the need for direct experience in "reality." We can plan, figure, devise, and act out quickly and safely in our personal virtual realities. Once the information is processed we can decide whether our virtual reality stories will play out realistically in the environment. If we don't like the results, we can simply revise the scenario.

Naturally, the process isn't foolproof. The first date can be a disaster, the surprise party can crash, and the brilliant intellectual analysis can be meaningless when tested in actual reality. Yet if that occurs you can chalk it up to "learning a new lesson." Either way, the process saved you quite a bit of trial and error.

We can rely more on our minds than on our bodies to adapt to our environments. We can constantly update, adjust, and extend our information to enable us to avoid dangerous or inappropriate scenarios. Of course, human psychology plays a distinct role in compelling us to *want to* make these distinctions. This falls under the aegis of mental health. We might end up with socially inappropriate choices, disordered thinking, or behavior that defies cultural norms. In other words, there's quite a lot of room for glitches in the program.

By the same token, virtual-reality simulations offer similar advantage with far less individual work—*they* provide the virtual data for us to process. The filmmakers, the actors, the writers, the camera people, the editors—they construct the virtual realities for us. What a powerful seduction! We get all the "goods" without the work.

INFORMATION STORAGE

Clearly, virtual realities are a critical part of information-processing. However, if we had to reconstruct a virtual reality every time we needed to process internally generated information, it would take an enormous amount of time. Why do you think it was so easy to visualize the rocking chair and the old woman with the frayed red afghan? Now try to picture something else. Visualize an *otus asio*. What do you see? Is it frightening? Does it make you smile? Or is there a blank in your mind—a void where there would ordinarily appear to be a mental image? Watch what happens when you find out what an *otus asio* is. It's the species name for the common barn owl. Now what's in your mind? Probably a picture of that strange, "wise"-looking bird with its large head, neckless body, round, forward-placed eyes, and tiny beak. Can you see it in the barn, way up there in the eaves? Can you see the barn? Stacks of hay, the familiar farm animal smell, and look—there's a gray dappled horse in the stall. Do you see the slightly rusty farm equipment leaning against the walls and the sun streaming in between the slats of wood? The difference between the two experiences is that you had no memory of *otus asio* (unless, of course, you have a strong background in animal biology). But you do have a virtual scenario of a barn owl and a barn. Perhaps you have never even been to a real barn, but maybe you've seen pictures, watched *Mr. Ed* in reruns, or experienced "barn" in the thousands of "barn" movies or television shows you've seen in your lifetime. Whatever the input, you processed the information about "barn" and stored a mental image in your mind. Now what would happen if you were asked the simple question, "What is happening to the owl in your barn?" Can you tell the story?

The power of an information-processing creature equipped with extensive information storage can stagger the imagination. Simply compare it to your computer. What would happen if your computer could do everything you wanted except store information? Each time you turned it on you would have to reinstall all your software; redo all your documents; reprogram all its functions. By the time you finished all the work, there would be no energy or time left to do additional information-processing. Memory in a computer is a critical component, one that has been increasing exponentially over the years. The newest computers can measure memory in terms of a terabyte, or a trillion bytes of information. It takes only eight measly terabytes to store all the data in the Library of Congress, yet they still can't come close to emulating the human information-processing utilized in sitting down to dinner with your family and figuring out who is in a good mood.

"SAFE" NAVIGATION

Brent zooms over the clouds, preparing to land. He checks his instruments—everything looks okay. Ready to land. *Brent grins. The airplane in his hands responds instantly to his commands.* Descend. *Remember, it's a tight landing with a short runway. Not much room to play around. Brent increases the angle without adjusting his speed. Suddenly the sirens go off, ringing loudly in his ears. Stall. The plane is in a stall. Brent breaks into a sweat as he struggles to regain control. It doesn't work. The aircraft spirals to the ground, crashing in an empty field, instantly becoming a huge fireball with billows of black, heinous smoke.*

I did it again, *Brent says to the flight simulator.* Damn.

Safe navigation is serious business. Without it, students like Brent would never survive their education. Instead, virtual-reality simulations afford the elbow room to make some very serious mistakes. In an evolutionary context, the ability to navigate the environment safely has an enormous adaptive advantage to protecting life. You avoid a lot of the risks.

Let's look at it another way. As information-processing life forms, humans evolved not only the ability to integrate data but also the desire to obtain it. For instance, what good is it to have a life form dependent on food (nutrients) without a corresponding mechanism that compels it to eat dinner? Likewise, what good is it to have an information-dependent species without a corresponding mechanism that compels it to seek and consume knowledge? Dr. Stephan Kaplan, professor at the University of Michigan, writes that "exploration of one's environment in order to know it well enough to range widely and yet not get lost was thus an important element in a larger survival pattern" (p. 584). Hunters and gatherers were programmed to wander and explore far enough to absorb new knowledge but not far enough where they would experience confusion and disorientation. This worked well for wandering peoples—they could follow the herds, move with the seasons, find new places and survive using the skills needed in their environment. For instance, a hunter-gatherer living in the mountains could readily adapt his or her skills to the foothills, but put that same person in the tundra and he or she would not know how to survive. In an age of fast and easy transport, we call this same phenomenon "culture shock." A New Yorker can survive in California, but put that same New Yorker in Lilongwe, Malawi, in southeast Africa, and she will probably have big problems.

The need to understand and explore was programmed into humans. Clearly, this is still very much a part of the human condition. Ideally, a system that would allow safe exploration or navigation would enhance human information-processing potential. Let's go back to that New Yorker in Lilongwe. How would the experience change if our New Yorker spent some time "safely" navigating Lilongwe? She might watch a video on the culture of Malawi, learning what the buildings, stores, and daily life looks like in the capital city. Then she might read a book on Chichewa, the Malawi language, and learn a few words. She might search the Internet to get an idea about the culture, political systems, and popular tourist spots in the country. Last, she might find the latest Malawi *kwacha* monetary exchange rates, learn what Malawians eat in their restaurants, and practice how to be polite and respectful of the people who live there. The same New Yorker would arrive in Lilongwe, after many virtual trips, knowing what to expect.

Whether going to Lilongwe, figuring out how to avoid the bear's den, or planning a strategy for corporate war, a virtual system for safe navigation offers enormous adaptive advantage.

THE CONSCIOUS SPIRIT

As discussed earlier, consciousness is generally seen as awareness—knowledge of what is happening to *you*. Consciousness equips us to change, grow, expand, exploit, and adapt to solve the problems of our environment. The conscious spirit refers to the experiences we perceive as transcending our environments—a virtual space where we maintain the illusion that "anything" can happen. In the conscious spirit we can experience deep spiritual and religious convictions, fantasy, illusion, transcendent visions and ideas that contain virtual content that clearly separates the body from the spirit.

Human history has repeatedly demonstrated the power of the conscious spirit. People have fought wars, given and taken human life, and created massive physical monuments to what they perceive as God. Individuals have produced great works of art, great works of thought, and great works of human invention. In the same context, humans have pursued great evil, designed psychological and technological instruments of torture, murdered other humans, and established an art out of a behavior demonstrated by no other animal on earth—war.

The conscious spirit maintains the illusion that there is a power that transcends human biology, giving us insight into a virtual place where the ordinary, mediocre, and concrete have no impact. The conscious spirit, by definition, has produced the very best and the very worst in individuals as well as in the species. It gives us the illusion that we can do and accomplish *anything,* move beyond the confines of our biological definitions and control what in actual reality is far beyond our power. While we walk on the street in the conscious mind, we fly in the clouds in our conscious spirit. It is truly ironic that the same seat of genius can give birth to great thought from Albert Einstein, wondrous art from Michelangelo, noble commitment from Mother Teresa, and flagrant evil from Adolf Hitler. Pinker describes it this way:

> In a well-designed system, the components are black boxes that perform their functions as if by magic. That is no less true of the mind. The faculty with which we ponder the world has no ability to peer inside itself or our other faculties to see what makes them tick. That makes us the victims of an illusion: that our own psychology comes from some divine force or mysterious essence or almighty principle. (p. 563)

The conscious spirit affords us a continuing sense of mystery about ourselves and our spirituality. The solution to this mystery can't be proven; instead, it compels us to continually search for answers. According to Kaplan, mystery is "the promise of information if one can venture deeper into the scene" (p. 588). It is a powerful force in evolutionary psychology, because "mystery" infers that one could learn more, absorb more information through exploration and the consequent alteration of vantage point. In other words, humans love mystery because it promises the potential acquisition of more information. And as information-processing systems, we need a constant data feed.

DENIAL OF DEATH

Who wants to think about death? We talk about it, we write about it, we read about it, and we watch it on television and in the movies almost every day. But it is always someone else's death—not our own.

Most people don't want to think about their own deaths or the deaths of their loved ones. Even those with the deepest spiritual convictions who believe firmly in life after death find that the concept of death presents a formidable obstacle. The paradox, as we all know so well, is that if we thought of death every day—if it were part of every step we took, every breath we breathed—we would never be able to live.

Consider the conflict inherent in that paradox. Death is a part of life. We all know that. We have all "lost" to death. We all "know" what it is like. The death of a pet brings on sadness, loss, and often the need to replace it as quickly as possible. The death of a loved one brings on a prolonged period of psychological grief. The thought of our own death terrifies us, yet there is nothing we can do. We can avoid, delay, and perhaps immortalize our work or our genes, but the person we know as "I" will eventually die.

It is the flip side to self-awareness. Self-awareness tells us we're alive, but it also gives us that intolerable piece of information—we will also die.

Ernest Becker, in his seminal book *The Denial of Death*, addresses this painful human paradox. His ideas, discussed further in Part II, help explain why virtual reality is an adaptive mechanism to promote survival of the human species. Consider this: in virtual reality we shed our bodies—we become part of an environment where we experience the illusion that biology does not count. And if we're not biological creatures, we don't have to follow the essential rule of biology: to live is to die. Perhaps cyberspace is the best example of our need to deny death. When we play a game we collect points and lives. We can easily "die" and resurrect ourselves with the click of a mouse. We can even enter wars, from martial arts confrontations to technological holocausts, and survive to play again. If we're not gameplayers we can give ourselves multiple identities and surf the Net. If one identity is "killed"—becomes undesirable or unpopular—all we have to do is recycle our "self" to another identity. Everyone is immortal in cyberspace because mortality—death—does not exist.

It is the perfect illusion to keep a self-aware species happily hunting and gathering.

BIBLIOGRAPHY
FOR PART I

Andersen, H. C. 1994. The emperor's new clothes. In *Twelve Tales*, translated by E. Blegvad. New York: Margaret K. McElderry Books.

Aronova-Tiuntseva, Y., and C. F. Herreid. No date. Hemophilia: "The royal disease." *Case Studies in Science* [Online], 7 pp. Available: http://ublib.buffalo.edu/libraries/projects/cases/hemo.htm [December 24, 1998].

Barkow, J. H., L. Cosmides, and J. Tooby, eds. 1992. *The Adapted Mind: Evolutionary Psychology and the Generation of Culture*. New York: Oxford University Press.

Becker, E. 1973. *The Denial of Death*. New York: The Free Press.

Bloom, H. April 12, 1997. Reality is a shared hallucination. *Telepolis* [Online], 9 pp. Available: http://www.heise.de/tp/english/special/glob/2227/1.html [September 12, 1998].

————. January 20, 1998. The conformity police. *Telepolis* [Online], 10 pp. Available: http://www.heise.de/tp/english/special/glob/2248/1.html [September 12, 1998].

————. February 26, 1998. The huddle and the squabble—group fission. *Telepolis* [Online], 8 pp. Available: http://www.heise.de/tp/english/glob/2278/ 1.html [September 11, 1998].

Bowlby, J. 1991. *Charles Darwin: A New Life.* New York: W. W. Norton & Company.

Caribbean lizards evolve independently. April 1, 1998. *ScienceDaily* [Online], 3 pp. Available: http://www.sciencedaily.com/releases/1998/04/980401074442. htm [December 24, 1998].

Carroll, L. 1994. *The Collected Stories of Lewis Carroll.* New York: Citadel Press.

Christensen, J. November 24, 1998. Teachers fight for Darwin's place in U.S. *New York Times Cybertimes* [Online], 4 pp. Available: http://nytimes.com [December 14, 1998].

Cosmides, L., and J. Tooby 1997. *Evolutionary Psychology: A Primer. Center for Evolutionary Psychology* homepage [Online], 29 pp. Available: http://www.psych. ucsb.edu/research/cep/primer.htm [December 1, 1998].

Darwin, C. 1859. *On the Origin of Species* [Online]. Available: http://www.literature. org/Works/Charles-Darwin/origin/preface.html [December 14, 1998].

———. 1871. *The Descent of Man* [Online]. Available: http://www.bio.bris.ac.uk/ resource/darwindm.txt [January 7, 1997].

———. 1962. *The Voyage of of the* Beagle. New York: Doubleday.

Gallant, R. A. 1972. *Charles Darwin: The Making of a Scientist.* New York: Doubleday.

Goodstein, L. December 21, 1997. Christians and scientists: New light for creationism. *New York Times Cybertimes* [Online], 3 pp. Available: http://nytimes. com [December 14, 1998].

Greenhouse, L. June 27, 1997. High court voids curb on "Indecent" Internet material. *New York Times Cybertimes* [Online], 4 pp. Available: http://nytimes. com [January 4, 1999].

Hartmann, H. 1958. *Ego Psychology and the Problem of Adaptation.* New York: International Universities Press.

Henahan, S. July 10, 1997. Neanderthal: No relation. *Access Excellence* [Online], 3 pp. Available: http://www.gene.com/ae/WN/SUA10/neander797.html [December 18, 1998].

Jung, C. G. 1934. The concept of the collective unconscious. *The Archetypes and the Collective Unconscious.* Collected works, vol. 9. [On-line]. Available: http:// www. geocities.com/Athens/158/collective.htm [January 22, 1997].

———. No date. Achetypes as defined by Carl Jung. *The Nature of the Archetypes* [Online], 4 pp. Available: http://www.acs.appstate.edu/~davisct/nt/jung. html [September 19, 1998].

———. No date. *Carl Jung* [Online], 13 pp. Available: http://www. oldsci. eiu.edu/psychology/Spencer/Jung.html [September 16, 1998].

———. No date. A definition of archetype. *The Archetypes and the Collective Uncon-*

scious [Online], 4 pp. Available: http://www.trinity.edu/~cspinks/myth/ motif.html [September 17, 1998].

Kaplan, S. 1992. Environmental preference in a knowledge-seeking, knowledge-using organism. In *The Adapted Mind: Evolutionary Psychology and the Generation of Culture*, edited by J. H. Barkow, L. Cosmides, and J. Tooby. New York: Oxford University Press.

Lampmann, J. March 25, 1998. A frontier of medical research: Prayer. *Christian Science Monitor* [Online], 4 pp. Available: http://csmonitor/com/durable/ 1998/03/25/us/us.1.html [September 15, 1998].

Milgram, P., and F. Kishino. 1994. A taxonomy of mixed reality visual displays. *IEICE Transactions on Information Systems* [Online], 15 pp. Available: http:// vered.rose.utoronto.ca/people/paul_dir/IEICE94/ieice.html [January 4, 1999].

Minsky, M. 1982. Why people think computers can't. *AI Magazine* 3 (4).

————. 1990. Logical vs. analogical or symbolic vs. connectionist or neat vs. Scruffy. In *Artificial Intelligence at MIT, Expanding Frontiers*, edited by Patrick H. Winston [Online], 21 pp. Available: http://www.ai.mit.edu/people/minsky/ papers/SymbolicVs.Connectionist.txt [December 24, 1998].

————. No date. *Society of Mind* [Online], 2 pp. Available: http://brainop. media. mit.edu/text-site/libretto/marvin.html [December 26, 1998].

Ornstein, R. 1991. *The Evolution of Consciousness: The Origins of the Way We Think.* New York: Simon & Schuster.

Overview of human origins. No date. *Long Foreground: Human Prehistory* [Online], 16 pp. Available: http://www.wsu.edu:8001/vwsu/gened/learn-modules/ top_longfor/lfopen-index.html [December 16, 1998].

Pinker, S. 1997. *How the Mind Works.* New York: W. W. Norton.

Quinney, P. No date. The last Neanderthal. *ScienceNet* [Online], 7 pp. Available: http://www.campus.bt.com/public/ScienceNet/publications/neanderthal. html [December 8, 1998].

Recer, P. April 28, 1998. Human ancestors may have spoken far earlier. *Nando.net* [Online], 2 pp. Available: http://www.nando.net/newsroom/ntn/health/ 042898/health6_24888_noframes.html [December 18, 1998].

Roszak, T. 1996. Evolution and the transcendence of mind. *Mental Health Net Perspectives* [Online], 5 pp. Available: http://www.cmhc.com/perspectives/ articles/art05964.htm [September 12, 1998].

Schuster, C. S., and S. S. Ashburn. 1986. *The Process of Human Development: A Holistic Life-Span Approach.* Boston: Little, Brown.

Spielvogel, J. J. 1991. *Western Civilization.* St. Paul, Minn.: West.

Stearns, P. N., M. Adas, and S. B. Schwartz. No date. The agrarian revolution and the birth of civilization. *World Civilizations, the Global Experience.* [Online], 7 pp. Available: http://www.stetson.edu/~psteeves/classes/agrrevolution.html [January 4, 1999].

Study finds link between religious faith and recovery from depression. April 30, 1998. *Mental Health Net Reading Room* [Online], 2 pp. Available: http://www.cmhc.com/articles/depress8.htm [September 12, 1998].

Toulmin, S. 1990. *Cosmopolis: The Hidden Agenda of Modernity.* New York: The Free Press.

TU biologist sees Darwinian selection in action. October 26, 1998. *ScienceDaily* [Online], 3 pp. Available: http://www.sciencedaily.com/releases/1998/04/980401074442.htm [December 24, 1998].

White, M., and J. Gribbin. 1995. *Darwin: A Life in Science.* New York: Dutton.

Wong, K. September 1997. Neanderthal notes. *Scientific American* [Online], 2 pp. Available: http://www.sciam.com/0997issue/0997scicit4.html [December 18, 1998].

PART II
TO BE OR
NOT TO BE

YOUR
VERY OWN SELF

Who am I? The question weighs heavy, gripping me unrelentlingly, haunting me when I least want to think. Am I the vicious, bestial creature of history, whose legacy has given me war and pain? Am I the gentle soul of philosophy whose legacy has given me the ability to love? Am I sibling to the primate, or parent to the computer? I look around and see the question, unanswered, in everyone's eyes. We get in our cars or climb on our trains, we go to work, we go to play, we sit mesmerized in front of the television watching electronic people dance in our imaginations. We live, we love, we lie through our complicated lives. What are we afraid of? Asking the questions or getting the answers?

*I*DENTIFYING THE SELF has been a constant theme throughout human history. Who am I? What is the self? Is it the same as or different from the soul? What does either of them have to do with occupying an organic body—a biological machine that lives, reproduces, and dies? Why is it even important to talk about the self? How does it shape our experience of reality and virtuality? Perhaps most important, what is the evolutionary purpose of having a conscious self? "What or where is the unified center of sentience that comes into and goes out of existence," Pinker asks, "that changes over time but remains the same entity, and that has a supreme moral worth?" (p. 558).

The very concept of *self* is virtual in nature and has been studied, discussed, and philosophized about since the dawn of human consciousness. Yet it isn't anything we can see, touch, or hear. It isn't something we can formulate in terms of molecules, cells, or biochemical responses. It isn't even something we can place neatly inside a mental module because it spans all modules, involves all neural networks, incorporates the very essence of "I."

"I," in fact, is very strange. Where does "I" live? Can you locate "I"? If so, how much brainpower does it take to generate an "I"? Is that brainpower bad, good, or something in between? Consider some intriguing aspects of "I."

You're walking down Seventh Avenue in Manhattan. Suddenly you come across a homeless man wrapped in filthy blankets. His face is smeared with dirt, his eyes dull and glazed. He looks at you directly. You pause. He pulls a dented coffee can from beneath the blankets, and his hand trembles as he shoves it in your path. In a small, slurred voice, the homeless man pleads, "Help."

You have two choices. You can ignore the plea, erase the glazed eyes from your mind, and continue on to the French restaurant where you're meeting a friend. Dinner will probably run you well over sixty dollars, including drinks, a bottle of your favorite Beaujolais, and the luscious specialty of the house, chocolate raspberry mousse.

The homeless man waits, staring. It's your choice.

Four quarters clink in your pocket. If you give him money he'll probably just buy drugs. You *know* that. After all, a recent article in the *Times* described how most of the homeless are dual diagnosis people—both mentally ill and substance abusers. So why pay for his crack?

On the other hand, what are four quarters? Nothing off your chocolate raspberry mousse.

The homeless man waits. You're confronted with a multitude of unanswerable questions. First, there is the issue of choice. Some call it free will. What does that mean? Pinker writes, "How can my actions be a choice for which I am responsible if they are completely caused by my genes, my upbringing, and my brain states?" (p. 558). The decision to toss those quarters into the dented coffee can is not preordained—but is it completely random either? Or is it something in between, something that is intrinsically linked to the "I" in you? Knowledge tells you otherwise. After all, there's that article in the *Times*. Will your quarters be tumbling into the dark and sinister world of street drugs? Where did you really get that knowledge? Just the newspaper? What about books, television, movies? Remember the movie you saw about Colombian drug lords, the one where the cartel shoots everyone, rich and poor, who doesn't cooperate? Is that where you want to toss your quarters? Yet there was that television show about the fourteen-year-old kid who got hooked. It was all about the horrific family struggle and all the people determined to get the kid off drugs. Is it a sinister world after all? And what does all your knowledge really mean? Maybe the most important aspect of the knowledge is that you *believe* it to be truth. Why? Why do you believe?

If you can't make the decision to part with your quarters based on free will or knowledge, how about old-fashioned morality? Doesn't a *good* person part readily with money to help those who can't have Beaujolais with their dinner? Good and bad, right and wrong: you're back into the quagmire of "I." Who am I? How do I construct the meaning of myself?

The self can be defined as a person's conception of what and who he or she *is*. Take that one step further. Self-awareness has a small but vital evolutionary function—it is an intrinsic part of consciousness, or the ability to make deliberate decisions, interpret environmental input, learn and process new information to solve adaptive problems. We recognize the "I" in behavior but turn to philosophies in order to attempt definition. And here is where philosophy has had such difficulty piecing it together. "We still haven't explained the inner forces of evolution that have led to the development of an animal capable of self-consciousness," writes Ernest Becker in *The Denial of Death*, "which is what we still must mean by soul—the mystery of the meaning of organismic awareness, of the inner dynamism and pulsations of nature" (p. 191).

Why is the nature of self so important in understanding reality in the age of psychotechnology? Self represents the core of who we are, the essence of how we perceive ourselves. In that context, understanding self sheds light on both reality and virtuality. It affects how we experience reality as a "shared hallucination" as well as how we experience virtuality as "consensus actuality." We need to know whether self is discernable or a concept that we are not designed to fully understand. Is it a divine spirit, something that defies human grasp? Is it a scientific construct that can be dissected into organic components? Or is it part of a system that creates what Pinker describes as "not a combination of body parts or brain states or bits of information, but a unity of selfness over time, a single locus that is nowhere in particular" (p. 564)? Perhaps, Pinker suggests, that not knowing the self, along with the other essential mysteries of life, is the price we pay for the vast diversity of our minds. In other words, we can know almost anything except our selves.

They are all virtual questions living in virtual realities.

You're back on Seventh Avenue, trying to decide whether to toss those quarters into a dented coffee can. There are still no answers. For a tiny moment there is a blank. Then one single question: "What should I do?"

"Help," the homeless man cries, his emaciated body shuddering beneath the blankets.

The four quarters crash against one another. No more time to think.

Quickly you throw three quarters into the coffee can. *Compromise.* You move beyond the homeless man. Behind you a muffled voice says, "Thank you." Without thinking, you turn the single, remaining quarter over and over in your pocket. The cool metal feels good against your fingers.

HOW DOES THE SELF COME TO BE?

We may not be able to fully determine the essence of self, but we can observe how it emerges. Humans are not biologically created as separate and distinct life forms but begin, in utero, as part of a symbiotic relationship with mother. In this context, life begins with separation. Separation refers to the process of disconnecting, of parting from mother to become an independent life form. Birth, seen as an event of emergence or trauma, is essentially the first human experience of separation.

Separation as a physical and psychological event is an intrinsic part of the human experience. The concept of separation involves all of us from scientists, artists, and philosophers to secretaries and truck drivers. From a global perspective, separation has led to vast changes in human civilization. Wars have been fought over separation, religions have been created from separation, and social mayhem has resulted from separation.

We begin as a part of someone else, in a place that's warm, dark, and supremely safe. Our needs are met without question. Our world moves in the deliciously slow, timeless motion of the womb. As fetal beings in utero, our only job is to grow. But growth is a double-edged sword. It brings us toward touch, feeling, and the use of our senses. It urges us into the experience of ourselves as separate, singular individuals. It reveals the fragile beauty of sunlight, the sweet harmony of music, the dizzying realm of taste, touch, and motion. At the same time, to grow is to be born, and birth removes us from the dark, safe, timeless world of the womb into the harsh, concrete light of reality.

When a baby is born, life must adapt. Inside the baby's body, things must change quickly. Baby must breathe on his or her own, cry, and learn to take in nourishment. Baby must adjust to the cold, the noise, and the piercingly bright light outside the womb. Outside the baby's body things must also change quickly. A couple is transformed into parents. A sibling's world is invaded by a new threat. Grandparents' position in the family is redefined. Maybe the baby enters a disordered world where he or she is whisked away from an addicted mother into the arms of social service.

The newborn nudges other players in the world. A pediatrician has a new patient. Another social security number is assigned. A community might have to alter its forecasts for school enrollment.

Mother's body changes too. She begins to lactate in preparation for feeding baby. Mental modules guide her, ideally, to bond with her child. If there are glitches in the "maternal" program, they begin to surface. Father changes also. Social and cultural roles take on new meaning. He too begins bonding with the new member of the family. Mental modules guide him, ideally, to seek to shelter and protect mother and child. Whether they live in a cave or a condo, the process unfolds.

Another process is initiated. This involves the harnessing of physiological and psychological development. Gradually, the newborn will learn to adapt to life outside the womb. Gradually, the newborn will begin a lifelong trek down a road that often pits the needs of the individual against the needs of the environment. Another "I" is born.

Look at it conceptually. The self emerges from physiological and psychological separation. The self, by definition, is individual—it cannot be conjoined. Developmental theorists have studied and written extensively about this phenomenon. While many argue about the meaning of the process, the content is essentially the same. When each human is born, he or she leaves the warm, safe environment of the womb and enters a cold, noisy world. The body is no longer attached to another; it becomes an information-processing machine of its own.

What has already occurred? When a human embryo is conceived it is simply a joining of egg and sperm cell. The result is a *potential* rather than a sentient being. As it develops in the womb, the embryo cycles through the evolutionary ladder until it arrives at the point that we would identify it as human. Where is this point in time? At conception? Four months into gestation? Six months? Even though science can describe what is happening, it can't tell us when that embryo becomes human. Perhaps that belongs to the realm of things we can never know. Either way, the embryo cannot exist without mother. It is essentially a parasitic relationship—it lives off of the body within which it's contained. Psychologically, this creates a symbiotic relationship, or one where there is no perception of separateness. How could there be? Physiologically as well as psychologically, the lives of mother and baby are *one* until the warm, comfy connection is severed and a tiny, helpless human being is alone in the world.

Is birth a coming out, a kind of debutante's entrance into the world? Or is it a trauma, a painful wrenching from warmth and security? Freud viewed birth as the latter, writing that "the first expression of anxiety which an individual goes through (in the case of human beings, at all events) is birth, and, objectively speaking, birth is a separation from the mother" (p. 591). This does not mean that all anxiety is correlated with separation. Freud argued that the human newborn, as a totally narcissistic creature, has no knowledge of mother as a separate person and thus does not, at birth, experience a subjective separation. This occurs later as the child goes through a development process that gradually diminishes the psychologically symbiotic relationship between mother and baby.

Psychologist Otto Rank, one of Freud's early followers and author of the seminal book *The Trauma of Birth*, also believes that human birth is a shock to the new baby. His conceptualization is far more dramatic than

Freud's. According to Rank, birth is not pleasant or uplifting. It is a horrendous shock to both body and mind. Birth is as painful to the child as it is to the mother. It begins by wrenching away the blanket, the protective amniotic fluid that kept baby warm and free from shocks. Then baby is forced down a cramped, inhospitable passage by merciless contractions that often distort its body. Birth ends in a painful burst of light, cold, noise, activity—shocking senses that had been soothed and regulated in the womb.

The psychological jolt delivered at birth heightens the trauma. Essentially, the fetus is forced to separate, cut loose, without choice, from all security. What was once a singular unit in the womb becomes two separate individuals in the world: mother and child. The newborn suddenly experiences intense anxiety and fear, exacerbated by total dependency. It is like being lurched from Eden into hell, ripped from warmth that offered totality into the chaos of cold, noise, light, and touch.

It's no wonder that newborns cry.

Rank argues that the first human separation (birth) is a basic, primal experience that leads to severe anxiety and fear. It is the terror of having to be separate, individual, and accordingly, isolated. Rank maintains it corresponds to the fear of separating from the whole, or the fear of becoming an individual. That fear expands to a more global emotion—the fear of life itself. In other words, the human is plunged into a terrifying world where he or she, at the moment of birth, is singular and alone. He or she is flooded with fear. What will happen in this unknown place? Why have I lost my safety? Please, *please* let me go back.

Slowly, as the newborn acclimates to life as a separate body, the opposite emerges—a fear of return, going back and losing the hard-earned individuality. It's not so bad after all. Please, *please* don't make me go back. Simply put, being afraid of losing individuality corresponds with a very primal terror of once again being dissolved into the whole, losing separation and self. In other words, the fear of death.

Rank's belief suggests that once humans have experienced psychological and physical birth (separation), they are terrified of losing it, because losing the self translates into death. This creates two opposing poles of fear, thrusting individuals into a conflict that continues throughout life.

Many scientists disagree. They maintain that human development is a process of connecting, not severing—a struggle to form attachments rather than tolerate separations. Obviously, attachment is a powerful and enduring force in nature. It is intrinsic to the survival of life—from cells that cling together to elephants that herd together to hunter-gatherers that live together. Species have evolved to connect to other members of their species, which is essential for reproduction and consequent natural selection. Attachment theorists argue that relating is critical to survival—relating first to the mother, then the family, and ultimately the people in the outside environment.

Does the self emerge from trauma and painful separation, or from attachment and a continuing struggle to connect? Possibly it's both. The self can be compared to a seesaw, with development as the fulcrum and separation and attachment on opposite ends. The balance between holding on and moving away becomes one of the most difficult and conflicting aspects of psychological life. People become "I" through their connection with others. No wonder we haven't been able to solve the mystery of ourselves. It's a virtual reality fraught with conflicts, ironies, and paradoxes.

STICKS
AND STONES

Excreting is the curse that threatens madness because it shows man his abject fini-
tude, his physicalness, the likely unreality of his hopes and dreams. But even more
immediately, it represents man's utter bafflement at the sheer non-sense *of creation:*
to fashion the sublime miracle of the human face, the mysterium *tremendum* of
radiant feminine beauty, the veritable goddess that beautiful women are; to bring
this out of nothing, out of the void and make it shine in noonday; to take such a
miracle and put miracles again within it, deep in the mystery of eyes that peer out—
the eye that gave even the dry Darwin a chill: to do all this, and to combine it with
an anus that shits! It is too much. Nature mocks us, and poets live in torture.
— *Ernest Becker* (pp. 33, 34)

O NE OF THE greatest twentieth-century philosophers was a social
theorist and professor of sociology, social psychology, and anthropology. Ernest Becker (1924-1974) took on the job of summing up the
meaning of human struggle. Drawing from evolutionary theory, psycho-

103

analysis, and anthropology, Becker attempted to make sense of what we already know. Unlike Darwin, Becker was not heard around the world. Although he received the Pulitzer Prize for general nonfiction in 1974 for his groundbreaking work *The Denial of Death*, Becker remains relatively unknown. Perhaps the reason is because his message is so unsettling, cutting through to the core of our most cherished illusions.

Becker felt, long before personal computers and the World Wide Web, that we were drowning in a morass of unconnected knowledge. We have so much information, so much data to process and no thread, no common philosophical core to guide us. It's like having a computer without a monitor—you know what it can do, you know what's there, but you have no means to *see* it. Becker maintains that our knowledge, in the context of the human condition, reflects a basic, unavoidable human paradox that he called the human existential dilemma.

It begins with evolution. We evolved as biological creatures, part of a naturally designed scheme that, before our species, shielded animals from self-awareness. The dogs and cats that live with us have no sense of time, no conscious awareness of their life as we would define it and subsequently no awareness of their own impending death. Fido simply doesn't own an "I" equivalent to his owner's. As Becker notes, you can shoot an animal in a herd and the others will go on grazing unless they sense danger, which usually translates into fear and subsequent action. While animals can acknowledge or sense loss, death has no real meaning. Bambi cries only in Disney animations.

This does not diminish the life or experience of an animal. It simply differentiates it from humans. It's why we own Fido and he doesn't own us. Animals are both a part of us and very separate from us.

The action an animal or herd might take when it senses danger is stimulated by fear. Fear is one of the most effective means of self-preservation. If horses did not experience fear, they would remain in burning barns; rodents would remain in the open grasses ready to be captured by eagles; deer wouldn't run from mountain lions or human predators. Fear preserves species at two levels: it protects the individual and it protects the species from extinction. Introduce a new factor—or predator—and the animal might not *know* to be afraid. This can lead to death and severe reductions in population that can wipe out the entire species. It has happened to animals all over the globe as human technology improved faster than their ability to see people as a danger. The American buffalo or golden eagle are good examples of unrestrained human decimation of animal life. There are also more subtle ways to create unseen enemies—things such as pollution, acid rain, and destruction of natural habitats.

Let's look at the concept of self-preservation. What does it actually imply? "To preserve a life" suggests that life is *worth* saving. Even in the simplest forms of life, self-preservation emerges from an essential narcissism or centrism about protecting one's own skin. *I must fight to live.* Each animal must protect its own integrity—it is designed for that purpose. From an evolutionary psychology view, this is essential to survival of the species. If each individual, as well as a species, did not have built-in narcissism to ignite self-preservation and protect life, it would not survive.

Apply that same concept to the animal that is self-aware: us. How does it manifest itself in human psychology? Narcissism becomes inseparable from self-esteem or a basic sense of self-worth. It is a necessary part of physiological *and* psychological life. Becker argues that human narcissism becomes symbolic, similar to other information-processing functions. It feeds on

> symbols, on an abstract idea of his own worth, an idea composed of sounds, words, and images, in the air, in the mind, on paper.... The single organism can expand into dimensions of worlds and times without moving a physical limb; it can take eternity into itself even as it gaspingly dies. (p. 3)

Human narcissism is a powerful force, recognized throughout history. One of the best-known fables from antiquity is the story of Narcissus, a beautiful young man who believed he had achieved perfection. In his world, all of the young women and graceful nymphs fell in love with Narcissus. He repeatedly and cruelly rejected them, breaking hearts over and over again. One day, a young girl who was a victim of his meanness prayed that he would know what it was like to experience unrequited love. Her prayer was heard.

Narcissus was walking in the forest when he paused to drink from a stream of water. As he bent over he saw his reflection. Staring back at him were beautiful, bright eyes, perfect skin, and seductive red lips. Narcissus was convinced that he saw an exquisite water spirit living in the pool. He immediately fell in love, but as he bent to kiss the spirit, the reflection fled. He backed away and the lovely water spirit returned. He stretched out his arms to embrace the spirit, but once again it disappeared into the water. Narcissus was smitten. He spent the rest of his days trying to capture the fleeting water spirit. Gradually he pined his life away, his love forever unrequited.

The story of Narcissus has appeared over and over again in literature, philosophy, social science, and art. What does Narcissus have to do with the newly born "I" discussed earlier? Many propose that human newborns experience a type of narcissism that is akin to a "grandiose myth." The child believes he or she is the source of gratification. *I cry, my bottle appears. I cry, my wet diaper disappears. I cry, warm arms comfort me.* It is a myth of omnipotence—of total power where *my cry* can magically produce relief, satisfaction, and pleasure. The myth of omnipotence affords a sense of utter control over a strange and hostile environment, helping the newborn to psychologically overcome the trauma of birth and the loss of the womb. The aim is to achieve a balance, or homeostasis, in the infant's new environment. As Rank proposed, this comes with a price: first the fear of separation, and then the consequent fear of reabsorption or death.

Life is designed to develop and adapt. By four or five months of age—long after baby walruses are swimming and baby wolves are running—the human infant is programmed to begin to differentiate between him- or herself and others. It is the first step toward psychological separation, the subsequent emergence of self, and, in healthy development, the moderation of infant narcissism.

In an evolutionary context, this narcissism or myth of grandiosity is as important to human self-preservation as an animal's ability to flee from danger. Its goal is to assure continued survival of the individual as well as the species. If the newborn were not narcissistic, demanding unquestioning care, and if the mother were not equipped with biochemical and psychological systems that stimulate her conscious response to "care for baby," the newborn would be abandoned. Helpless to care for itself, that very same newborn would soon die. In a more pragmatic context, a larger, highly complex brain needs more time to develop. The human child must be sheltered and nurtured to assure healthy physiological development. Designing a narcissistic system handily resolves the issue of time.

Practical experience as well as scientific research supports the scenario. We know that human newborns do not survive without care—we see glitches in the program every day when babies are abandoned or neglected by their mothers. Health care workers have long recognized the symptoms of neglected babies as a "failure to thrive." More recently, the new diagnosis of children suffering from "attachment disorder" has shed light on problems caused by infants who did not receive early appropriate psychological care. One study examined children adopted from Romanian orphanages. Many of the babies went straight from the hospital to the institution, never having any contact with their birth mothers or consistent care from a single caretaker. The longer the children spent in the orphanage, the more likely they were to show attachment disorders or difficulty connecting appropriately with adoptive parents. The children adopted at eight months or older had the most problems. They had trouble bonding with adoptive parents, sometimes completely avoiding them, showing little emotion, or the opposite, getting angry and interpreting even the simplest separation as abandonment. The developing human brain needs other people in order to be properly "wired" (DeAngelis 1997).

Narcissism and its early childhood demands are essential ingredients for healthy human psychological development. When human children are wired incorrectly during those early, psychologically fragile years, glitches in the program can affect them for the rest of their lives. Consider the problem of narcissistic adaptation. We are born with narcissistic needs that are slowly moderated to enable us to live in social groups. Clearly, the process can go wrong. We all know about the infamous narcissists—people, like O.J. Simpson, who believe they can literally get away with murder. If narcissism is essential, then where are the glitches in the program? What causes the disorders? James Masterson, in his classic book *The Narcissistic and Borderline Disorders*, writes about the child who develops narcissistic pathology:

> The fantasy persists that the world is his oyster and revolves about him. In order to protect this illusion, he must seal off by avoidance, denial and devaluation those perceptions of reality that do not fit or resonate with this narcissistic, grandiose self-projection. Consequently, he is compelled to suffer the cost to adaptation that is always involved when large segments of reality must be denied. (p. 13)

Simply put, when the narcissistic child reaches the stage in development where he or she recognizes that omnipotence is a myth—that grandiosity does not work—the truth is avoided. Instead, the child simply cuts off that knowledge of reality, refusing to believe that the kid next door can be just as important. *I'm always number one.*

We all know adults who suffer from narcissistic disorders. They are the people who always have the "best"—the best cars, the best homes, and the best clothes. They can be extremely charming because they give off an aura of arrogance, looking and acting the part of one who is sublimely in control. America *loves* narcissists. It gives permission for some of the best—and worst—behavior in today's society. The narcissists who live next door are always more entitled, like the neighbor who deserves the most expensive landscaper or the latest sexy car. It's also the coworker who surreptitiously courts the boss in hopes of snagging his job, the buddy who has to wear only the finest designer clothes, the parent who has the smartest child, the young adult who can graduate only from an Ivy League university. The same grandiosity catapults politicians, actors, and athletes into the heated limelight of the media. It thrusts businessmen, lawyers, and professionals into the steely seats of backstage power.

Narcissism is also dangerous business. Along with the arrogance comes haughtiness, a sense of entitlement, a willingness to exploit people. There is little or no empathy for other people. Narcissists tend to chew up people quickly in social relationships. The parents who tout their child as the best in the school discover that he has a serious drug dependency. The buddy who has to wear the best clothes ends up in bankruptcy. Politicians imbued with their power to make laws that control others end up breaking those laws themselves. Athletes bloated with the worship of adoring fans gamble on the very games they're supposed to play. Businessmen giddy with their control of other peoples' money find themselves in jail from insider trading or tax evasion. Actors and actresses kill themselves.

What hovers beneath the veneer of narcissism is a fragile sense of self. "Underneath this defensive façade is a feeling state of emptiness and rage," writes Masterson, "with a predominance of intense envy" (p. 15). Put a nick in the veneer of his or her narcissism, and everything lets lose.

Yet narcissism is essential for healthy human survival. "A working level of narcissism is inseparable from self-esteem," writes Becker, "from a basic sense of self-worth. We have learned ... that what man needs most is to feel secure in his self-esteem" (p. 3). Without it, we could not survive.

A self-aware life form, with the ability to manipulate both actual and virtual realities, interprets healthy narcissism and the subsequent self-esteem as a virtual experience. A virtual hierarchy emerges—the self must be of great value in the universe, must have purpose, must *count* for something. Lodged in a pitiful body, the value of the self emerges from virtual standards, psychosocial constructs that imply wealth and singularity. As Becker puts it, we compile a rap sheet to prove our own heroics and, consequently, our self-worth. By being heroic we elevate the self beyond the mundane—giving it a one-of-a-kind quality that gives us a virtual definition far beyond that of biological life form. Heroics can range from blindly plunging into battle to leading the PTA to compiling a weighty bankbook to getting on the dean's list. The means to achieve heroism can range from mythical to scientific, from spiritual to mundane. Method is not very important. The goal, Becker argues, is to achieve "a feeling of primary value, of cosmic specialness, of ultimate usefulness to creation, of unshakable meaning." Becker describes all of society as a "symbolic action system" establishing status, hierarchy, roles, customs, behaviors, and norms with the underlying goal to perpetuate the illusion of heroics and cosmic specialness (p. 4). To illustrate, consider the following scenarios:

- A young professional enters the work force with one goal: to climb the corporate ladder. Why? To make more money. What will more money bring? Power. What will more power bring? Better clothes. More trips. More things to *do*. Why? It makes her feel better. Why? Others will feel respect or envy when thinking about her. Others will want to be near her, knowing that she will be going places. How does that make the young professional feel about her *self*? Very, very good. Very important. And, of course, very valuable.

- A social worker struggles to assure that poor families get fed during the holidays. He puts in extra hours, searches for donations in the community, convinces volunteers to work Christmas morning. Why? He doesn't get more money, but he *helps*. Whom does he help? The less fortunate. He gives of his own time and energy, assumes a stoic position about the concrete needs of his self so that others might have more. He is a very fine social worker. In fact, he is one of the best—maybe even one of the best in the entire city. Everyone knows that. They all admire his altruism, compliment him on his dedication to others. How does that make the altruist feel about his self? Very, very good. Very important. And, of course, very valuable.

The end result is the same. It doesn't matter whether the "cultural hero-system is magical or religious, primitive or secular, scientific or artistic" (Becker, p. 5). It can be a title in a corporate system, an act of altruism, a courageous crusade, a work of art or science or technology, as long as it affords that feeling of importance and value of self. In that context, society is all a "mythical hero system in which people serve in order to earn a feeling of primary value, of cosmic specialness, of ultimate usefulness to creation, of unshakable meaning" (p. 5). The feeling is essentially a virtual reality that perpetuates the belief that the self has carved out a place in the world, has transcended actuality. By doing so the self goes beyond its biological destiny, preserving the illusion that the things created in human society are of "lasting worth and meaning, that they outlive or outshine death and decay, that man and his products count" (p. 5).

The circle is complete. Underlying all of this need to transcend actuality and psychologically dwell in a virtual reality are Rank's polarizing fears—the fear of life versus the fear of death, what Becker refers to as an existential dilemma.

"Heroism," writes Becker, "is first and foremost a reflex of the terror of death" (p. 11). It is the result of the essential human paradox. The human self and the human experience is half virtual—defined by mental images, symbols, metaphors, and histories of virtual realities. We have the innate ability to soar above the clouds, to think, to fantasize, to devise, and to invent technology that alters our relationship to actuality. As many spiritual people believe, each of us contains a spark of the divine, harboring the ability to transcend multiple dimensions, ride the stars or the waves, dream in vivid colors and music, invent both the beautiful and the ugly. Yet at the same time, we move from ashes to ashes, dust to dust. We live in a body that must be fed and watered, or it will suffer painfully and then die. We gasp for air, have aches and pains, urinate, and expel body fluids that many of us find foul-smelling and repulsive. We bleed, we decay, and, eventually, we die. "This is the paradox [for humans]: he is out of nature and hopelessly in it; he is dual, up in the stars and yet housed in a heart-pumping, breath-gasping body that once belonged to a fish and still carries the gill-marks to prove it" (p. 26). Our uniqueness is also our albatross, for at the same time we know that we tower above the other animals that inhabit earth, our bodies will ultimately end up in the same place—decomposing in the ground. In our virtual realities we are worlds apart from other earthbound life; in our actualities we share the same destiny.

The dogs and cats, whales and dolphins, gazelles and rhinos are all spared the knowledge of that basic conflict. They are not aware of themselves; they do not experience consciousness in the same manner as humans. They do not share our virtual realities, but they do not suffer our contradictions. They do not have to find a way to survive the knowledge that all the beauty and joy and grief and pain that we experience will end with every animal's fate: death.

Becker maintains that we are plunged into an excruciating dilemma. The only solution is to deny fate; in other words, create a synthetic oblivion of "social games, psychological tricks, and personal preoccupations" (p. 27), anything from politics to philosophy that will help us avoid acknowledging the inevitability of the death of the self. The duality can never be reconciled; it can only be denied.

Society, then, is essentially a human design to maintain the ongoing illusion of human life. Religion maintains a power that supercedes biology—a plane where heaven and its divine ruler offer succor to spiritual immortality.

"Is it not for us to confess," Freud asked, "that in our civilized attitude towards death we are once more living psychologically beyond our means and must reform and give truth its due?" (Becker, p. 11).

But the truth is paralyzing. Biological imperatives can shatter human illusion, create predictable psychological obstacles that will not allow us to proceed. Like a computer, the always-present conscious knowledge of organic death would crash the entire information-processing system. We need to be protected against ourselves and our dangerously dual self-awareness. Mind and body, although both parts of a human gestalt, are experienced as separate and distinct.

I think, therefore I am. I breathe, therefore I live.

The remaining chapters in Part II will explore the most popular means used by humans today to harness virtual realities that sustain illusion and, by definition, deny conscious knowledge of biological death.

THE CYBORG
METAPHOR

T HE GRIM-FACED CAPTAIN stared into the eyes of the
judge. A tribunal had been assembled to decide on a strategic issue
of property.

The captain sighed deeply, his bald head smooth and shiny in the synthetic glare from the overhead lights. "Data is a machine," he said softly.
"We, too, are machines of a different type."

It was an unusual event, even for the crew of the starship *Enterprise*,
whose continuing mission was "to boldly go where no one has gone before."
Stopping briefly at Starbase 173 for crew rotation, Commander Bruce
Maddox, Starfleet Associate Chairman of Robotics, came aboard. He
quickly made it known that *his* mission was to disassemble Lieutenant
Commander Data, the beloved android. The goal was pure research—he
needed to learn the intricacies of the Starfleet officer's positronic brain so
he could reproduce, and hopefully in the future create, a whole new collection of humanlike androids such as Data.

The disassembly had the potential to destroy Mr. Data's existence. Everyone *knew* an android could be taken apart but, like Humpty Dumpty, no one was sure one could be put back together again. Mr. Data's possible demise was too much to bear for the crew who had made distinct emotional attachments to the machine. The android was a favorite not only among his living peers, but also among the millions of viewers who eagerly tuned in to spend an hour each week with *Star Trek.*

The episode, aptly called "Measure of a Man," explored a metaphor known to humans since the first rock was picked up off the ground and used as a tool, as far back as 3 million years ago. What is the relationship between humans and machines? Why is there a relationship at all? How has this relationship served the adaptation of an information-processing life form? What happens to the self when it is housed in human-designed mechanics?

Data unsuccessfully attempted to convince Maddox not to dismantle him: "I am the culmination of one man's dream," he explained in his child-like logic. "When Dr. Soongh created me, he added to the substance of the universe. If by your experiments I am destroyed, something wonderful will be lost."

Maddox persisted. He maintained that the android was a machine, the property of Starfleet. As such, *it* had no more rights than a computer.

Viewers grew restless. Data, an "it"? It was unfathomable. Data was the charming, plastic-skinned, synthetic-eyed innocent who protected everyone against all odds. The ultimate in machinery—an immortal with a soul.

A hearing was called with Captain Phillipa Louvois, Judge Advocate General in the sector. Even in the far future, the way to fight back is through litigation. And in this specific courtroom scene the goal was to determine whether Data was a machine or a new human-designed life form entitled to all the rights reserved for life forms within the Federation. It reflected a deeply rooted human fantasy—to have a self and be immortal all in the same body.

In a dramatic defense, Captain Jean-Luc Picard pleaded eloquently for Data's "life": "The decision you reach here today will determine how we regard this creation of our genius," his voice resonated through televisions in every living room. "It would reveal the kind of a people we are—what he is destined to be. It could significantly redefine the boundaries of personal liberty and freedom, expanding them for some, savagely curtailing them for others."

Star Trek: The Next Generation had made a spectacular entry into television in 1987. The new series emerged, phoenixlike, from a media legend. The original *Star Trek* ran twenty-one years earlier, from 1966 to 1969. When it was taken off the air, devoted fans would not let it go. Clubs, groups, and conventions met throughout the country. Reruns appeared year after year on television, until Gene Roddenberry reactivated the concept. Within a few years *The Next Generation* went warp speed into movies; *Voyager*, with a female captain, took to the universe; and *Deep Space Nine* settled in next to a newly discovered wormhole.

The Next Generation was different from its predecessor. Although the crew still traveled on the *Enterprise*, the new series reflected a different ideology. The original crew sported a diverse human population with a sprinkling of aliens whose mission was to explore new worlds. They were known for their highly evolved human crew, periodically plagued by remnants of a primitive biological nature. Sex and violence lived happily beside logic and cybernetics. These were very sixties issues—how to tame the beast by superimposing noble intent. The next generation was less interested in these conflicts. "Self" was more in vogue. Their crew tackled issues involving cultural, psychological, legal, and ethical battles that bore an uncanny similarity to the emerging struggles of the Information Age. Cybernetic questions were repeatedly raised, apparent in characters such as Geordi LaForge, the blind engineer who wore a computerized VISOR (Visual Instrument and Sensory Organ Replacement) that enabled him to see better than humans, and their most formidable enemy, the cybernetic collective Borg.

"Measure of a Man" concludes with a wrenching decision made by the judge. "He sits there looking at me, and I don't know what it is," the judge stared at Mr. Data. "Is Data a machine? Yes. Is he the property of Starfleet? No. We've all been dancing around the basic issue—does Data have a soul? I don't know that he has. I don't know that I have. But I have got to give him the freedom to explore that question himself."

A *machine* exploring the question of possessing his own soul?

As the Information Age becomes more entrenched in our lives, we move to consciously redefine the self. It feels like a revolution in human thought, what William Mitchell describes in *City of Bits*: "The border between exteriority and interiority is destabilized. Distinctions between self and other are open to reconstruction. Difference becomes provisional" (p. 31). The new millennium hunter-gatherer no longer makes decisions between when to eat and when to roam. Instead, he is controlled by a computer on his wrist that keeps constant track of the passage of time; by machines that propel him to and from structures where light, temperature, transportation and security are maintained by computers tucked secretly in a back room; and by virtual realities created *within* machines. As a species, we wear synthetic teeth; see through plastic lenses that clarify our vision; have fake hips and kneecaps installed when our own wear out; rely on pacemakers when our hearts run down; live, love, and lie with machines that partner with our selves in cyberspace—the list grows each day as our machines become more intrinsic parts of who we are. How could our Stone Age computers have taken us *here?*

The twentieth century was cluttered with visions of social-scientific partnerships between humans and machines. To our time-limited observations, it seems like an inevitable revolution in human design. But take a closer look. Technology has leaped to places nineteenth-century designers could hardly imagine. We devised the very best and the very worst implements for human civilization and any environment that it might touch. Yet inside all of it, beneath the silicon chips and massive mechanisms that drive our world, we are still those hunter-gatherers looking for ways to control and manipulate our environments.

In *1984* George Orwell drew a grim picture of a society controlled by the telescreen broadcasting images of Big Brother and maintaining constant, invasive surveillance of party members. Was it more or less disdainful than the hunter-gatherers who refused to adapt to the Neolithic agricultural revolution or the people who felt the world would end with the use of telephones? What about the naysayers who claimed that putting humans in space would irrevocably change Earth's climate?

No one can argue that twentieth-century cybernetic media heroes proliferated, including individuals such as the Six-Million Dollar Man, Bionic Woman, Lawnmower Man, and Power Rangers. In an ironic coincidence, William Gibson published his prophetic novel *Neuromancer* in 1984, introducing a terrifying electronic environment that used simulation in place of reality. He called it cyberspace.

> On the Sony, a two-dimensional space war faded behind a forest of mathematically generated ferns, demonstrating the spacial possibilities of logarithmic spirals; cold blue military footage burned through, lab animals wired into test systems, helmets feeding into fire control circuits of tanks and war planes. "Cyberspace. A consensual hallucination experienced daily by billions of legitimate operators, in every nation, by children being taught mathematical concepts.... A graphic representation of data abstracted from the banks of every computer in the human system." (p. 51)

It took less than ten years to illustrate that truth could be stranger than Gibson's fiction. The Internet became accessible. The World Wide Web started to build the global online village. *Star Trek* found that the question could no longer be avoided: what happens when you merge the "genius of man" with machine?

The implements were new, but the press for technology—the often blind pursuit of mechanized ingenuity *at all costs*—is very much a part of human mental programming. From hunter-gatherers to Internet surfers, we are designed to invent, adapt, improve, and reinvent technology. For better or worse.

Look at it this way. The human species is an information-processing life form that must use intellect rather than teeth, claws, or brute strength to survive. One of the most basic, distinguishing features of the newly evolved humans was their ability to create tools. Through tools they could survive as well as manipulate the environment to suit their needs. This is the essence of Hartmann's concept of adaptation—we create to adapt and then adapt once again to our creations. The first stone tools enabled early humans to manipulate their environment. They were key to the qualitative separation between ourselves and non–information-processing animals who had no option but to coexist with the harsh vagaries of nature. We didn't have the incisors of a saber-toothed tiger to attack our prey, so we invented spears. We didn't have the coat of a woolly mammoth to protect us from cold, so we invented tools to make fire. We didn't have the hump of a camel to store our water, so we developed containers. Tools also encouraged the growth of abstract thought, opening the door to Hartmann's progressive style of adaptation. Once you construct a spear, someone will always come along and figure out how to improve it. The environment became a force that could be challenged and even conquered to improve the quality of human life. It's programmed right into those Stone Age computers.

Early humans were designed to create technology. Technology was first, and always, the accumulation of knowledge available to humans so they could fashion tools, practice manual arts and skills, and extract or collect materials. Technology was a innate part of the species, setting the pace for adaptation. Darwin firmly believed that humans were able to eventually dominate life on earth because they had hands to obey their will. Hands replaced the deficit in natural weapons; humans used intellectual and social abilities to develop their technologies. Humans learned that this combination enabled them to master their environment *and* all the other life forms that lived there. A rock, picked up and thrown at an enemy, was a machine for survival. Similarly, a stone, chipped and carved into a spear and aimed at an unsuspecting animal provided dinner. The metaphor was clear: human-with-machine/tool was invariably better than human-without-machine/tool.

A STONE AGE CYBORG?

The idea of human-is-better-with-machine/tool evolved along with the social, intellectual, and psychological development of the species. From spears to computers, human history is marked by the great technological discoveries. Although various forces have struggled to thwart the growth of technology, they invariably lost to the confirmed, often unstated belief that humankind is better with machines. Philosophers, artists, poets, and other thinkers mourned the loss of the natural world. Henry David Thoreau wrote in *Walden* that "our inventions are wont to be pretty toys, which distract our attention from serious things. They are but improved means to an unimproved end" (p. 52).

Yet evolutionary designs persist. Just as we are compelled, as information-processing creatures, to gather and integrate data, we are compelled to create, use, and improve technology. It is part of who we are. Whether a wheel or a disk drive, technology drives the Stone Age computers in our minds. We are programmed, as a species, to survive through our tools and machines. Without that assumption the first stone used as a weapon for dinner would never have been tossed. And without that assumption, cyberspace would still be a fantasy in Gibson's imagination. Beneath that hovers a very virtual reality. The more machine we are, the less biological we become. The less biological, the easier it is to deny the existential dilemma. If half of "me" is nonorganic, then only half of "me" can suffer life's ultimate fate: death. Machines are not buried in the earth to rot and decay. They are repaired, recycled, and improved.

It's called the cyborg metaphor. Humans are better with machines because our mental modules are programmed to follow that critical pathway in species survival. Humans are better with machines because they allow us to live longer and better. Humans are better with machines because we can create cyborg bodies—part human, part machine—and unconsciously deny the essential human duality between the powers of the mind and the destiny of the body. The cyborg metaphor has, and will always be, an intrinsic part of who we are.

In another episode of *Star Trek*, the Borg, an alien race of cyborgs, kidnap Captain Picard. They inform him that they need a human voice to speak for them and he has been chosen for the job. The captain will be incorporated into the "collective," the system that links all Borg with each other. "Strength is irrelevant," they inform the Captain. "Resistance is futile."

Perhaps resistance is futile when attempting to curb the evolving cyborg metaphor in human species. The press of technology seems to have a life of its own—even the most powerful naysayers have never been able to thwart what has been identified as progress. Yet humans have repeatedly made attempts to stem change brought by technology. Perhaps the first protesters were the Neolithic hunter-gatherers who avoided the new technology of agriculture. It's been written that Socrates told a story about a king who saw the invention of writing as a technology that would diminish the human ability for memory. For nearly fifty years after Gutenberg invented the printing press, people continued to read the large, handmade books, avoiding the dramatic new technology in word processing. One of the most infamous collections of antitechnologists were the Luddites, a group of skilled craftsmen in England who in 1812 physically attacked the machines they felt were threatening their livelihood. More recent were individuals who attacked the advent of the telegraph, felt the automobile would be the end of civilization, and warned society of the dangers of watching television over listening to the radio. The list is as long as technological innovations themselves. Today's neo-Luddites decry the computer age, predicting that we will lose our humanness in bytes, bits, and silicon. Steven Talbott, author of *The Future Does Not Compute*, writes, "And today the needful work is to distinguish ourselves from our machines. It is to rediscover, for example, that all knowledge is knowledge of man, and that nothing worth calling an ideal can be found in the engineered world, but only in ourselves" (p. 18).

Does Talbott touch a painful nerve in our neural programming? Are the Luddites so wrong? The same technology that brought us the pyramids, covered wagons, and cell phones also brought us gunpowder, air pollution, and nuclear bombs. The cyborg metaphor operates without a concomitant conscience, something or someone that tells us that it can be wrong, dangerous, or even murderous to utilize human ingenuity in a specific manner. Obviously, human technology is as capable of producing evil as of producing good—and everything that falls between. As the pace of invention speeds up we seem to manufacture increasing threats to ourselves, other life forms, and the environment. Is it too much power for mere mortals? Do our Stone Age computers know how to discriminate? Are we further fragmenting the self—creating a system of recycling identities in exchange for the illusion of biological obscurity? When does our philosophy catch up with our technology?

ARE WE BECOMING A RACE OF CYBORGS?

Ever meet a *real* cyborg? Most of us would say no. When we hear the word *cyborg* we tend to think about the Borg that kidnapped the *Star Trek* captain, Arnold Schwarzenegger's *Terminator*, Robocops and bionic people with super powers.

Think again.

The cyborg is no longer restricted to science fiction, television, and film. It has become a social reality. A cyborg, as the combination of human and machine, is really quite common. Most of us already fit the qualifications. George Landow, professor at Brown University, estimates that at least 10 percent of the U.S. population can be considered fully endowed cyborgs because they have pacemakers, artificial joints, drug implant systems, implanted corneal lenses, or artificial skin. This does not include what Landow refers to as "metaphoric cyborgs," or people who join with machines for specific purposes, such as playing a video game, surfing the Net, using fiber optic microscopy to perform surgery, or working with computer-generated images to make movies. It is a "merging of the evolved and the developed," he explains in "Cyborg: Some Definitions, Descriptions, and Exemplications." "This integration of the constructor and the constructed, these systems of dying flesh and undead circuits, and of living and artificial cells." Artificial organs, prosthetic limbs, chemical agents that alter our physical or psychological processes, computer chips embedded beneath the skin to regulate everything from medications to birth control make cyborgs of us all.

Do you wear a "machine" called contact lenses? Did you have a knee or hip replacement? Do you have a watch strapped to your wrist or a Disc-Man connected to your ears? Do you go on the Internet in order to do business through e-mail, talk to friends, play in chat rooms, or wander through your virtual community? Do you take human-designed medications to alleviate the symptoms of a cold, the grip of an infection, or the debilitation of a depression? Then you too must be a cyborg.

This is only the beginning. Bioengineered body parts from skin and organs to bone and blood will be grown in labs. Living tissue and electronic devices will merge to overcome biological frailties as well as to augment human capability. All over the world companies are building prototypes for devices such as LVES (pronounced "Elvis"), a low-vision enhancement system that uses wide-angle cameras, zoom lenses, and other video and computer feeds to enable people with poor vision to see. The military is enthralled with the idea of cyborgian battle gear, such things as headgear that collects and disseminates information, equips soldiers with night-vision sensors, video panels, and voice activation of a computer built into the lumbar region of body armor. It's not the stuff of science fiction. Steven Mann, assistant professor of electrical and computer engineering at the University of Toronto, is using a line of "wearable computers" that can be installed in clothing. He has created devices such as eyeglasses that sport an embedded computer monitor and "smart" underwear that regulates room temperature. New millennium technology is making cyborgs of us all. Landow, in "Four Kinds of Cyborg," suggests that with our present knowledge we can identify categories of cyborg technologies:

- *Restorative*, where lost functions, organs, or limbs are replaced. These cyborgs are created from devices such as prosthetic limbs, knee or hip replacements, and other synthetic body parts such as heart valves and shunts.

- *Normalizing*, where a life form is restored to its standard configuration structure or appearance. The man with a pacemaker fits into this category. He has many peers—people with insulin pumps, surgical reconstruction, contact lenses, corneal implants, hearing implants, and anyone who uses pharmaceuticals to cure, treat, or control physical or mental illness.

- *Reconfiguring*, where modifications are made to create a "posthuman" or "protohuman." We all fit into this category. These are the "metaphoric" cyborgs who exist (in an electronic environment) only through the mediation of a machine. You "talk" on the telephone, communicate through e-mail, "live" on the Internet only when the button is switched to "on." Turn it to "off," hang up the telephone, take e-mail off the computer, and "I" is no longer there.

- *Enhancing*, where superhumans are created. We are only beginning. But the birth of superhumans or supercyborgs is upon us. Tiny microchips embedded in human flesh and genetically engineered designs have already shown us it's possible. Imagination and technology are our only limitations.

As the self becomes more embedded in technology, it grows more scattered. What began as essential and unanswerable philosophical questions become confounded by an intimate relationship that is clearly not controlled by divine intervention or even the slow, reliable forces of nature. In the body-machine duality, strange questions arise—which one made which? Which one controls the other? Who is better? How does one hate—or love—one machine over the other? Can evolution proceed when machines, not life forms, are involved? Where does that leave us when it comes to adaptation? These are not random questions for another generation to answer. Consider what has already occurred:

- A cyberneticist "wires" himself with a temporary, surgically implanted chip. It transmits signals to a computer that tracks his movements, turns on his PC, checks his e-mail, and greets him as he enters a room.

- A paralyzed stroke victim, unable to speak, is implanted with a tiny device that transmits electrical signals from his brain to control a cursor on a computer screen, conveying simple messages.

- Engineers construct computer chips containing DNA to diagnose genetic mutations.

The cyborg metaphor is another virtual reality that has become, with increasingly sophisticated technology, widely accessible. Will the cyborg metaphor take over more and more of our bodies and imaginations? Will it lead to total immersion into virtual-reality simulation and the consequent erosion of actuality? Or are we all like Mr. Data, witnessing the evolution of a new psychosocial life form? Rob Fixmer, in the *New York Times*, warns that

> without safeguards...the enhancement of our brains could easily destroy our minds, leaving us unable to distinguish reality from virtual reality—maybe even self from non-self. Powerful software would have to be developed to help us sort, sift and prioritize the constant deluge of information lest our brains degenerate into data landfills.

MEDIA MAYHEM

"Seeya."

It begins innocently enough. A pretty young teenage girl. A soft, seductive male voice on the telephone. Wrong number. Cut to the house. The American Dream—a cozy colonial with trees, a swing hanging from a branch, windows aglow with warm, friendly lights. Cut back to the kitchen. She puts popcorn on the stove, and the telephone rings again. It is the same wrong number.

"Why don't you want to talk to me?"

"Who is this?"

"You tell me your name and I'll tell you mine."

In her young, perky way she moves around the house—making the popcorn, absently touching the knives in their natural wood holder on the kitchen countertop, getting ready to watch a video. She talks to the wrong number because he's clever and she's innocent. But then he pushes. Ever so slightly.

"You never told me your name."

125

"Why do you want to know my name?"

"Because I want to know who I'm looking at."

There is an icy pause in the action. Your fists tighten. Your heart beats faster. No. *Music rumbles in the background like a distant roar of thunder. The storm is coming.* No. *The music grows more eerie, more ominous in tempo. The camera closes in. The scene changes come faster. The music is louder, and suddenly the teenager and the telephone caller are screaming at one another. Before you know it, the teenager is terrified, the music out of control and the tension unbearable.*

I T DOESN'T MATTER that you're watching Drew Barrymore on a screen, that the popcorn burning on the stove is a picture and not the acrid smell in your nose. You believe. And that's what makes it so horrific when Drew Barrymore ends up, in the opening minutes of the movie, bloodied, gutted, and strung from a tree that looks just like the one with the swing. You still believe.

Director Wes Craven's movie *Scream* held audiences spellbound. People drew their breath in horror, they groaned, cried, winced, some even screamed in the darkened theaters. Yet it was only a movie.

We all know what it feels like. How many films have induced the familiar lump in the throat and embarrassing tears? Do people watch pornography because it's an interesting exercise or because it sexually arouses them? Have you ever yelled out the answers at *Jeopardy*, cursed the referee on *Monday Night Football*, or laughed when Robin Williams cavorted across the screen? Can you go to a 3D or Imax movie and not flinch when the ball, animal, or water is thrown "directly" into your face? Do you get motion sickness when you climb aboard a simulated ride like Universal Studios' *Back to the Future* or Disney's *Star Wars* or play a virtual-reality game with a headset?

Something happens when we watch television, movies, stare at a computer monitor or venture into virtual-reality simulations. We *believe*. We believe they are real.

What did Wes Craven do to make people believe in *Scream?* Many of his film techniques were classic: the rising crescendo of music; a subjective camera that makes the viewer feel as if he or she is part of the scene; speeding up the edits (scene or viewpoint changes) as the climax nears;

using metaphors, like the expanding tin of popcorn on the stove, to serve visual cues for increasing tension. They were all devices to further entice the viewer, yet something had to be there before Craven even started, or we would never believe that Drew Barrymore could be murdered on screen when we saw her interviewed on television that very morning.

Byron Reeves and Clifford Nass from Stanford University conducted research that spanned over a decade, studying how people relate to the media. They formulated *The Media Equation*, proposing that people experience the media as real. They surmise that our Stone Age brains evolved "in a world in which *only* humans exhibited rich social behaviors, and a world in which *all* perceived objects were real physical objects. Anything that *seemed* to be a real person or place *was* real" (p. 2). These assumptions were essential for information-processing life forms. How else could they learn to discern differences among individuals, families, and groups—as well as objects in their environment? Keep in mind that Stone Age humans were the only life form capable of complex social behaviors—no species could compete. They were programmed for social interaction.

The complexities of human social relationships are far too lengthy to fully discuss here. What we need to understand is the depth of our conflicts and the impossibility of a global or generic solution. Our conflicts are essential and threatening, good and bad, happy and sad—there is an endless supply of adjectives to describe them. They begin at birth and increase throughout our lives. In order to negotiate social relationships we need some basic, irrefutable assumptions. Family and kinship systems serve as an example of one of our many programmed social assumptions. In the same manner, we have many basic assumptions that guide our social lives. For example, how do we determine humanness to begin with? It might sound simple, but the concept is really quite complex. How does a dog know another dog? How does a fish tell the difference between a squid and a fish of its own species? In the case of humans, our brains are programmed to accept some very essential information. If the life form *looks* human, he or she *is* human; if the life form behaves humanly, he or she is human, and so forth. Thus, when a parrot "talks" we know it isn't human because it doesn't look or sound human. It served our ancestors well.

These assumptions are so basic they seem almost ridiculous. Of course we know that what looks like a person isn't a horse. Let's take it one step further. We need these basic assumptions—the groundwork must be built in so we're free to negotiate the really tough stuff. Compare it to a computer. Every computer needs an operating system that provides the basic rules and regulations for it to work. The most popular operating system is Windows. What would happen if every time you turned on your computer it would have to reconfigure itself to use Windows, and every time you ran a program it would have to return to the operating system, load it up, and then reconfigure all over again? Turning off or rebooting the computer would force you to start the whole procedure once again. It would be a colossal waste of time.

Windows, with all its power, does not have the computing ability to distinguish the difference between a happy smile, a sad smile, and a nasty smile. It does not have the ability to recognize a facial expression, identify a smell, or interpret the meaning in a voice. It cannot identify a subjective difference between your sister and your friend, your mother and your boss, your lover and the guy that owns the sports bar down the street. These things are built in to the human operating system. We learn them very early in life and don't have to reconfigure our program each time it comes up. It frees us to consider more complex issues, such as whether that sad smile on the boss's face is about him losing his job or you losing yours. Perhaps the human social program looks like what Reeves and Nass describe:

> During nearly all of the 200,000 years in which *Homo sapiens* have existed, anything that acted socially really was a person, and anything that appeared to move toward us was in fact doing just that. Because these were absolute truths through virtually all of human evolution, the social and physical world encouraged automatic responses that were and still are the present-day bases for negotiating life. Acceptance of what only *seems* to be real, even though at times inappropriate, is automatic. (p. 12)

We arrive at the Media Metaphor. Human mental modules are programmed to assume that what appears real *is* real. It is a powerful and automatic assumption. Consequently, simulations of people and environments easily deceive our Stone Age brains—particularly if we don't think about it, if our minds are running on cruise control, or if we are only semi-involved in what we are doing. It's simple. We can't and don't overcome the assumption that what appears real *is* real, because we don't want to, don't need to, or don't gain anything by it. This is where the real power of virtual-reality simulations lies. "There is no switch in the brain," write Reeves and Nass, "that can be thrown to distinguish the real and mediated worlds" (p. 12).

That's why we scream at the movie *Scream*; cry when the heroine dies; believe that the finely groomed politician on television doesn't curse, belch, or break the laws he has created; and make passionate love in cyberspace. That is also why, when a pretty, innocent-looking teenager in *Scream*, played by Neve Campbell, says softly, "But this is life. This isn't a movie," *we believe*. And when her teenage lover responds gently, "Sure it is, Sydney. It's all a movie. It's all one great big movie," we continue to believe.

ENTER TELEPRESENCE

Ultimately, *Scream*'s appeal lies in its candor—its appealing way of stating the obvious. The rules of scary movies are discussed throughout the plot, a movie within a movie, constantly revealing the outcome. Many films use these devices because they enhance our experience—information-processing life forms play with symbols in the same way tigers toy with their prey, dogs toss around their chew bones, and young bucks smash their antlers against one another. In *Scream* the metaphor is the rules. Randy, the gawky film nerd and video store worker, states it definitively: "There are certain rules that one must abide by in order to successfully survive a horror movie: Only virgins can outsmart the killers in the chase scene. You can never have sex—sex equals death. You can never drink or do drugs— it's the sin factor. Never, under any circumstances, say, 'I'll be right back,' 'cause you won't be back."

Knowing the rules, knowing the outcome, even guessing who the killers are doesn't diminish the tension in *Scream*. After all, people have been reading and viewing Shakespeare's plays for almost four hundred years. We know the characters, the stories, and the endings, and we still love them. Hamlet is still a powerful, conflicted character, and Lady Macbeth still reminds us of our own obsessions and compulsions. *Shakespeare in Love*, a postmodern film version of *Romeo and Juliet*, built on another story within a story, brought audiences and romantics to tears. We feel and believe it.

This phenomenon is described by a psychological construct called *presence.* Presence is a natural attribute of consciousness, one that gives definition to our immediate environment. It refers to an individual's perception of his or her surroundings, being in the here-and-now. Look around you. Where are you? Maybe you're sitting in your favorite chair with a light over your shoulder and a blanket across your legs. Maybe you're on a beach with the ocean wind blowing across your face. Or maybe you're in a subway, train, or bus commuting with thousands of other people. Take a moment and look around you. What do you see? What do you hear? What do you smell? That's presence—the perceptions you experience in your immediate environment. But wait. Maybe the sun went behind the clouds and your bright beach darkened and cooled. Maybe the kid playing music on the boom box next to you got off the train. Maybe someone went into the kitchen and cooked up some popcorn, and its smell drifted over to your favorite chair. Your environment changed and, accordingly, your perceptions of it. Presence, then, is not a stable, inflexible state but a constantly shifting phenomenon. Presence is a function of the human information-processing system that harnesses highly reactive sensory receptors to pick up and process a continuous input of environmental data.

Now that you have noted your immediate presence, try this simple exercise. You are no longer in the surroundings you just observed. Instead, imagine yourself in the High Sierras. You're dressed for hiking with good shoes and a warm jacket. Do you see the redwoods? They stretch like giants above you, their huge, graceful trunks reaching to the sky. The smell of the forest fills your nose—the tangy pine, mellow earth, the wildflowers scattered across the deeply carpeted forest floor. A cool wind blows across your face. It feels so good! You gulp the thin, fresh air—it's like an icy drink on a hot day. Your deep breaths invigorate you. It's as if the mountains breathe life and energy into your body. You pause to fill your eyes with the woods around you. Beneath the redwoods, tiny trees and bushes struggle to survive in the shadow of their towering brethren. Lilliputian spiders weave delicate webs around the leftover dinner of nocturnal animals. At the massive foot of one redwood several tiny seedlings have taken hold. They are the delicate children of the mammoth that looms before you, their thin branches struggling to survive. Suddenly you hear a familiar *swish* of water. A mountain stream! You break off the dirt trail, letting your ears lead the way. The sound of the water gets louder as you crunch through pine needles, leaves, and cast-off branches. Your heart quickens. You can taste the water, feel it against your skin. All around you the sounds and smells of the forest encourage your pursuit—birds cawing, small animals scurrying, an owl hooting incongruously. Look over there! Just beyond a ridge of gray, ancient rock there is a break in the woods—it must be the stream. You run the final steps and stop reverently to watch the water race down the mountain, writhing over flat, worn stones and making tiny whirlpools and trails of white water. You can't help it. You're a little kid again and you *have* to be in that water. Without thinking, you rip off your shoes and socks and plunge your feet into the stream, balancing on rocks slick with moss. The icy water assaults you, instantly numbing your toes. The frigid stream is excruciating—tears come to your eyes and you cry out, your laughter rising above the treetops and getting lost in the calls between a pair of golden eagles.

Where did you go? If you were able to put yourself in the High Sierras, then the presence that you noted earlier had clearly changed. It receded. Taeyong Kim and Frank Biocca, media theorists, have suggested that there are three basic categories of presence:

• Presence in a physical environment.
This is the "default" sense of presence—the feeling of being there that serves as a basic attribute in human consciousness. It is what you experienced when you stopped reading and looked around your environment—the place that you occupied for that moment in time and space. Presence in a physical environment is such an ordinary experience that most of us never really think about it.

• Presence in a virtual environment.
Kim and Biocca define this as the experience of "being there" in any environment created by communication media. It is what you encountered when you read about being in the High Sierras and for the moment forgot, paid no attention, or temporarily suppressed your sense of presence in your physical environment. In other words, you shifted your focus to the virtual-reality environment created by the words. The more powerful subjective sensation of being present in a mediated remote or virtual environ-

ment (and not in the immediate surrounding physical environment) is
called *telepresence*. Telepresence is what happened when you screamed
during the movie *Scream*, cried over the cinematic death of Private Ryan,
or got lost in the Body Wars ride at Disney World.

• Presence in an imaginal environment.

This type of presence refers to those virtual-reality environments
where we experience the sense of being there in a place created only by
internal dreams, mental imagery, or fantasy. That's where we "go" when we
daydream, when we wake up in the morning and can't figure out whether
our dream was real or not, when we create fantasies that are far more
absorbing than our physical environments. Unlike physical or virtual presence, imaginal presence is completely internal, not relying on outside
stimulation or media.

It is not, however, a simple dichotomy. "As individuals experience sen-
sations coming from the physical environment or the virtual environment,
their sense of presence, or being there, may oscillate moment-to-moment
between these two senses of place," write Kim and Biocca, "or they may
withdraw their attention to these stimuli and retreat into the imagination.
Therefore, at any moment users might feel 'present' in one of [the above]
three places."

Let's look at it another way. You walk into the bedroom to watch your
favorite television drama. Obviously, your first sense of presence is in a
physical environment. You fluff up the pillows, put the glass of soda and
bag of pretzels on the night table, and dim the lights. Next, you stretch out
on the bed and make yourself comfortable. You reach over and grab the
remote control, turn on the TV, and flip to the right channel. The show
starts and the lives, faces, and worlds of the TV characters fill the screen.
You listen carefully, and before you realize what's happening, you've
entered their virtual world and are struggling, along with the characters, to
resolve their dilemmas. Your sense of presence has shifted to the environment in the virtual-reality simulation, and the pillows on your bed and
glass of soda on the night table have receded from your focus. But then
there's a break—commercial time. The cavorting teenagers in an ad
pushing a popular brand of blue jeans bore you. You've seen it too many

times. You drink your soda, munch on the pretzels, and your mind wanders. Yeah, there's that vacation you want to take to Europe. You always wanted to wander through the streets of Paris, dining in fine restaurants, visiting the Eiffel Tower and exploring the Left Bank. You imagine yourself strolling down the Champs Élysées, the Arc de Triomphe looming before your eyes. Maybe you'll stop for a moment at a romantic sidewalk café to sip demitasse or nibble on a croissant. Your sense of presence has once again shifted, and now it's presence in an imaginary environment that supports the daydream. But then your stomach might rumble for something more than the pretzels in your physical environment, or the commercial is over and you go back to the drama on television, or you ignore everything and continue down the Champs Élysées. It happens to all of us. We shift our sense of presence at will, focusing on different environments with the innate knowledge that at any given time we can return to our former place. The sense of presence in an information-processing life form functions like windows on a computer. You can maximize or minimize many windows at once, keeping them running, but hidden, on your active desktop.

The media metaphor is about the second sense of presence—the feeling of "being there" in a virtual environment. Kim and Biocca call it telepresence, a "state of presence in a remote environment." As such, telepresence is a powerful psychological feature in virtual-reality environments. Telepresence can be experienced in books, newspapers, cartoons— in fact, many theorists maintain that the quest for increased telepresence has been a critical part of all human media. Telepresence has evolved along with our virtual-reality environments from caves to cyberspace.

Telepresence lies at the emotional heart of cyberseduction. Why? Because we are information-processing machines, and telepresence offers an efficient, preprogrammed system to expand our ability to utilize virtual realities. We are self-aware beings that need to psychologically deny our biological destiny in order to survive, and telepresence encourages us to believe in other "realities." We are conflicted creatures, and telepresence offers relief from unsolvable dilemmas. We are social creatures, and telepresence allows us to "experience" other lives and by doing so broaden and protect our own domains. Perhaps most important of all—we love telepresence because it simply *feels good.*

TELEPRESENCE TEKKIES

We're all tekkies in telepresence. The technology appears in the toys, gadgets, tools, and entertainment that dominate our new millennium pleasures. Telepresence technology makes virtual-reality simulations a significant part of daily conscious life. It's the television in the bedroom, the big screen at the movies, the world of cyberspace, burgeoning telecommunications, the simulated rides in the amusement park, and virtual-reality games where you wear gloves, headsets, or body suits. Telepresence technology works because we don't have to struggle to establish a sense of being there. No time in the history of humankind has virtual reality and the psychological experience of telepresence been so widely and readily accessible. Matthew Lombard and Teresa Ditton, media experts at Temple University, write that telepresence has "an intensifying effect on media users, increasing or enhancing enjoyment, involvement, task performance and training, desensitization, persuasion, memory, and parasocial interaction." Our Stone Age minds are easily duped into believing. So what does it do to engage us?

We have fun. Suddenly we're transported to another place. We can scream, cry, laugh, and be angry—and then leave the movie theater. We can chuckle at the antics of a sitcom couple or shout at the injustices delivered on the eleven o'clock news. It's so obvious a response that most of us don't think very much about it. And the more we're involved, the more fun it is. Just think how the entire country was mesmerized for a year attending the drawn-out trial of O. J. Simpson, or the incredible numbers of people who religiously tune in to *Monday Night Football.* If it weren't fun, no one would bother. Telepresence gives us a sense of what Lombard and Ditton call "social richness," or the feeling that we are an immediate and intimate part of the action. As such, we become the judge and the jurors, and if we so choose, any or all of the participants. Depending on the medium, the user, and the context, we perceive either ourselves being transported *there* or the action being brought to us *here.* We can commune with the characters, commune with others communing with the characters as in a movie theater or a baseball stadium, or commune with the vast, virtual collective in cyberspace.

We're doused in virtual reality. Telepresence has the intriguing quality of embracing our interests—getting us deeply engrossed in the virtual-reality simulation we're attending. You don't have to go any further than a video arcade to observe this phenomenon. Players are "lost" in their virtual worlds, often oblivious to the light, sound, and noise that surround them. They interact with the computer more than with the friend playing the game next to them. And when they lose, make a mistake, or confront something they don't like, the computer is held responsible. Just think about what it is like to go to an IMAX movie where all eyes are focused on the screen, bodies tensed for visual assault, hands often gripping railings or armrests for balance. Naturally, the degree of involvement depends on the type of media, the content, and the user. This quality of telepresence is referred to as immersion. Lombard and Ditton discuss that "the most compelling virtual reality experiences [are when] the senses are immersed in the virtual world; the body is entrusted to a reality engine." Interestingly, many people in the field of special effects view their work as a synthesis of reality with the intent to dupe the human brain into believing that what it sees is logical and believable.

We get better. Telepresence gives us the illusion of progress. Play a few games and you get better. Watch a few television documentaries and you get smarter. Catch the evening news and you are better informed. Whether these improvements are quantifiable or subjective, they afford the illusion of being more involved, more aware, more a part of the action. If you miss the Sunday afternoon baseball game on TV, you might be "behind" in the race-for-the-pennant discussion around the water cooler at work. If your son doesn't have the latest, blood-curdling game machine and can't compare scores with his classmates, something must be wrong with him. If your teenager can't socialize in the online chat rooms, something is seriously missing in her life. And if you don't know how to send e-mail . . .

We make friends. Parasocial relationships permeate the virtual roads traveled in telepresence experiences. Research has shown that people often respond to characters on television as real social entities, not actors on a set. The opposite is also true. "Real" people on television, such as politicians, activists, business promoters, and other representatives of special interests, play the roles that will entice viewers to believe they have certain characteristics. Consider the presidential speeches with the American flag in the background, the photos of the family on the desk, and the sincere, unblinking eyes that stare directly into the camera—affording the illusion that *he* is talking only to *you*. Or the highly subjective news reports that imply you are experiencing headline news when stories are selected by the amount of interest, sensation, and, accordingly, viewer loyalty they will generate. According to Lombard and Ditton, when users, transported by telepresence,

> perceive a medium (e.g., a computer) as a social entity, at least some of the users' perceptions, thought-processes, and emotional responses are similar or identical to those found in human-human interaction. The psychological effects of this kind of presence are therefore potentially as diverse as those generated by nonmediated social interaction.

Perhaps most important, parasocial relationships require far less emotional and psychological commitment, provide easily resolved or contained conflict, and enable us to insulate ourselves against the pain of social disappointments, failures, or anxiety.

The tools to accomplish these telepresence qualities are constantly improving. Essentially, their goal is to increase immersion, to involve as many human sensory and psychological receptors as possible to captivate and transform physical presence into telepresence. Science-fiction writers have described future worlds where telepresence dominates presence—where virtual-reality simulations become originals. Perhaps this is the essence of postmodern culture. We have reached a point in time where natural selection no longer serves our need to adapt. Instead, we rely on technologies that are carrying us into dimensions that have never been documented, filling our lives with virtual-reality simulations until it becomes almost psychologically impossible to distinguish that copy from the original.

JURASSIC JABS

Suddenly the power went down. Ten thousand volts in the electric fence was rendered useless. They sit in their brightly colored electric jeeps, waiting. Waiting for the lights and the power. There are two cars: the kids are in one, the scientists in the other. The storm assaults them, rain beating so hard that the first ominous rumbles sound like thunder, not the deep roar of a giant prehistoric beast. Then abruptly, without warning, you're in the car with them, watching the twenty-foot-tall Tyrannosaurus Rex rip away the impotent electric fence like it was paper fluttering in the wind.

"Keep absolutely still," Dr. Grant hisses to Dr. Malcolm in one of the jeeps. "Its vision is based on movement."

But in the other jeep the kids use a flashlight to see what's happening, so it's only minutes until the T-Rex is ripping their car to pieces, its bloodthirsty jaws breaking through the glass roof to hover inches away from their heads . . .

URASSIC PARK, STEVEN Spielberg's famous 1993 film, was
one of the most elaborate productions in cinema history. It introduced innovative technical devices that combined sophisticated computer
graphics and remote-controlled models to bring the extinct dinosaurs back
to life. It spawned books, toys, and a sequel—in an unforgettable journey
that transported viewers in a time machine back 65 million years.

The story was adapted from Michael Crichton's novel about a business
venture to create a live animal park where scientists had cloned dinosaurs
using DNA extracted from prehistoric insects trapped in amber. Ironically,
two weeks into the production of *Jurassic Park*, the Associated Press wire
service carried a real story about a team of California scientists who *had*
cloned a fragment of genetic material from an extinct bee preserved in
amber over 25 million years ago. "If the midge [stingless bee]," the news
story reported, "consumed dinosaur blood, the researchers said they may
be able to unlock the secrets of the mysterious extinct reptiles and their
evolution" (Shay, p. iii).

Truth can be stranger than fiction. Or, in the case of virtual-reality
simulations, truth and fiction can merge.

So what did we really see in that gripping *Jurassic Park* scene? The
Tyrannosaurus Rex began life as a series of drawings by Mark "Crash"
McCreery. It evolved into a twenty-foot-high, 13,000-pound mechanical
creature with foam rubber skin and hydraulic technology powered through
a computer control board, somewhat akin to a flight simulator. Most of the
other dinosaurs in the movie were computer graphics—virtual creations
built in cyberspace. In the gripping scene described above, everything took
place on a 135 x 240-foot sound stage—one of the largest in Hollywood. It
was designed to look like Hawaii. The car sat on inner tubes to give the
impression of being in a mud pit, and ferocious rain machines created the
downpour. The panting of the T-Rex was created by taking the sounds of
whale blowholes and looping them into a breathing rhythm. Its roar came
from layering the sounds of an elephant, alligator, penguin, tiger, and dog.

And we bought it.

TELEPRESENCE TRICKS

The process of transporting ourselves into virtual realities is as natural and preprogrammed as the process that assumes that what looks human *is* human. When we need a mediating device to induce the virtual-reality, in this case, the virtual reality simulation, our minds have to be tricked. When we see a person on the street with his or her back to the sun, the shadow will fall in front. We *know* this to be true—it is one of the many sensory bits of information we have stored in our minds. If we take that same person, with the sun behind, and the shadow falls behind him or her and not in front, our brains will tell us it is impossible. It will be much harder to believe that what we are seeing is true or real and accordingly, much more difficult to induce telepresence. If you question this premise, simply turn on your television and adjust the video controls to make all human faces green. Is the serial killer on the *Lifetime* movie still as frightening? Is Dan Rather still as convincing? How funny is David Letterman? Our brains know that what *looks* human *is* human, and people don't have bright, lime-green skin, unless, of course, that is part of the story. This simple concept challenges the best special-effects people in the business. The rule is crystal-clear: you have to use a wide variety of telepresence tricks to reproduce what people will experience as "real" in order to increase immersion (and thus, believability) in the virtual-reality simulation. These tricks roughly fall into the following five categories:

1. What you believe you see is what you get.

Everyone has seen the classic movie *The Ten Commandments*. During this momentous film, Charlton Heston raises his arms and, with the help of God, "parts" the Red Sea. Audiences gasp as the Hebrew people cross the dry riverbed to the other side, free from slavery. What the audience does not know is that it really wasn't the Red Sea being parted or a wondrous miracle being observed. Instead, they were seeing a very clever special effect created by using two slabs of Jell-O to represent the diverted shores.

The most important ingredient in creating psychological immersion—or maximizing telepresence—is visual manipulation. The rules are rigid. Like the lime-green faces described earlier, you can't violate what the eye, or the human brain, doesn't expect. Jon Boorstin writes in *The Hollywood Eye*, "We can be fooled, but we mustn't feel fooled. The visceral world is very unforgiving of stunts and special effects that feel hokey, so Hollywood has finely honed these skills" (p. 118).

If you want to heighten telepresence you have to follow the rules with whatever tricks you can devise. The process involves a deep understanding of how we see, how we interpret what we see, and how we integrate it into our Stone Age minds. Once again, the overriding concept is that our brains believe that something is human or real if it *looks* that way. The Jell-O in *The Ten Commandments* does look like a parted Red Sea, so we believe it.

Researchers, filmmakers, special-effects professionals, sound designers, and others involved in virtual-reality simulations know the basic elements in creating visual illusions of reality. The most important factor is to create a simulation that enables you to believe. Lombard and Ditton note that ways to increase the level of telepresence involve visual cues such as color, sensory richness, vividness, contrast, resolution, and the similarity to the natural world. The quality of the image and the absence of distortions further convince us that it is real. Thus, we have no problem believing that Tom Hanks as *Forrest Gump* shakes the hand of President John F. Kennedy in a scene where separate images have been digitally cut together. Rationally, we know that it could not have happened. After all, Tom Hanks was not even ten years old when JFK was in office. But it doesn't matter. We're not watching Tom Hanks after all—we're joining Forrest in his incredible trip through life.

Interestingly, researchers have found that two other visual qualities unrelated to content also significantly affect telepresence: image size and viewing proportion. Larger images, as well as being close (without excessive proximity), make people feel more involved in the action. This is clearly demonstrated in the trend to buy larger televisions. A related feature is the proportion of the visual field occupied by the image. For example, a large movie screen in a small theater can be as effective as a giant movie screen in a giant theater (unless you are sitting at a comfortably close distance). The IMAX theaters, as well as theaters-in-the-round, have taken full advantage of this to strengthen telepresence. To illustrate, ask yourself a simple question: Do you feel more like you're *there* when watching a movie screen placed in the front of a theater, or when watching a wrap-around movie screen where you can face front and see where you're "going" and face back to see where you've "been"?

The newly developing industry in individual computerized virtual-reality simulations use headsets and other optic devices placed close to the eye to take advantage of this concept. In this manner they monopolize the visual field, increasing the proportion of viewing area without the need to create larger, more expansive screens.

As technology improves, these visual techniques will be utilized more in cyberspace applications, communications devices, video games, and other virtual-reality simulations. The increasing levels of immersion have the potential to further blur the lines between physical presence and telepresence, opening a Pandora's Box of questions, risks, and psychological implications. It has been only in recent years that researchers have tackled the issues concerning the effects of violence, sex, and aggression on young children watching television and movies. New technologies increase this exposure. Video games, for example, often have more graphic, interactive violence than television. We need to consider the implications of our visual presentations *before* suffering the consequences. However, as with all human technological adaptations, we move far faster than our philosophy, ignoring the potential destructiveness of our own powers.

Consider this: television news programs eagerly air reports of American bombings. It doesn't matter which "war"—the visual is the same. To make it more graphic, the news provides a "bird's-eye view" of how a bomb is dropped. On television it looks like a window with vertical and horizontal scoring. The target is where the two lines cross. You can't see much below except for shaded gray areas. In the background a voice tracks what is occurring. Suddenly you see it happen—a switch is flipped and the bomb drops, leaving billows of smoke rising in its wake. You don't see the homes, you don't hear the people scream, you only know the hit. Score!

It's chillingly similar to the video games at the local arcade.

2. The hand is quicker than the eye.

Movies don't really move. They are simply a series of still photographs that are run together quickly so the eye connects them into a moving image. We have all seen those little books where you flip the pages quickly and the pictures miraculously have motion. Yet how many of us think about the phenomenon when we're in a movie theater?

The proof is in almost every movie we've seen. Would it make a difference if we knew that the tornado in the original *Wizard of Oz* was a specially built muslin stocking, or the doomed H.M.S. *Titanic* that we watched plowing through the seas was actually a forty-five-foot model? For the length of the movie we gave in to telepresence. But what if they were still pictures on the screen? Would we have believed them?

Industrial Light and Magic, the special-effects company that worked on *Star Wars*, has created one of the most intriguing and convincing illusions of motion. They built the first Dykstraflex camera for the original *Star Wars* movie—a system where the camera could pan, tilt, and track around a constructed model without ever losing focus. The camera could repeat the same movements from shot to shot, building visual sequences in layers. Artists then constructed tiny, minutely detailed models of starships built to scale. More than seventy-five models were built. When they went to shoot the "action" scenes, the only ship that ever moved in *Star Wars* was the Dykstraflex camera.

3. What Spielberg never told us.

Director Steven Spielberg has convinced us to believe in the most bizarre creations, such as a kindly alien named ET, evil little gremlins, and fierce dinosaurs hatched by people. And that's just the beginning. There are many more ways to fool us. Consider some of the camera techniques employed in virtual-reality simulations of all types. By manipulating the camera, or the scene that is presented to the viewer, telepresence can be greatly enhanced. We saw that in *Scream*, when the camera increased tension by closing in on the victims and making quick cuts between images. "Subjective camera shots create a view through an actual or implied entity's eyes," write Lombard and Ditton, "and so transform the viewer from an event spectator into an event participant."

Think about what makes the televised baseball game exciting. The camera doesn't remain at one wide-angled view of the field. If we want to feel part of the game, we can't remain a distant observer. The camera cuts into a close-up of the pitcher, and we carefully watch his routine—he rolls the baseball in his hand, he touches the brim of his cap, he does a ritual tap on his left forearm. His eyes narrow, his lips are set and his face takes on a fierce grimace. He winds up, ready to throw the pitch. We really *feel* there. How many of us admit that we would rather watch the game on television than be in the ballpark?

One of the most widely used tools to enhance telepresence in virtual-reality simulations is the blue screen, an essentially simple concept used in films, video, and computers. A subject is photographed in front of an evenly lit, bright, pure blue background. When the shot is completed the blue screen is replaced with another image. While the concept is simple, the execution is far more complex, involving sophisticated technology necessary to create completed images that will appear visually accurate to the highly discerning human eye. For example, take your favorite hero and have him "run" away from a train, automobile, or evil aliens pursuing him. Add some action music and a lot of noise, and you have a great scene. No one in the audience will realize that the hero is running in front of a blue screen.

Think about the blue screen the next time you watch the weather report. The weather person is cheerfully pointing to the national weather map, indicating fronts, large clusters of clouds and heavy storms. "In the west," she might say, pointing to California, Washington, or Oregon, "there will be heavy rains, while the other side of the country," she gingerly swings an arm eastward, "is experiencing hot, sunny weather." You don't think anything of it; in fact, you're probably patiently waiting until she points gleefully to *your* part of the country. In actuality, your weather person is pointing to a very bright blue screen. The weather map is added on in the composite that you see on your TV screen. It's only an approximation where the hand should be, based on an off-camera monitor playing the composite. So now, if you watch carefully, the hands of your favorite weather person might be slightly off base.

Another common, highly deceptive device is the TelePrompTer, a clear, nonreflective surface that displays words for reading. Picture this: you're watching a televised speech of a political figure. He or she stares unflinchingly into your face, relaxed, almost intimate, words mouthed only for *your* benefit. The politician leans closer toward you as if there were no one listening but the two of you. It looks and feels like a private conversation. There are no notes, no awkward words, and no stumbles. How can you *not* believe such a direct and open plea? What you don't see is the TelePrompTer, a device placed strategically by the camera so it *appears* that your candidate is looking directly at you and not reading the digitized words that move slowly, at the speed of speech, across the screen. Even if you are aware of the fact that the TelePrompTer exists, it still tends to fade from consciousness. It's like trying to keep in mind there's a camera between you and the film or the television screen. When we become more aware of mediating devices, our telepresence decreases.

We are not alone in the duplicity. The best actors will tell you that in order to give a good performance, they, too, must believe. "Generally," Boorstin writes, "actors have to convince themselves the scene is centered on them, and they rewrite their scenes in their minds from their own point of view. This is not simply ego, but a necessary step in taking possession of a role . . ." (p. 86). The best performances *look* real, as do the best virtual-reality simulations. Perhaps this is why so many people who are prominent in the media are quite adept in acting skills—from performers to news-people to politicians. A recent poll found that 25 percent of people surveyed, and 40 percent of people under thirty, learned about the presidential campaign from "comic" news sources such as Jay Leno and David Letterman. Thirteen percent cited MTV as their source for political information. "Whatever their degree of irreverence," writes journalist Howard Kurtz in *Newsday*, "these programs impart serious information amid the yuks. And for many people, they're the primary source of political information" (p. A24). This is a steadily growing phenomenon, as crossovers between media stars and government become more common. Consider some of the people who have entered office since Ronald Reagan was president: Sonny Bono, Clint Eastwood, Fred Thompson, and, of course, Jesse "The Body" Ventura. The opposite is also true—former New York City mayor Ed Koch has been on television and radio and later sat as the judge in TV's *People's Court*, and Bob Dole, former Senate Majority Leader and presidential candidate, as well as Tip O'Neil, former Speaker of the House, have appeared in several television shows and commercials. Perhaps most amusing was the Lays potato chips commercial aired during Super Bowl XXIX, featuring two defeated incumbent governors—Ann Richards of Texas and Mario Cuomo of New York.

Possibly the best politician/actor in U.S. history showed his stuff when, during a critical speech, the TelePrompTer ran the *wrong* words. It was September 24, 1993, and President Bill Clinton was giving a nationally broadcast speech on health care. Suddenly the TelePrompTer began to scroll the wrong speech, taken from the February 17 address Clinton had made before a Joint Session of Congress. Perhaps his predecessors might have fumbled, yet an Information Age president has very different qualifications. President Clinton made a quick comment to the vice president, seated behind him. Gore immediately alerted aides, and Clinton winged it, with the help of his notes, for the next five to seven minutes, looking straight into the camera. No one watching Mr. Clinton on television knew what happened until long after the speech was over.

4. The sound of music and everything else.

We rarely consider the possibility that a sound can be an illusion. Ask yourself that old philosophical question: If a tree falls in the forest and there's no one to hear, does it make a sound? When mulling over the answer we never consider that the sound, the perception of the sound, or the manipulation of the sound, can be inaccurate. Either it *is* or it *isn't.*

Even the earliest video-game makers knew that. Without sound, telepresence is greatly impaired. With sound, telepresence is greatly enhanced. Close your eyes. Now define where you are by the sound. If you're in that favorite chair, maybe you can hear the whir of the air conditioning or the hiss of a heater. The rumble of a car or whine of a siren may drift in from the street. If you're on the beach you'll hear the soothing, rhythmic pounding of the surf, maybe a radio being played on the blanket next to you, or the laughter of a young child as she digs sand castles. And if you're on a subway, train, or bus—well, the sounds are so loud and so varied that you're literally assaulted by noise. Our aural lives are filled with such a vast range and variety of sounds that, like our visual systems, we must select, filter, and interpret them to assess our physical environment. Not surprisingly, the art form with the largest human audience has always been music. Anyone can enjoy it, from singing a lullaby to the primitive rhythms of rock to the complex crescendo of a symphonic orchestra. The designers of Pong, one of the earliest electronic video games, were well aware of the importance of sound. Pong consisted of a tiny point of light that bounced back and forth on the screen. The goal was to hit it with the "paddle," a small line that was manipulated by the player. Every time you hit the "ball" there was a satisfying "pong" sound, an electronic replica of one-way ping pong.

Sound *creates* images associated with emotional responses. We don't often consider this psychological aspect of sound; most of us think of it as an accompaniment. Sound enables us to see things, to summon up mental images and emotions that are associated with it. For example, close your eyes and locate a specific sound in your environment, such as rain on the rooftop, footsteps on a creaky floor, a dog barking. You mental modules are programmed to enable you to pair the sound with an image, a memory, or an emotional response. Is the rain heavy, making you feel somewhat glum? What does the dog look like? Does it remind you of the puppy you loved as a child? Who is walking across the floor? Do you get a shiver of expectation or of fear? Creators of virtual-reality sound environments use this in many popular devices. Think about those "environmental" sound machines designed to help you relax or go to sleep. They reproduce a variety of sounds, including such things as the ocean surf, rain, waterfall, forest sounds, wind, birds, animal sounds, country-evening sounds and the ubiquitous "white noise" that emulates a mix of "all" sounds.

Similarly, audiotapes use a wide variety of sounds to induce everything from meditation to motivation to diet and exercise. Of course music, as an artistic arrangement of sounds, has been accomplishing this throughout the history of humankind. What emotions or images does the pounding of a drum summon, in contrast to the sweetness of a flute or the piercing tones of an electric guitar? Why do some people prefer classical music over rap, or jazz over pop? Now take the music, add words, and a new set of images, emotions, associations, and virtual-reality environments is opened up.

In virtual-reality simulations, sound is used to guide our perception, enhance our illusion, and serve a specific contextual function. It amplifies our visual perception and helps us shape and interpret what we are seeing. Think what happens when we turn off the sound as we are watching a movie or television show. The visual components seem stilted and obvious. The action appears flat and unreal. The movements of the actors come off as awkward, even amusing. While sound is usually undervalued by audiences, it's critical to sustaining the illusion. Simply put, we hear in three dimensions, and, accordingly, enhanced telepresence requires the inclusion of that very powerful and affective sense. Boorstin writes,

> The tone of a movie, its level of abstraction, is set as much by its sounds as its pictures. Fight scenes without the sound of fist on flesh have a curious, insubstantial quality; fight scenes with fist effects that sound like a truck hitting a bridge abutment are ludicrous. . . . Multichannel surround-sound, so distracting from a voyeuristic standpoint, packs a wallop here—being enveloped by the sound only adds to the sick roller-coaster thrill of swooping over a Vietnamese village on an air cavalry chopper in *Apocalypse Now*, napalming it to hell. (p. 131)

Human ingenuity has developed the difficult art of sound simulations in many different ways to enhance telepresence. The most critical factors are quality and dimensionality: do we believe the sound, does the music enhance the action, does the sound change and adjust to our senses as it would in actuality? Our libraries of sound are impressive—we hear the exaggerated and discrete sounds when suspense is being built or the irregular staccato music that tells us a shock is approaching. A powerful cacophony of sound and music intensify action. Imagine what a car chase would look like if there were soft music in the background or how a tender love scene would come off with a roar of fire engines.

Sound can be created in a simple and straightforward way or in layers, dimensions, and superimpositions to achieve new sounds. The illusions are intriguing. For instance, the background sounds in the shower scene in Hitchcock's classic movie *Psycho* were the collective screeches of violins, repeated over and over again. The noises made by Linda Blair as the young girl possessed by the devil in *The Exorcist* were a blend of screams, animals thrashing, and English spoken backward. The Wookie voice from *Star Wars* was created by recording the sounds made by a four-month-old cinnamon bear and mixing it with other bears, a walrus, seal, and badger. And they all sounded "real."

5. Coming to your theater soon.

Telepresence technology continues to grow at lightning speed, enhanced by the dramatic ongoing developments in computer technology. The near future will see an increase in the virtual inclusion of other sensory outputs such as smell, body movement, touch, and force feedback. Interactivity will also increase, bringing virtual-reality simulations into all aspects of daily life. These features will expand telepresence as well as potentially *replace* face-to-face contact. Telepresence technology is used in such varied areas as communication between individuals or groups, conferences, education, meetings—even surgery. One of the most far-reaching telepresence experiences occurred on July 4, 1997, when the Mars Pathfinder, using a remote system controlled by earth-bound scientists, transported us all to the surface of the Red Planet.

It's not difficult to imagine a world where virtual-reality simulations dominate our consciousness, controlled by the inventors, designers, and policy-makers who direct the content. Who are these people? Can we trust them to make the correct presentations, enhance the healthiest metaphors? Or do they, consciously and unconsciously, proliferate the biases, prejudices, and conflicts of human social relationships? These are serious questions. We already know the power of virtual-reality simulations to stimulate copycat behavior, set social trends, sell products, and convince people to think and act in redesigned ways. One study found that people who experienced a greater sense of telepresence expressed more confidence in the products they were going to buy. They were persuaded to feel *good* about their purchasing behavior. Don't we see, hear, and experience this ourselves each day? Other studies suggest that telepresence experiences are encoded into memory in a similar way as nonmediated experiences, confusing what is actual and what is virtual. *I know what cops are like—I've seen them for years on television. What more can you expect from the FBI? I've skirted them for years in the movies.* Increased immersion into virtual-reality environments might take us further and further away from subjective consciousness, putting us at risk of becoming the psychological "puppets" of those very same media inventors, designers, and policy-makers. Do you recognize any of the following slogans? How have they affected our behavior as a society?

- We do it all for you. (McDonald's)
- It's the real thing. (Coca-Cola)
- Better ideas driven by you. (Ford)
- Good for the body, good for the soul. (Campbell's)
- Do one thing. Do it well. (GMC)
- Don't leave home without it. (American Express)

How do we control these highly persuasive virtual-reality simulations and protect ourselves and our children against the powerful potential influence? Is free will or psychological manipulation the inevitable result?

Perhaps, as Ornstein writes, "we are going to need a lot of help in the next few decades to refashion and rethink our world. . . . Our progress depends more on consciously directing adaptations than on improving rationality" (p. 267). Virtual-reality simulations are here to stay. We need to control them, not allow them, or their designers, to control us. As Marshall McLuhan predicted almost forty years ago, the medium has *become* the message. If we don't participate in that message, then we inevitably surrender our consciousness to a stronger will with far more questionable motives.

VIRTUAL KIN

*I*T WAS A familiar scene in the 1950s: three kids in the family, a home in the suburbs. Dad gives Mom a kiss and goes off to work. The kids dash off to school. Mom remains home to vacuum, dust, and bake chocolate chip cookies for the warm and fuzzy three-o'clock after-school snack.

Advance the tape to *now*. Dad gives Mom a kiss and goes off to work. Mom takes the kids to daycare or gives the nanny instructions and goes off to work. The warm and fuzzy three-o'clock snack consists of soda, a bag of chips, and a fierce battle with aliens on the video-game machine.

Today kids come home to virtual-reality simulations. They play with joysticks instead of baseballs and compete against digitized warriors instead of the kids next door. We still live in families, but they tend to be isolated, broken, and multitiered. We still live in communities, but they tend to be scattered and transitory. We still hunt ferociously for mates, per-

151

petuating the age-old gender wars, even as they move toward serial rather than lifelong marriages. What is it all about?

Let's go back to nature to sort out a few basic concepts. Primates, unlike some other mammals, live in groups where they cooperate. Primates recognize their kin and form "family" associations and "friendships." At the same time there is competition between groups for such things as food, mates, and shelter. Early humans continued these social relationships because, from an evolutionary standpoint, they *worked*.

Consider some basic facts about life. If you want your genes to carry on into subsequent generations, you have to favor those individuals who transport them. Narcissism is one technique—preserve yourself and you preserve your genes. Yet you also share genes with your parents, brothers, sisters, and children. It would be critical to protect those individuals as well. Extended family—uncles, aunts, cousins—also carry some of your genes, so you would also be invested in protecting them, although not with the same vigor that you would use with immediate family members. This is a basic description of what evolutionary psychologists believe underlies human family and kinship relationships.

A critical part of this scenario is *spreading* your genes—making sure that they continue to survive in new offspring. Sexual relationships are an integral part of nature's strategy, and are discussed further in the next chapter. Robert Wright, in *The Moral Animal*, writes:

> The various members of a Stone Age society were each other's rivals in the contest to fill the next generation with genes. What's more, they were each other's tools in that contest. Spreading their genes depended on dealing with their neighbors: sometimes helping them, sometimes ignoring them, sometimes exploiting them, sometimes liking them, sometimes hating them—and having a sense for which people warrant which sort of treatment, and when they warrant it. (p. 27)

Natural selection is a highly competitive process. As discussed earlier, the dark-winged moths died when the tree bark was light, allowing the light-winged moths to proliferate. When the environment changed, the rules of competition shifted and the light-winged moths died off. The analogy is clear. If there is only one piece of meat for dinner, not everyone can eat it. If there is only a limited amount of water, not everyone can drink it. Essentially, the earth has limited resources that can support only a limited amount of life. Overpopulate and you starve. Look around you. People starve in third-world countries because resources are limited. Maybe there's overpopulation or an unexpected drought or other disaster and suddenly already depleted resources can't be stretched. People starve in American cities because symbolic resources—money—are also limited. Fierce competition for survival breaks out in both environments with many subsequent victims.

How do self-aware life-forms protect their genes in such a competitive climate? *Blood is thicker than water.* We all know the words. And we all know that their truth is irrefutable. Human mental modules are programmed to view kinship differently than their other associations. Most parents will unquestionably sacrifice themselves for their children. Siblings who fight bitterly with one another at home will fight even harder to protect their brother or sister from "outside" bullies. Our history is filled with stories of powerful families, fierce kinship rivalries, and carefully guarded genealogies that can be traced for hundreds, even thousands, of years.

All societies have families, marriage, and kinship systems that are held as sacrosanct. Most traditional families follow well-established roles differentiated by gender: the female is the nurturer, the primary caregiver who offers unconditional love; the male is the connection to the outside world, the primary breadwinner who offers conditional love based on a child's ability to successfully negotiate his or her environment. *Both* roles are critical in healthy human development for establishing a crucial psychosocial balance. Ironically, society has assigned values to designate which role is more important. Consequently, a man's role as dad carries financial, emotional, and social status, while a woman's role as mom is held in much less esteem. Interestingly, sometimes the best moms are male and the best dads are female. This role reversal can result in severe consequences which we see in custody courts every day. Rigid role definitions based on gender severely limit both men and women. Nonetheless, to believe that the traditional role of dad is more *valuable* than the traditional role of mom, or vice versa, destroys the spirit of parental caregiving. Even today, when families are redefining themselves, when there are working moms and stay-at-home dads, when complex systems of stepfamilies and serial marriages are being created, the need for both men and women in a child's life is indisputable.

Our mental modules, as discussed earlier, are programmed to nurture an emerging self. In a similar manner, we are programmed to nurture a self within the context of an expanding family. We are born to a mother. Our first bond is, ideally, with her. Then the self begins to expand, bonding with father and subsequently brother and sister. More genetically removed individuals enter our social awareness and attachment systems—maybe grandparents, aunts, uncles, close cousins. These bonds are well established before we have close contact with the "outside" world—usually when we enter school somewhere between ages three and five. And then the process further unfolds. Paradoxically, as our worlds expand, our need for attachment to primary (family) groups persists. It's no surprise that we refer to our best friend as being like a sister or brother, or our favorite adults as being like a mother or father. We are programmed, psychologically and emotionally, to define ourselves first through our family relationships. Family values, although clichéd, are still very much alive. From an evolutionary standpoint, human beings were never designed to live in cubicles by themselves, commuting to work and having limited or no intimate contact with other humans.

Too often, particularly when forced into the isolated, often adversarial conditions of modern life, the glitches in "family" genetic or psychological codes become prominent. Children are taught or act out unrestrained behaviors that will hinder development and impair socialization. In general, families don't have to be flawless—it would be difficult to find any to fit that description. Families only need to be *adequate*—good enough to provide the basic needs that enable a child to grow and develop—in order to produce healthy offspring. By that definition, the vast majority of families are okay; they do their jobs along with the many idiosyncrasies, mistaken messages, undesirable behaviors, and inconsistencies that their adult children carry into their lives. Whatever the scenario, the vast majority of families raise children to seek out mates who will enable them to replicate the process—create their own family. Even after suffering through the most agonizing relationships, surviving the most bitter divorces, or being victimized through physical, emotional, or sexual abuse, people still seek to find new mates and create new families.

The concept of kinship does not, obviously, negate the basic conflicting and competitive nature of social relationships. We are programmed to compete, argue, defy, fight, and even kill if necessary. Murder is a crime punishable by death in many states, but self-defense is an acceptable "excuse" to kill. Murdering a stranger is a horrific crime, but a parent murdering his or her children is unspeakable and arouses shock, anger, and a cry for vengeance even from strangers. And, of course, along with infanticide is matricide, patricide, and other crimes against one's family.

Clearly, human nature is programmed for unresolvable conflict. Perhaps that is why we are so easily drawn into movies like *Scream*, stories of violence and angst and games that unmercifully pit one player against the other. Research in evolutionary psychology has found that mystery, defined by Kaplan as "the promise of more information if one can venture deeper into the scene" (p. 588) is the most consistent predictor of environmental preference. We love mystery and are obsessively drawn to virtual environments like Stephen King novels and movies, and we find enormous pleasure in vicariously participating in the acts of violence and aggression that permeate our lives in the form of sports, entertainment, and virtual simulations. They satiate the frustration of unfixable internal conflicts.

These inner conflicts emerge from our human existential dilemma, from Rank's (1972) polarizing fears, and from the constant tension between separation and attachment. Within and outside of our families we undergo physical and psychological development, only to create edifices that deal with a disharmony that can never be set straight. Part of us is driven to compete, to ruthlessly protect our own kin, to hunt and forage in a world where others are hunting and foraging to protect their own. Part of us is also driven to cooperate, to live with one another because we have to, to share, exhibit kindness and altruism, to work within a society that ultimately assists us in denying our most terrifying destiny. Which is the more powerful force? We all know about the stories of women being attacked and raped in the middle of urban rush-hour traffic and everyone ignoring the screams. We also all know about the tragedies that have struck entire communities and the thousands of people who have offered time, help, money, and succor to those in need. We have all hated our enemies and loved our friends. We have all been deeply disappointed by some and wonderfully uplifted by others. We protect our families and at the same time demonstrate our very worst behaviors when in their midst. Our lives are permeated with unresolvable conflict.

VIRTUAL KIN

Virtual-reality simulations, as copies of actuality, can become our new reality. We can "play" with our conflicts, rehearse and reenact them with the fantasy of achieving a resolution. Families can be perfect, enemies can be murdered, and we can rise to become (or identify with) the heroes and heroines of our worlds. Add telepresence, and *believing* becomes easy. It's easy to believe—or to be convinced—when the copy is more "real" than the original. Put it in the context of relationships and you can find yourself in a chilling Orwellian scenario.

Does it sound far-fetched? We start the training early. Information Age babies are wired into virtual-reality simulations. Consider the devices that aid the most primary relationships between parent and baby. Mommy Bear is a soft, cuddly brown bear billed on its packaging "to help provide the easiest and most natural transition between the security of the womb and the unfamiliarity of life outside the womb." Simply hang the stuffed animal on a crib rail or place it strategically next to your infant, turn on the switch, and baby is surrounded by the strange, rhythmic sounds of the womb. If parents are more hi-tech, they can buy a Slumbertime Soother, complete with a remote control that provides soft music, nature sounds, and lights while baby takes a nap. Parents can keep track of baby from anywhere in the house or yard by using monitors that pick up the smallest infant sounds, scramble outside signals for familial privacy, provide comforting sounds and lights, and, for the upwardly mobile, work via a five-inch television. When one considers the decreasing amounts of time shared by babies and their working parents, these devices are stand-ins for the real thing—virtual mommies and daddies. They're a far cry from our early ancestors who strapped babies to their backs and brought children to their work.

As the new-millennium baby ages, he can be treated to more mature virtual companionship in the form of Radar: The Talk 'n Listen Robot, toddler laptops, and activity boxes, highchairs, and desks that talk, sing, coo, count, and recite numbers. Perhaps the most prophetic "toys" are the interactive creatures that fill the shelves of children's stores. There's My Best Friend, a doll complete with voice recognition that actually responds to you, or e-mail board games that connect you with disembodied online competitors. ActiMates are a series of stuffed toys that move, play games, tell time, remember names, sing songs, and accomplish a whole host of peer activities. They come in several versions that are preprogrammed with 4,000 words each. Take these "friends" to the family television, and kids can "hook up" with their special shows and videos. Better yet, hook them up to the family computer, and their vocabulary jumps to 14,000 words with software that will, as the packaging claims, "guide, compliment and encourage your child." ActiMates claim to teach kids a whole host of lessons such as sharing, empathy, good citizenship, comprehension, and following directions. Who needs mommies, daddies, sisters, brothers, or friends?

The virtual-reality simulations that pervade the lives of our children take on an intriguing meaning. As brilliant visionary Marshall McLuhan wrote, "In this electric age we see ourselves being translated more and more into the form of information, moving toward the technological extension of consciousness" (p. 15). Accordingly, when kids play with virtual-reality simulations, they create virtual kin. In this context, the copy of the kin has the potential to become as "real" as the original, blood kin. The mechanical teddy-bear heartbeats substitute for the genuine throbs; exhausted, hard-working moms and dads let virtual reality do the babysitting; interactive playthings offer recorded statements of love . . . there's no limit to the metaphor.

The transition to virtual-reality playthings is not a revolution but an evolution, an adaptation to the latest technology. Child's play has always been critical in human development. Classic psychoanalytic theory maintains that play is the way the human ego deals with the angst of reality. A child's fragile, developing ego must find a way to inhibit or sublimate primitive drives for pleasure with the reality of increasing social demands and expectations. In the process of playing, kids assimilate and master specific skills and roles. It helps the child adapt to his or her culture, offering a framework to explore, experiment, identify strengths and weaknesses, and emulate adult roles. Clearly, games reflect the culture—only a capitalist society could produce such classics as Monopoly and Risk. Essentially, play reflects human biological, psychological, and cultural attributes—a forum where conflict, mastery, narcissism, and social identity can be rehearsed.

But what happens when the play involves such deep psychological immersion that it has the potential to replace the original? With the crushing power of telepresence, can family and friends be substituted with virtual-reality simulations that affect the emotional, cognitive, social, and psychological growth of children? If so, how do we define the new, emerging electronic family? How do we define the new, emerging electronic child? And, perhaps most important, what kind of adults will grow from these new psychological configurations?

Think about what is already happening today's families:

- Kids play "house" with interactive dolls programmed to say all the things they want to hear.

- Kids make friends with children they never see.

- Children surf the Internet by themselves instead of watching television with their families.

- A pick-up ball game involves throwing curve balls to digitized batters.

- Toddlers cuddle warm and fuzzy stuffed toys that profess their undying love for them. Then throw them away when the battery goes dead.

- Third-graders battle aliens instead of Little Leaguers.

- Buddies share stories in virtual hangouts.

- Kids own virtual pets instead of real dogs that you have to feed, entertain, and walk.

- The babysitter is a television set or video-game player instead of the teenager next door.

- Children play Monopoly against people around the world instead of the kids from their school.

- A teenager meets his or her first adolescent love in a chat room.

Is it bad? Is it good? Or does it simply reflect another aspect of cyberseduction and our new reality in the age of psychotechnology?

GENDER WARS

No human behavior affects the transmission of genes more obviously than sex. So no parts of human psychology are clearer candidates for evolutionary explanation than the states of mind that lead to sex: raw lust, dreamy infatuation, sturdy (or at least sturdy-feeling) love, and so on—the basic forces amid which people all over the world, including Charles Darwin, have come of age.
                                   —Robert Wright, The Moral Animal, p. 28

*C*HILDREN ARE NOT the only ones immersed in virtual- reality simulations. Cyberseduction has brought a new twist to relations between the sexes with what cyberfeminists profess is the potential to finally break down the inequalities assigned back in the good old days of the Neolithic agricultural revolution.

Ever wonder why we have sex at all? It's a central theme in our lives— we're always talking about it, thinking about it, or worrying about it in one

way or another. Most of us spend our time choosing, changing, com-
plaining, or complying with our partners. From real to virtual life, from
caves to cyberspace, sex, mating, and its outcome permeates all aspects of
our lives. What's the big deal? The passion of sex is fleeting, the positions
can be backbreaking, and the innovations are often ludicrous. We spend
excessive money, time, jokes, drama, and tragedy on our genitals. The sex
business spans time and heroics. We have more people, objects, stories,
double meanings, and unconscious urges devoted to sex than to anything
else. When you consider, proportionately, how much physical space the sex
organs occupy on our bodies, you can't help but wonder what all the
hoopla is about.

That is exactly the reason evolutionary psychologists have spent enormous amounts of time, research, and thought on the subject. Using the
reverse-engineering approach, they have studied it in great depth, seeking
to understand why sex exists at all. In the scheme of things, it would be
much easier *not* to have sex. We could just clone ourselves and get rid of
the gender wars completely. Nature could evolve a fit life form that survives well in the world and then stick to it, without modifications. Like a
living copy machine, we could just reproduce what works over and over
again. Why be forced to constantly mix new genes, each time risking new
bloopers in the pool?

John Tooby, William Hamilton, and other evolutionary psychologists
have proposed a fascinating theory as to why nature's more complex life
forms evolved requiring sexual rather than asexual reproduction. In the
days before antibiotics, microorganisms ruled. Large, long-living life forms
are great caves for germs; they're warm, they're wet, and they're around for
a very long time, so bodies have to work very hard to keep the bad life
forms out, or they won't survive. The human disease defense force is
impressive—we have skin to protect everything, a multitude of filters to
oust invaders, and, when all else fails, a tough immune system to do battle
against wily infiltrators. However, the attackers are nasty bugs. They have
all sorts of ways of getting inside, hijacking the mechanisms in a cell, gob-
bling up the good tissue, and bypassing the body's radar. We respond by
modifying our defenses for better security. The problem lies in the fact that
microorganisms are smaller, evolve more quickly, and find new, more
fiendish methods to attack. What's the best solution? If we establish an

unchangeable prototype and clone it over and over again, the bugs will be victorious. The microorganisms will figure it all out, bypass the body's security, and divide and conquer. It wouldn't be long until all those cloned life forms were completely wiped out. After all, there's no diversity.

Now draw a different scenario. Create a body that is constantly changing, an enemy that reinvents itself in each offspring. Genes are re-arranged each generation. The potential diversity in sexual reproduction is staggering—there are literally trillions of genetic combinations that can result from a single human coupling. Those are tough odds. Even the hardiest germs will find it difficult to wipe out the species. Consider some of the devastating epidemics in the history of humankind: bubonic plague, smallpox, influenza, AIDS. The germs waged a fine war, but in the end they were never able to obliterate the species. In the long run, the cumbersome process of sexual reproduction is worth the tradeoff.

If the theory is correct that sex serves as a defense against parasites and pathogens, then why specialize and have *two* sexes? Only two different individuals are needed. Pinker suggests that "it is because the cell that is to become the baby cannot be just a bag of genes; it needs the metabolic machinery of the rest of the cell" (p. 462). The ideal method is to fuse a big cell with a half-set of genes and all "the necessary machinery" with a small cell that contains a "half-set of genes and nothing else" (p. 463). The big cell is precious and sheltered, the little cell is fast and plentiful. We call the big guy an egg and the little guy a sperm. And that's really where all our problems begin.

Look at it from a purely biological view. The big guy, or egg cell, needs to be protected and nurtured so it can take its time to develop and grow into a new human being. The best way is to keep it *inside* the body, unlike other animals, such as fish and birds, which develop in far less protected environments. "The egg is big and precious," notes Pinker, "so the organism had better give it a head start by packing it with food and a protective cover" (p. 463). Consequently, human eggs are designed to lodge *inside* a body, to be fed, nurtured, and protected by their host, the mother. This is an "expensive," time-consuming project that requires an investment of nine months just to get the baby *out.*

The other half is designed with a completely different blueprint. "A sperm is small and cheap," observes Pinker, "so the organism might as well make many of them, and give them outboard motors to get to the egg quickly and an organ to launch them on their way" (p. 463). There have to be a lot of sperm cells swimming around to make sure that at least one will hit its mark. The investment is in quantity—quick in and out—rather than in time. But consider what those sperm have to accomplish. To reach their goal they must furiously battle their competitors, all the other sperm swimming around with the same intention. It's tough enough if all the other sperm carry the same genes. What if there are other, more ruthless competitors—sperm with different genes fighting to reach the target? The battle is fierce, with a deadly outcome. Only the sperm that wins gets to keep the genes intact.

When one considers that the basic goal of natural selection is to spread genes and thus assure the survival of the species, these are formidable wars. Clearly these ideas validate the critical roles of genetic diversity and intraspecies conflict in natural selection.

PARENTAL INVESTMENT

In 1948, A. J. Bateman, a British geneticist, conducted an interesting experiment. He put fruit flies in a special chamber and watched what happened. His observations verbalized a distinct pattern in reproduction. The females all had roughly the same number of offspring—it did not matter how many males they mated with. The males were different. The more females they mated with, the more offspring. However, not many of us look at this obvious phenomenon in an evolutionary psychology context. How has this well-known fact affected human behavior?

Robert Trivers, one of the world's leading sociobiologists, put the pieces together in a theory that he called parental investment (Pinker 1997; Wright 1994). Parental investment refers to anything that parents must do in order to increase the chances of survival and reproductive success in their offspring while simultaneously decreasing their own ability to produce additional viable offspring. Simply put, it refers to what it takes to get junior out on his or her own. In the human species, the female clearly begins with a far greater investment. First, her egg is larger and scarcer, whereas male sperm are a dime a dozen. Since every offspring requires one egg and one sperm, the female's investment is far more costly. Like Bateman's fruit flies, it doesn't matter how many mates females couple with—the number of offspring remain the same. Males, on the other hand, have a very different scenario. The more matings, the more offspring. In other words, a male leaves his sperm and he is gone, free to deposit elsewhere. His total parental investment is far smaller. But that's only the beginning of the story. A woman is stuck—human females have to nurture and carry the fetus for the next nine months. And with most mammals, the female continues the bulk of the investment, raising the offspring until it can survive on its own.

This fact is not true for all species. The male yellowhead jawfish guards the eggs by holding them in his mouth. Grey heron males help females incubate the eggs for twenty-six days and then, after the babies are born, look after them. Another fish, the male gobi, guards the eggs in a nest until they are born, while both the male and female Great Tit, a very common small bird that lives in Europe and Asia, share early-childhood care for the nineteen days in the nest after hatching. For most species, however, the kids are the mom's responsibility. Obviously, her investment is far greater than the dad's. Nature is filled with deadbeat dads who become very scarce after sex. This is not a feminist issue; it is actually very practical behavior. A single male can fertilize many females. Male reproductive success, like the fruit flies, depends on how many females he can mate with. He has to spread his sperm around in hopes of spreading his genes. Females, in contrast, have a much bigger investment, so they have to be a lot more careful about who they choose to father the kids. While it may be a lot of fun for the guys, it isn't always that easy. If there is a finite supply of females, some of those studs might not find their women. They are forced to compete for what's available. So natural selection has made sure that males, for the most part, are programmed to hunt for multiple sex partners even if they get beaten up in the process. They're always looking to invest their sperm.

Primates, for example, follow the formula of high female and low male parental investment. Orangutan males drift into areas where females live. They may settle down to dominate the female ranges, but once the babies are born, they are gone. Gorillas fight to become leaders of their packs, groups of females, their offspring, and maybe a few obligatory young males.

The leader is the combative king in his harem until his strength wanes and he relinquishes dominance to a younger male better able to fight off invading males. Similarly, male chimpanzees fight their way up a masculine hierarchy that works feverishly to protect the females and, like the gorillas, to be the sole provider of sexual favors. In all three species there is clearly a sexual competition for access to females, determined by the dominant male's ability to ward off interlopers and maintain his position. Wright maintains,

> Amid the great variety of social structure in these species, the basic theme … stands out, at least in minimal form: males seem very eager for sex and work hard to find it; females work less hard. This isn't to say the females don't like sex. They love it, and may initiate it…. Still, female apes don't do what male apes do: search high and low, risking life and limb, to find sex and to find as much of it, with as many different partners, as possible; it has a way of finding them. (p. 50)

THE REST IS HISTORY

Imagine that you have $10,000. It's all the money you have in your savings account, the only money you managed to accumulate after several years of hard work. You can't afford to lose the money, but it's doing nothing for your future sitting in a low-interest savings account. The only solution is to invest it. How? You don't want to do anything too risky because you can't afford to lose the money. Nor do you want to stretch yourself too thin. The solution is to put it into one very safe place. That means being very careful what you buy. Maybe you want a conservative mutual fund, blue chip stock, or U.S. Treasury Bill where it's a safe bet that the money will work for you. Certainly you don't want to throw it away on a speculative investment where you can lose the whole amount. Once it's invested, you watch it carefully. Sure, it's fun to watch the other stocks go up and down, even *pretend* that you own one, but that's only because you know that your $10,000 is safely invested, protected against the economic vagaries that make other choices so risky.

Now take the same $10,000. However, in this scenario it doesn't represent your hard-won savings. It doesn't even represent your future. The

$10,000 is only a piece of your annual bonus—money you never particularly count on getting. It isn't even that important— $10,000 is only a fraction of your yearly earnings. You don't want to dump it into the bank where it won't do anything for you. After all, with your income, bonuses, and generous pension plan, $10,000 is just a drop in the bucket. But you need it to make you look good. You want everyone to *know* how you can turn $10,000 into $50,000. It buys you respect, status, and power. Along with that you can buy a nice car, wear good clothes, and attract the hottest lovers. So you decide to invest. How? Well, you can invest in something that's a safe bet, but you'll never make a bundle of money that way. If you put it in something highly speculative—penny stocks, commodity futures, or options, you can make a lot more money. Sure, you also have a better chance of losing it all, but who cares? The $10,000 was not that important to begin with. If you don't make your fortune this time, there's a lot more where that came from. So maybe you split it up into several purchases, playing the market just to have fun. And you watch *everything*—because it's a lot of fun and you really don't have to worry about hoarding that ten grand.

Apply the same concepts to sex and courtship and you have Trivers's theory. In the first scenario there is the female, with a finite amount of money (eggs) and the need to protect it (spread her genes). She chooses carefully and limits the possibilities (avoids speculation), selecting the option that would provide the most security (the fittest male). In the second scenario there is the male, with a vast supply of money (sperm) and the need to look good by making more money (beating out the competition). He speculates, taking his chances in many different places (women), hoping that if he invests his money (sperm) in so many different locations, he will eventually score (spread his genes). In both scenarios, the goal is the same: produce viable offspring. It's only the process that's different.

If this theory is true, then our mental modules governing mate selection are clearly programmed based on gender and subsequent parental investment. It doesn't mean that we're confronted with a hard-and-fast rule, but rather it's the place where we begin (and often remain). Accordingly, women would be more discerning about their mates, more choosy about sex, more interested in a monogamous relationship and the fitness or ability to provide demonstrated by the male. Men would be far less discerning, more sexually eager, more likely to aggressively compete for their females, more protective and jealous of their conquests, and more interested in potential reproduction capacity of the women they mated with.

How does one translate fitness into the dating game? In a hunter-gatherer society, a woman might be attuned to a man's size and physical power, which would enable him to better protect her. Equally important would be his social status, which would enable him to get the better cave and the larger portion of the animal the clan brought home for dinner. Today this translates into wealth, status, and power, male attributes that women usually find attractive. Consider the annual media choice for the "most desirable" bachelor. These are usually the richest, most handsome, and most powerful single men around. Do teenage girls fantasize about famous rock stars and actors, or sanitation workers and laborers?

Human males usually display a high *male* parental investment relative to other species; therefore, women may also tend to look for the attributes that suggest kindness, love, and affection. While sex is important, it is generally the emotional accompaniments that appeal more to women. Thus, hardcore pornography tends to be a male domain, while women favor romance novels and love stories. Pinker writes,

> Women do not seek the sight of naked male strangers or enactments of anonymous sex, and there is virtually no female market for pornography. ... In all societies, it is mostly or entirely the men who woo, proposition, seduce, use love magic, give gifts in trade for sex, pay bride-prices (rather than collect dowries), hire prostitutes, and rape. (pp. 472–73)

The ultimate "payment" for sex, fidelity, and reduction of competition is, of course, marriage. This is not to suggest that females choose men based entirely on these qualities. Nor does this imply that women don't *like* sex, but rather, their priorities are very different from men's. Instead, it is believed to be the genesis of mate selection as defined by evolution. Both men and women are adept at deception in the dating game. There are also glitches in the program when childhood traumas involving sexual, emotional, or physical abuse affect choice.

How do men select their mates? As with women, males are looking for sexual fitness, but their definition is quite different. First of all, men are far more willing to have sex with *any* women. Consider an interesting study conducted by R. D. Clark and Elaine Hatfield on a college campus (Pinker, p. 470). They hired good-looking men and women to approach strangers of the opposite sex and tell them that they were very attractive. Then they asked questions, including the following:

1. Will you go out with me?
2. Will you come to my apartment tonight?
3. Will you go to bed with me tonight?

Fifty percent of both men and women accepted a date. Six percent of the women and 69 percent of the men agreed to go to the apartment. None of the women and 75 percent of the men consented to sex. It makes evolutionary sense. If your job is to spread those genes around and your investment is small, while competition is fierce, you're more likely to choose quantity rather than quality. Your priority, then, should be the reproductive fitness of your mate.

How does one assess that? The guidelines are relatively simple. Women can reproduce only when they are fertile. Fertility, however, declines steadily until menopause. So age matters—the younger the woman, the more children she can have. The best way to assess youth is through what is popularly viewed as physical beauty—clear skin, perky step, shiny hair, and tight body. Consequently, age and physical attraction are more important to men than to women. "Women can afford to be more open-minded about looks," observes Wright. "An oldish man, unlike an oldish woman, is probably fertile" (p. 65). Predictably, a male is more apt to be less reluctant than a woman when choosing *sex* partners and more reluctant than a woman when choosing *marital* partners.

Many of these theories appear irritating, even far-fetched. Perhaps, as discussed in the next section, these evolutionary programs are less influential when simulations replace real bodies. Can we, with our Stone Age minds, ever be completely free of such programs? Consider the work of psychologist David Buss, who examined mate selection preferences in a sweeping cross-cultural study involving thirty-three countries located on six continents and five islands with a total of over 10,000 subjects. The results overwhelmingly supported the preferences discussed above (Pinker, pp. 469–70). Buss reports that "males and females show consistent sex differences in mate preferences across cultures in two major clusters":

a) females prefer mates with resources and attributes that are correlated with resource acquisition more than males do, and

b) males prefer youth and physical attractiveness, two correlates of reproductive capacity, more than females.

In another cross-cultural study, Buss found that men prefer women who are, on average, 2.66 years younger than they are, and women prefer men who are, on average, 3.42 years older. Buss later concluded that males use "resource display tactics" to attract as well as retain mates. In other words, they show off their stuff in fancy cars, high status, money, expensive dates, and gifts. Females, on the other hand, use "appearance enhancers" to attract as well as retain mates. In other words, they make themselves look pretty, sexy, and appealing, using such things as makeup, clothing, and jewelry.

VIRTUAL GENDERS

Obviously this works when we know who is female and who is male. In an Information Age, however, the issues are not quite that clear. Cyborgs, media mayhem, and virtual kin have all clouded the issue. Kenneth Gergen, psychologist and author of *The Saturated Self*, writes, "A once obdurate and unquestionable fact of biological life—that there are two sexes, male and female—now moves slowly toward mythology" (p. 143). Why? New-millennium gender definitions are blurred, confusing even to the most discerning eye. Consider yesterday's gender icons. John Wayne, Gary Cooper, and Humphrey Bogart were clear cultural examples of maleness. Similarly, Donna Reed played the classic cultural female role of mother, Annette Funicello played the virgin, and "sex objects" such as Marilyn Monroe and Sophia Loren played the prostitutes. It was the old Madonna-whore dichotomy, and everything was crystal clear in those good old days.

Not anymore. Cross-dressing antics by men such as Howard Stern and Dennis Rodman, female styles such as cropped hair, baseball caps, and tuxedos erode cultural conventions. Robin Williams is Mrs. Doubtfire, and Wesley Snipes is a drag queen. Thelma and Louise outrun the entire male police department, and Whoopi Goldberg plays the male lead in a Broadway show, *A Funny Thing Happened on the Way to the Forum*, and no one even blinks. Social consciousness concerning homosexuality and transsexuality has further distanced us from the fixed, immutable sexual definitions of the past. Actress Anne Heche is very heterosexual on the screen and openly gay off. This leaves us in a quandary. Has the virtual metaphor had an impact on our genitals? If physiology and sexual preferences no longer tell us who is male and who is female, what does? Where do we put those inescapable evolutionary preferences?

The answers often cause more confusion, continuing to obscure what we once considered so obvious. Biological criteria seem adequate until we document and televise a whole population of people with penises who describe themselves feeling like women trapped in male bodies. There are heterosexuals, homosexuals, bisexuals, transsexuals, asexuals . . . the categories move further and further away from a two-gender species. Western medical professionals often use the criteria of chromosomes: XX is female, XY is male. However, even those definitions are confusing when one considers sex chromosonal anomalies—genetic conditions that confound the issues:

- Turner's syndrome: Only one X chromosome is present (or functional), leading to the development of a female without ovaries.

- Klinefelter's syndrome: There are two X chromosomes in addition to one Y, leading to the development of a male with small genitals, lack of sperm, and possible breast development.

- Fragile X syndrome: Believed to be the single most common genetic cause of mental impairment. There is a defect in the X chromosome that can shut down the gene.

Further complicating these definitions are findings that an excess of sex chromosomes, in combinations such as XXY, XXX, and possibly XYY, suggests an association with people suffering from psychosis.

Maybe the only answer is one that most people can't accept: there is no such thing as pure female and pure male. Instead, gender lies on a continuum that reflects multiple characteristics—physiological, psychological, and cultural—defined by the owner of the body or personality. Yet if we can't identify male from female, what will happen to our blue and pink baby clothes? Mom and dad? Segregated bathrooms? How will we define our sexual affiliations? How will we identify our selves—or our multiple selves? What will we do about those Stone Age impulses?

Our latest virtual-reality simulations in cyberspace encourage us to fantasize in prefabricated environments, testing gender definition and stretching the limits. Utilizing high levels of telepresence, you can readily turn Mary into Marty and Peter into Penny without anyone the wiser. "On the Internet," reads the classic cartoon, "no one knows you're a dog." Perhaps, in our increasingly virtual futures, we will no longer even *need* gender definitions. In *Sleeper*, Woody Allen's 1973 movie about the future, sexual satisfaction is achieved in a contraption called the orgasmatron. With medical technology we can already bypass the act of sex, replacing it with a sperm and an egg that meet romantically in a petri dish. If we don't like the results, a little genetic engineering will straighten things out. And after that? Mommy Bears can replace parenting, Talk 'n Listen Robots can replace teachers, ActiMates can replace friends . . . there's no limit to our technological dehumanization. Or maybe evolution will persist. And with all our tomfoolery, the old bodies will remain intact, wandering in some very strange new virtual realities.

TO BE
OR NOT TO BE

The winter desert surrounds you. Its stark beauty is breathtaking—the colors seem impossible in such a lifeless place. In the far distance, purple mountains rise into a cloudless blue sky. Directly in front of you is a conclave of irregularly shaped red rocks with a sign telling you that once, in this very place, was a raging ocean. Impossible. You move on with your plastic insulated water bottle on your hip and your electronic compass in your pocket. The sun relentlessly bears down on you, hot in the cool air. As you continue down the trail you stare at the dry, gold-colored earth. What are you looking for? But then you think, Why am I seeing green? Yes, it's life in the desert, strange, clinging plants that have adapted to one of earth's most inhospitable environments. Fascinated, you look closer. Your ergonomically designed walking stick falls to the ground. Your long-range cellular phone is silent. The computer watch you wear on your wrist quietly ticks away the minutes. But it is the green that fascinates you, and as you peer into its tiny world a miracle occurs. A brown lizard dashes between the leaves. You would have never noticed it without looking so closely.

L IFE ON EARTH continues to adapt. Natural selection is a powerful force, keeping our environment intact for millions of years.
Human life is now in the dangerous position of conquering the process of
life itself. How? Not through genetic engineering or super computers, but
with *time*.

Introduce a new design, and natural selection will take over. The process
will slowly weed out the life forms that cannot survive in the environment.
Build a camel without humps to store water, and it will die in the desert.
Construct a fish without gills, and it will drown in the ocean. Fabricate a
microorganism that can't evolve quickly, and it will become extinct after the
first effective round of human medication. The key is in the balance—the
harmony that is created when nature is allowed to take her time, correct her
mistakes, and continue the miracle of evolution and natural selection.

Yet there's no longer enough time. Our technology has developed a
pace and a life of its own. We change ourselves and our environments long
before the forces of natural selection even have a chance. It took us almost
5 million years to get where we are today, but it has taken us only one hundred years to invent cars, planes, and the space shuttle. And the pace is
accelerating. Computers have been around for only fifty years, and super
computers far less. Artificial intelligence is around the corner, along with
a whole host of technologies that we have yet to imagine. We will be
changing ourselves physically through genetic engineering and psychologically by introducing more intimate wiring to virtual realities. At the same
time, we risk blowing ourselves up with a nuclear bomb or polluting our
environment in a nuclear accident. We might starve ourselves out by
raping our forests, polluting our waters, and overpopulating our planet.
Even the climate, seemingly out of human control, is shifting as the ominous and still controversial greenhouse effect takes hold. We live longer,
keep more newborns alive, and continuously threaten the life forms that
share our environment. We defy nature to protect our physical and psychological integrity, relentlessly seeking to prove that we can outprocess
our own biological identities. In other words, our information-processing
is out of control. And nature doesn't have the time to correct it.

How do we adapt to our human-designed environments while protecting the life forms that nature evolved? How do we prevent extinction

of plants and animals due to human intervention? Consider the story of one small spot on the planet. Long Island Sound is an 8,000-year-old estuary whose shores were once home to the largest concentration of Native American tribes anywhere in North America. It stretches from northern Manhattan to the Atlantic Ocean, from Long Island's north shore to Connecticut and, via the Connecticut River, to southern Quebec. At one time it was swarming with life—dolphins, flounder, clams, oysters, turtles, bluefish, and porgies. But slowly, Long Island Sound changed.

It had been born in a different world, the child of massive fields of retreating blue glacial ice. It was one of nature's finest works of art, supporting endless cycles of life that made it more precious by their very existence.

When colonists came, they initiated its long, tragic decline. In the beginning it worked well with the new settlers; there was enough food for all. But then came the overfishing. When more fish are caught than are spawned, populations become depleted. The situation grew worse when houses were built, factories erected, and the wetlands drained. Sewage was dumped. Chemicals, toxins, and other pollutants were pumped in. There were oil spills. Fishermen exploited the underwater life until species not decimated by pollution were eaten away by human greed. The numbers were horrific: in one four-year period between 1989 and 1993, bluefish populations declined by 30 percent, porgies by 72 percent, winter flounder by 80 percent, and surf clams by 89 percent.

The government awkwardly stepped in and treated the sewage and reduced the bacteria, making the water clearer. More sunlight penetrated, stimulating massive algae blooms. And when the algae decomposed in the summer, it consumed what little oxygen remained. The result is what we see today—a natural body of water overloaded with both nutrients and contaminants, split in a bizarre balance between suffocation and survival.

Long Island Sound is only one small estuary on our ailing planet. What about the Amazon rain forests, the hole in the ozone layer over Antarctica, the long-term effects of oil spills like the one in Alaska? What about Chernobyl or Love Canal? It's been estimated that the richest natural environment on the planet—tropical forests—are being destroyed at the rate of over 50 million acres a year. Each year more plants and animals are added to the endangered species list, yet even as environmentalists struggle to stop it, governments and business clear more land, destroy more habitats, and ignore poachers who continue to decimate animal populations.

Ornstein believes that we need to proceed with conscious adaptation. He argues that biological evolution is essentially complete.

> We have to take command of our evolution now and begin a massive pro-
> gram for conscious changes in the way we think, the way we relate to
> others, the way we identify with the rest of humanity. The pace of
> change is far too great for us to try to adapt unconsciously. We have to
> take our very evolution into our own hands and do for ourselves what
> biological evolution has done for all life: adapt to an unprecedented new
> world. (p. 267)

The facts are simple. Our technology has robbed nature of time. We do not have millions of years to wait until our bodies and our environment can adapt to our new worlds. Like Long Island Sound, we can smother ourselves with both good and bad intentions, overload ourselves with both nutrients and contaminants, and ultimately create a schizoid fusion of real and virtual. Clearly, that was the result of our attempts to "cure" Long Island Sound. We also run similar risks in our attempts to "cure" our cultures. Consider what happened in China when traditional, harsh tactics were used to "cure" one of the most serious problems facing the country and the world: overpopulation.

The People's Republic of China (PRC) faced a life-threatening problem. It is the largest country in the world, with 22 percent of the world's population but only 7 percent of the planet's arable land. By 1970 the population growth was out of control—each woman had an average of six children. It was a major economic problem, with a projected new-millennium population of nearly 2 billion people. Experts acknowledged something had to be done, but as we have seen, there is a widening gap between human philosophy and technology. So when the government attempted to limit each family to one child in 1979, it chose traditional, heavy-handed tactics to enforce the new laws.

The government was battling thousands of years of human adaptation. Since antiquity, the traditional Chinese family often included three or four generations living under the same roof. Religion, civil law, and social

custom—including ancestor worship—reinforced the power and dura-
bility of the family. The teaching of Confucius from the fifth century B.C.E.
stressed the importance of maintaining the family, particularly the raising
of male children. A young wife's main duty was to produce a son. If that
did not occur, the husband could take a second wife or mistress to assure
continuation of the family line.

The PRC thought they could change it all. Instead, they created a cultural swamp similar to the problems in Long Island Sound. They set up a
system of rewards for one-child families—including additional medical,
housing, food, employment, and retirement benefits. Income deductions,
medical, economic, and employment penalties were established for those
who defied the policy. Hardships were imposed, including refusal of sub-
sidies, food ration coupons, and extra housing space. Pregnancies were
rationed, pregnancy permits were demanded, and the legal marriage and
childbearing ages raised.

People—mostly in the rural areas—ignored it. Traditionally, Chinese
women married into their husband's family and left their own biological
family. Only sons were considered important. Until about a century ago,
rural girls were not even named, often referred to as "eldest daughter" or
"number two daughter." Sons grew up to help in the fields and provide for
aging parents. The continued emphasis on sons created an additional
dilemma for the one-child families: what happened if they had a girl?

In the early 1990s the PRC came down even harder. No one under the
age of twenty-four could legally have children. Women were forced to
obtain "pregnancy permits." If they disobeyed, they were forced by government "early birth shock brigades" to clinics where labor was induced.
All over China families were being attacked, homes destroyed, and earnings confiscated for those who broke the law. Families faced huge fines, job
loss, incarceration—the tactics were ugly. Abortions and physical force
were replaced by a system of compulsory sterilization. Perhaps the most
ominous were the techniques used to assure that if a family only had one
child, it would be a boy. Some midwives were instructed to keep a bucket
of water at the feet of the mother while she gave birth. If the baby was a
girl, the midwife was supposed to drown it and report a stillbirth. Other
baby girls were given away or simply abandoned.

And then technology arrived. Families discovered that the most efficient way to eliminate the problem was with a piece of high-tech equipment: the ultrasound scanner. In a Third-World country where modern technology is scarce, the ultrasound machine became widespread. After all, it revealed the sex of a fetus. A girl could be aborted; a boy would go to term. Natural balances plummeted. The normal ratio of 105 boys born for every 100 girls was seriously skewed. One survey found it had increased to 118.5 boys for every 100 girls born. It was a dangerous imbalance, the result of a much-needed "cure."

Today, things have eased up in China. The PRC now uses more education, contraception, and "additional citizen" taxes to limit families to one child. Of course, now each woman has, on average, two children. On the one hand, the PRC succeeded. But what will happen tomorrow when all those boys grow up to a shortage of girls? Will China end up like Long Island Sound—a population overloaded with both nutrients and contaminants, split in a bizarre imbalance between genders?

We can no longer rely on natural selection to normalize our planet. Our knowledge of genetics will enable us to do things we cannot psychologically integrate. As with both Long Island Sound and China's one-child policy, the old paradigms don't work. We need to understand that the most ominous threat to humankind does not lie in our technology. Instead, it waits, ready to pounce, in the gap between human technology and our philosophy. As Ornstein suggests, we need to consciously catch up to what we are really doing—shift our thinking so we can accommodate our virtual realities to nature and our planet. Perhaps if we continue the way we're going, technology will eventually collide with nature and end the environment we know as earth. One can speculate that it might be the inevitable end of the program we call evolution. However, we *are* information-processing life forms with the ability to reshape our systems. We are programmed to adapt, to adjust our philosophy to protect both new and old environments. As Hartmann observed, "Human action adapts the environment to human functions, and then the human being adapts (secondarily) to the environment which he has helped to create" (pp. 26–27).

Conceivably there's a *third* adaptation that involves consciousness and a responsive philosophy that closes the dangerously looming gap between who we are and what we create. Nowhere is this more apparent than in the emergence of cyberspace and the subsequent possibilities of new virtual dimensions that we are only beginning to explore. The goal of this book is to connect the past and the present with the future, to put in perspective the power of today's technologies. Part III examines this latest technological environment, suggesting ways to guide human adaptation in cyberspace without destroying what nature, outside *and* inside, has taken so long to design.

Maybe in cyberspace we can learn to dream better dreams.

BIBLIOGRAPY
FOR PART II

Barkow, J. H., L. Cosmides, and J. Tooby, eds. 1992. *The Adapted Mind: Evolutionary Psychology and the Generation of Culture.* New York: Oxford University Press.

Becker, E. 1973. *The Denial of Death.* New York: The Free Press.

Boorstin, J. 1990. *The Hollywood Eye: What Makes Movies Work.* New York: Harper-Collins.

Bordwell, D., and K. Thompson. 1997. *Film Art: An Introduction.* New York: McGraw-Hill.

Buss, D. 1992. Mate preference mechanisms: Consequences for partner choice and intrasexual competition. In *The Adapted Mind: Evolutionary Psychology and the Generation of Culture,* edited by J. H. Barkow, L. Cosmides, and J. Tooby. New York: Oxford University Press.

Clark, R. D., and E. Hatfield 1989. Gender differences in receptivity to sexual offers. *Journal of Psychology and Human Sexuality* 2: 39–55.

DeAngelis, T. 1997. New research sheds light on attachment disturbances in adopted and foster children. *APA Monitor* [Online], 3 pp. Available: http://www.apa.org/monitor/jun97/trauma.html [January 16, 1999].

179

Dery, M. 1993. Flame wars. *South Atlantic Quarterly* 92 (4): 559–68

Dunn, A. November 19, 1998. Science fact: Line between machine and human blurs. *The Philadelphia Inquirer* [Online], 4 pp. Available: http://www.phillynews.com/inquirer/98/Nov/19/tech.life/CYBO19.htm [January 22, 1999].

Ellis, B. J. 1992. The evolution of sexual attraction: Evaluative mechanisms in women. In *The Adapted Mind: Evolutionary Psychology and the Generation of Culture*, edited by J. H. Barkow, L. Cosmides, and J. Tooby. New York: Oxford University Press.

Fagin, D. July 23, 1995. What's ailing the sound? *Newsday*, A4.

Fixmer, R. August 11, 1998. The melding of mind with machine may be the next phase of evolution. *New York Times* [Online], 3 pp. Available: http://www.nytimes.com [January 22, 1999].

Freud, S. 1959. *Sigmund Freud: Inhibitions, Symptoms and Anxiety*. New York: W. W. Norton & Company.

Gergen, K. 1991. *The Saturated Self: Dilemmas of Identity in Contemporary Life*. New York: Basic Books.

Gibson, W. 1984. *Neuromancer*. New York: Ace Books.

Hartmann, H. 1958. *Ego Psychology and the Problem of Adaption*. New York: International Universities Press.

Implant transmits brain signals directly to computer. October 22, 1998. *New York Times Cybertimes* [Online], 2 pp. Available: http://www.nytimes.com [January 23, 1999].

Kaplan, S. 1992. Environmental preference in a knowledge-seeking, knowledge-using organism. In *The Adapted Mind: Evolutionary Psychology and the Generation of Culture*, edited by J. H. Barkow, L. Cosmides, and J. Tooby. New York: Oxford University Press.

Kim, T., and F. Biocca. September 1997. Telepresence via television: Two dimensions of telepresence may have different connections to memory and persuasion. *Journal of Computer Mediated Communication* [Online] 3(2): 27 pp. Available: http://jcmc.huji.ac.il/vol3/issue2/kim.htm [September 24, 1998].

Kurtz, H. January 27, 1999. Getting news with comic spin: Serious matters amid the yuks. *Newsday*, A24.

Landow, G. P. Last updated January 21, 1997. Cyborg: Some definitions, descriptions, and exemplications. *Cyberspace & Critical Theory* [Online]. Available: http://www.stg.brown.edu:80/projects/hypertext/landow/cspace/cyborg/definition.htm [February 28, 1997].

————. Last updated January 21, 1997. Four kinds of cyborg. *Cyberspace & Critical Theory* [Online]. Available: http://www.stg.brown.edu:80/projects/ hypertext/landow/cspace/cyborg/4categ.htm [February 28, 1997].

Lombard, M., and T. Ditton. September 1997. At the heart of it all: The concept of telepresence. *Journal of Computer Mediated Communication* [Online] 3 (2): 39 pp., Available: http://jcmc.huji.ac.il/vol3/issue2/lombard.htm [September 16, 1998].

Mahler, M. S., F. Pine, and A. Berman. 1975. *The Psychological Birth of the Human Infant.* New York: Basic Books.

Masterson, J. F. 1981. *The Narcissistic and Borderline Disorders.* New York: Brunner/Mazel.

McLuhan, M. 1994. *Understanding Media: The Extensions of Man.* Cambridge, Mass.: MIT Press.

Mendels, P. December 8, 1997. Seminar explores effects of technology on humanity. *New York Times Cybertimes* [Online], 3 pp. Available: http://www. nytimes.com [January 20, 1999].

Mitchell, W. J. 1996. *City of Bits: Space, Place and the Infobahn.* Cambridge, Mass.: MIT Press.

Mizrach, S. 1996. What is anthroFuturism? [Online], 8 pp. Available: http:// www.clas.ufl.edu/anthro/cyberanthro/AnthroFuturism.html [November 10, 1996].

Napoli, L. October 15, 1997. That computer in his pants is more than a fashion statement. *New York Times Cybertimes* [Online], 4 pp. Available: http://www. nytimes.com [January 21, 1999].

Ornstein, R. 1991. *The Evolution of Consciousness: The Origins of the Way We Think.* New York: Simon & Schuster.

Orwell, G. 1949. *1984.* New York: Harcourt Brace Jovanovich.

Pinker, S. 1997. *How the Mind Works.* New York: W. W. Norton & Company.

Pollock, D. 1990. *Skywalking: The Life and Films of George Lucas.* Hollywood, Calif.: Samuel French Trade.

Professor gets first chip implant. 1998. *Reuters. ZDNet* [Online], 3 pp. Available: http:// www.zdnet.com/zdnn/stories/news/0,4586,2131717,00.html [January 19, 1999].

Rank, O. 1952 *The Trauma of Birth.* New York: Robert Brunner.

————. 1972. *Will Therapy and Truth and Reality.* New York: Alfred A. Knopf.

Reeves, B., and C. Nass. 1996. *The Media Equation: How People Treat Computers, Television, and New Media Like Real People and Places.* New York: CSLI Publications.

Ronningstram, E., and J. Gunderson. 1996. Narcissistic personality: A stable disorder or a state of mind? *Psychiatric Times* [Online], 6 pp. Available: http://www.mhsource.com/edu/psytimes/p960235.html [January 16, 1999].

Shay, D., and J. Duncan. 1993. *The Making of* Jurassic Park. New York: Ballantine Books.

Snodgrass, M. M. 1989. Measure of a man (R. Scheerer, director). In *Star Trek: The Next Generation* (B. Armus, producer). New York: Fox Broadcasting.

Talbott, S. L. 1995. *The Future Does Not Compute: Transcending the Machines in Our Midst.* Sebastopol, Calif.: O'Reilly & Associates.

Thoreau, H. D. 1971. *The Writings of Henry D. Thoreau: Walden*, edited by J. L. Shanley. Princeton, N.J.: Princeton University Press.

Wright, R. 1994. *The Moral Animal.* New York: Vintage Books.

PART III
BACK
TO THE FUTURE

UPGRADING
STONE AGE
COMPUTERS

It was just one of those days. You got to work late and everyone knew it. Mid-morning the computers went down. Lunch was a tuna fish sandwich soggy with too much mayonnaise and stale bread eaten at your desk. Your boss showed up ten min-utes before it was time to go home to tell you that the company lost "your" client. If things don't shape up, then you'll also be "lost" from the company.

So you stayed late to make it look good. By the time you get home everyone has eaten dinner. The nanny is upset because the baby got sick and she's worried about catching a virus. Your spouse is angry because you forgot to pick up the dry cleaning and now it's too late. There won't be any sex later to help you fall asleep. To make matters worse, your in-laws call to say they're flying in for the weekend and will be staying with you.

You gobble some leftovers and head for the computer. First, you arm your joystick and battle alien invaders that bear a striking resemblance to your boss. Then you go to your casino game where, after a few hands of blackjack, you're up $5,000. Who needs a job? Feeling better, you check the e-mail. One buddy across the country is sending her in-laws on an extended cruise. Another buddy just opened his own busi-

ness and doesn't have to worry about a boss any more. A third is getting a divorce.
Things are really heating up. Your "lover" sends an instant message to you: "Let's
have sex." That sounds even more appealing than shooting your boss. If the president
of the United States can have virtual sex, why not you? You go to a private boudoir
and steamy, passionate words fly between you. Your heart pounds as you climax in a
virtual frenzy. You take a deep breath. Satiation. It feels wonderful. A good way to end
an awful day. You turn off the computer and go to bed.

I T'S A PERFECT world. Fight or flight? No problem. We stay
and kill the boss—each night if we feel like it—without any consequences. Wealth? We set the casino game to make sure the odds are with
us—and then pile up the bills. Sex? We have it only when, where, and how
we want. No problems satisfying our mates.

We, as a species, have waited 5 million years for a place where we have
no existential dilemma, where life is measured in points and can be resur-
rected at will, and where death is merely a click of a tiny hand-held creature incongruously called a mouse. Cyberspace offers the ultimate illusion—it quickly resolves all those conflicts when we wander in its disembodied parameters. Who cares about bodies and evolution? We can be
whoever we want to be.

Or so we like to believe. We're at the beginning of a technology that
promises to revise human thought and behavior, leading to adaptations we
can't even imagine. But is it really such an idyllic place? Or is it an
advanced virtual-reality simulation with the ability to vastly increase
telepresence and immersion, bringing us further away from the original
into an even more deceptive copy? If so, as a species, what kind of price are
we willing to pay for such a luxury? And which genes do we really carry
into its deceptive arms?

Technology has always come with lofty promises. Because we are programmed to believe that humans are better with machines, we eventually
embrace the inventions of human ingenuity. Too often we take on innovative technologies like a new coat—it's good looking, it feels comfortable, so
let's put it on. Rarely do we take it off, once purchased. Rarely do we pause
and consider the far-flung implications of our new ventures. As a species,
we tend to act far sooner than we think.

That's the way we're built. According to Ornstein, we tend to allow automatic routines to take over, shifting from one immediate situation to another. This enables us to encapsulate our worlds into something that's readily handled. In this context, we have adapted by evolving rules that explain ourselves and our world. We may not particularly like how our minds set priorities: (1) keep out of trouble, (2) mind the store, and (3) organize around short-term contingencies. But this is the system that got us here. The implications of these evolutionary priorities are sobering. They compel us to keep the world small, within our immediate perceptions, amplifying the tiny shifts in our daily routines and, for the most part, ignoring the major ones. In the past, people could do little about major changes in the world. It was simple: move, die, or tolerate everything.

This type of behavior is all around us. The media tells us there is a civil war in a country that has nuclear weapons technology, yet we're far more concerned with what we're going to eat for dinner than with the potential for global catastrophe. People in disaster areas are always getting "caught" in their homes trying to rescue photographs or personal items instead of their lives. When we're stuck in a traffic jam, rarely do we consider the serious, life-threatening problems of automotive overpopulation, the pollution from exhaust, or road rage. We think about what to say when we arrive late for work.

While our minds are programmed to be alerted to "newness," novelty fades quickly. Today's headlines are tomorrow's old news. Our minds are constantly shifting, adjusting to the here-and-now, and overriding material that doesn't have immediate impact. "The unconscious shifting of the mind's works is what salesmen as well as scoundrels try to take advantage of," (p. 210) writes Ornstein. Simply put, it's a lot harder to think things through, to use our limited consciousness to negotiate our worlds. As discussed earlier, if the hunter-gatherers paused to think things through when faced with a woolly mammoth, they would have been dinner long before any conclusion was reached.

Now we live in a world where our challenges are more cerebral than physical; where our wealth is based on the symbolic system of money rather than on the concrete value assigned to gold; where our most precious commodity is information, not physical goods. We have designed a human-centered world where our environments are dominated by machines rather than geology and fellow life forms that share our planet. Yet our Stone Age computers persist: Our systems of information-processing have not varied substantially since the days when weather shifts were more significant than political shifts. We are programmed to automatically respond to the here-and-now, so it's no surprise that when the car was invented, no one predicted the gridlock it would bring in the future. And it's no surprise that when television was invented, no one predicted the influence it would have on children watching endless hours of violence, aggression, and sex. And it's certainly no surprise that we're doing it all over again by not concerning ourselves with the consequences of a pervasive cyberspace where much of human life is conducted within a machine-generated dimension.

Perhaps it's time to go through the painful exercise of forcing our consciousness to take hold. We can't stop the new technologies—but we need to consider where they're taking us and how they're redefining who we are. We're here by natural selection where adaption to the environment designs change. Let's not allow the technological designers to take over. If we don't bridge the gap between our philosophy and our technology, we're destined to become Borg drones where resistance is futile.

Part III is about exercising your consciousness and taking control of cyberspace—for yourself, your children, and your genes. It's about learning the psychological implications of disembodied space *before* you hit the automotive gridlock and television copycats of the future. The goal is not to stop the wheels of "progress." Clearly, this is beyond your power. Instead, you need to control, guide, and direct the wheels to make technology work for you and not the other way around. Neither resistance nor coexistence is futile when your consciousness is leading the way, edging your thinking beyond what most of us already use—a tiny fraction (less than 10 percent) of the cognitive potentials in our brains. If we don't bring our consciousness and our philosophy up to par with our machines, then we might find ourselves in very deep psychosocial trouble.

WHERE
IN THE WORLD
IS CYBERSPACE?

C YBERSPACE IS ANYWHERE *a computer goes,* yet it goes far beyond that. Perhaps Robert Louis Stevenson defined it best back in 1886. He wrote the classic *Dr. Jekyll and Mr. Hyde,* a story that dramatically portrays what he believed to be the conflict between good and evil residing in every human body.

> Think of it—I did not even exist! Let me but escape into my laboratory door, give me but a second or two to mix and swallow the draught that I had always standing ready; and whatever he had done, Edward Hyde would pass away like the stain of breath upon a mirror; and there in his stead, quietly at home, trimming the midnight lamp in his study, a man who could afford to laugh at suspicion, would be Henry Jekyll. (p. 100)

Stevenson proposed that each of us is made up of many identities, a "polity of multifarious, incongruous and independent citizens" (p. 104).

Freud agreed. He designed a model of the psychic apparatus of the mind: the id, the ego, and the super ego, maintaining that there was no single self but rather a decentralized collection of mental modules functionally related to one another. Later theorists proposed that there was a collective library of human archetypes shared by the species. More recently, developmentalists argue that our "selves" are really the ongoing internalizations of other people and things. The concept of self, similar to the concept of gender, has undergone a gradual erosion from a single, stable identity to a collection of identities and finally, in cyberspace, to a concept that appears more like cycling, multifaceted groupings of "I." Human science, philosophy, and technology adapted new definitions of self. Why?

Technology and cyberspace have created an environment where multiple selves are concretely possible—a place where many "you's" can be designed, accepted, and acted out within permissible social parameters. Sherry Turkle, psychologist, MIT professor, and author of *Life on the Screen*, contends that people "cycle" through many selves in cyberspace, moving from one virtual community or environment to the next, mixing and matching roles, surfing the Internet as if it were a "social laboratory" filled with experiments that construct and reconstruct the self. In other words, a global Jekyll and Hyde. Do today's netizens find it as difficult as Stevenson's character to maintain the balance between good and evil, right and wrong?

Let's look at it another way. We go outside and our world is very defined. Up is the sky, down is the earth. All we need is to see the clouds and the sun or the grass and the road, and our bodies are placed in space. We stand upright because of gravity and move or don't move because of inertia. The basic rules are simple: take a step and move forward, backward, or sideways. Expend some energy and there's a corresponding response. If it's summer in the Southern Hemisphere, we're cold in North America. If it's winter in the Southern Hemisphere, we're hot. These are only a few of the automatic assumptions that govern our lives. As discussed earlier, more complex ones are generally left to our mental modules where automatic information-processing does the job for us. There are rhythms all around us—in our bodies, our cultures, and our environments. Personal physical experiences are the highlights of our days—hunger and subsequent satisfaction when we eat; relief when we defecate; satiation after good sex; pleasure with happy emotions and sadness with unhappy emotions. Although we know it's far more complex than stated here, the basic knowledge of these events clearly defines who we are and where we are going. Cyberspace, however, throws it all out the proverbial windows.

Cyberspace is a virtual-reality simulation where space is intangible, existing on a viewing screen and psychosocial constructs rather than dimensions. Time, distance, and place are relative, determined by the design rather than by the environment. There's no gravity to tell us how to stand up or sit down. There's no sky to look up at, no motion to experience, and, at least for the time being, limited sensory input for our mental modules to process. Cyberspace exists because of machines and because we *want* it. It exists because we project human emotions, behavior, psychological need, telepresence, and significance into a world created by electronic magic. We give our machines permission to define our selves.

Consider what happened to Chip Morningstar and F. Randall Farmer, designers involved in the creation of Lucasfilm's Habitat, a large, commercial multiuser environment. They had a lofty dream—to build a simulated world where users "communicated, played games, experienced adventures, fell in love, got married and divorced, started businesses, found religions, waged wars, protested against them, and experimented with self-government" (Morningstar and Farmer 1990). It didn't quite end up that way. They discovered that cyberspace "is defined more by the interactions among the actors within it than by the technology with which it is implemented." In other words, the technology, as with other virtual-reality simulations, became invisible while the illusion took precedence. The here-and-now quality of human information-processing surfaced, conceding to the automatic response of "what looks human is human." Whether it's words on a screen (typed by an unseen hand), anger in a chatroom, or war in an online game, the technology is able to present enough symbols to activate the media equation. And we're only beginning. What happens when technology offers holographic views instead of screens, widespread video conferencing instead of textual chats, sound illusions that expertly copy voice, background noise, and aural expectations? If we can believe that a Tyrannosaurus Rex on a two-dimensional screen is real, what is the future potential of such a powerful virtual-reality simulation as cyberspace?

Identifying the location of cyberspace in psychosocial terms leads us out on very thin ice. If there is no such concrete thing as cyberspace, then where are we surfing? If it's just another human projection, a basic simulation of reality, then what are we creating? Can we look at cyberspace as an altered state of consciousness, akin to meditation or hypnosis? Or is it an imaginal telepresence—where we dream, fantasize, and create internal images? Maybe it's a political tool—a psychological despot that dooms us to Orwell's age of uniformity, solitude, double think, and Big Brother. Perhaps the future will tell us that cyberspace is all of the above and more —a place where we can reach multiple dimensions and defy, at least temporarily, the aura of death. Let's not wait to find out.

We can begin with simple parameters, knowing that with technological sophistication these features will change and expand, requiring more conscious thought to maintain psychological control. Cyberspace occupies a psychological space that enhances telepresence with a device conspicuously absent from most other forms of today's highly immersive virtual-reality simulations—interactivity.

"Interactivity" refers to the multidimensional concept where users can influence the presentation of a simulation and subsequently, their experience. In other words, they can be part of the action. Compare it to film and television. Viewers are just that—they watch the action. Eating a bag of popcorn, having a headache, or wanting to go to the kitchen for a snack doesn't affect the action. It continues whether you're there or not. The most viewers can hope to do is to buy or copy the simulation on their own tape and play it back at their own leisure. Of course, we all know that tapes are nothing like the original—which is actually a copy in itself. Sound convoluted? It is. The fact remains that the best control we have over film and television media is constructing a copy of a copy—and reducing the viewing quality (and telepresence) to boot. The best solution? Watch that movie on the big screen in the neighborhood theater. Catch that television show when it's aired—and don't answer the telephone during the show.

Interactivity is a very different story. You *are* part of the action. According to Lombard and Ditton, "Most writers have either implicitly assumed or explicitly suggested that a major or even primary cause of presence is the ability to interact with a mediated environment." Telepresence increases when you're a participant in the simulation. Accordingly, Lombard and Ditton maintain that there are several variables that determine interactivity and the subsequent depth and range of telepresence:

• *The number and extent of inputs that can be controlled.* Inputs are the aspects of a simulation that respond—such as hand commands (haptic input) from a mouse, joystick, or keyboard; speech or sound recognition (voice/audio input) such as voice commands; body movement and location (kinetic input) such as gloves and headsets; and physical processes (psychophysiological input) such as heart rate, muscle tension, and brain waves. Think of this in terms of a video game. In the old games, like Pong, all you could control were the movement of the paddle, the speed of the ball, and the reset button. In newer games you have a multitude of options that allow you to design a customized game, change sounds, determine play by movement in your hands or your body suit, "converse" with the game through voice recognition . . . the possibilities increase each day. And with each progression our "involvement" and accordingly, telepresence, is enhanced. This is all before some of the new technologies that generate signals directly from the brain further enhance the illusion that there is a mediating device between you and the virtual-reality simulation. In a similar context, video conferencing in cyberspace increases telepresence more than voice e-mail. And voice e-mail increases telepresence more than text e-mail.

• *The range and depth of inputs that can be controlled.* The more you can do and the less effort it takes to control a virtual-reality simulation, the greater the telepresence. This is so obvious that many of us have never even registered it. In a traditional pinball machine, all you could do was release balls and flip paddles. In video pinball you can design the whole layout, choose the length, speed, and rules of the game, and control the number of paddles as well as where they are located. The simulation of physically playing a pinball machine is very powerful.

Now take that one step further. Some video games utilize haptic input—you feel the tension in a fishing rod or the vibrations in a motorcycle or race car. And they change as you "speed" up, incur obstacles, or try to reel in that giant virtual fish. How is the sense of "being there" affected when you put on a headset that excludes visual and auditory input from the environment and replaces it with a virtual-reality simulation that changes as you move your head and peer into crevices? How does it feel when you move your feet and you experience the sensation of walking through the virtual environment? Or what about a video arcade game that puts you into a first-person starship where you feel the tension in the pilot's control, the resistance of the throttle, and the impact of attacks from other ships careening toward you across a simulated star field complete with the twists and turns of the enemy, the danger of asteroids, and the scream of laser weapons—all encapsulated in a machine that places you in a cocoon-like vehicle? We might not have it on our desktops yet, but it's coming.

• *The speed and user reactivity of the machine.* "Real time" is a popular goal in cyberspace. "Real time" refers to something that is actually happening as we see it without any built-in time lag. It enhances interactivity by deluding us into believing that there is absolutely nothing between us and the person or event happening. As discussed earlier, we're programmed to respond to the here and now. If you feel rain on your head, the storm is not occurring yesterday—it's happening now. If you feel ice cream in your mouth, you're eating now, not tomorrow. If a virtual-reality simulation can teleport you to the illusion that your experience is in the here and now, then it's much easier to believe. A telephone is highly interactive for this very reason—it gives you the distinct sense of being there, conversing with someone on the other end of the line without mediation of the plastic devices, relays, and signals that simulate a voice. Consequently, the psychological experience of communicating in a chat room is very different than e-mail; "watching" a live performance via the Internet is very different from viewing online video. This, of course, is regulated by the technological manipulation of speed, reducing sensory delays and subsequently producing the illusion that you are in fact, *there.*

The power and psychological space of cyberspace is in its infancy. Without physical parameters to limit it, our technology has the potential to create any simulated space, thrusting us into virtual realities far beyond our present imaginations. But what does this do to our Stone Age computers? how does it affect the parts of us that still remain, by definition, connected to the old-fashioned concept of body?

"RELATIVES" IN THE AGE OF PSYCHOTECHNOLOGY

*T*HE DAY BEGINS with breakfast.

It's a choice from among hundreds of brightly packaged cereals, from honeyed seven-grain flakes to sugar-free, fat-free puffs bioengineered to lower cholesterol. You eat from a bowl designed in New York and manufactured in Malaysia. The television, poised precariously above the kitchen table, broadcasts the morning news: the latest riots in the Middle East, human-rights violations in China, and the mugging that took place down the block. Choosing between a synthetic waterproof trench coat and a soft leather jacket that blatantly violates animal rights, you rush out the door. Going to work involves some serious choices. If you live in the suburbs you might climb aboard a high-speed train built in France, drive a car manufactured in Japan, or ride a bus made in Detroit. If you live in the city you might catch an elevator maintained by union workers who leave state-required inspection stickers on the wall, stand next to visiting businesspeople from Germany, green-card workers from Korea, or illegal aliens from China. If you work on a ranch or farm you might be grappling with the latest genetically altered life forms, speculating whether competition from Third-World agriculture will cut already narrow profits. And if you're really lucky, you're a telecommuter who does business from the early American den in your home, with a Siamese cat in your lap and a Siberian husky by your feet.

Once at work, you receive telephone calls from the other side of the country, e-mail from the other side of the world, and a sad letter from your college buddy who just lost his job due to federal cutbacks. You fax a report to a customer who lives in a time zone three hours earlier and telephone your daughter's school to find out the exact dates of the second-grade play next month. The day continues with more information assault: sales are down in Europe because of a new initiative passed by the European Union; workers in the factory in Bangladesh want a fifty-cent increase, so you have to hike your prices; Hong Kong wants to talk about a new investment in the Pacific Rim; and your best friend wants to play tennis before your community-action group meets tonight to discuss the rising crime rate in your neighborhood. The computer on your desk is acting up because there was a fire in the manufacturing plant in Japan that makes the part you need to repair it, and the Internet moves infuriatingly slow because bandwidth is clogged. Your son calls from school and he is near tears because you said you might miss his Little League game Saturday afternoon, scheduled at the same time you planned to see the new Spielberg film. And all you really want to do is sit down for a few minutes, spend some time with your spouse over a cup of coffee from Columbia, surf the Net, look at video footage from the latest natural disaster in Africa, or catch the international soccer scores while munching on strawberries shipped from Chile.

S O C I A L   S A T U R A T I O N

Our Stone Age computers have been thrust into a world they were not designed to negotiate. We're pelted with an unending flow of information that can crash the most stable mental modules. We connect with one another through machines instead of eye contact; we play in virtual-reality simulations instead of on the beach; we're packed into dense concentrations of human bodies instead of in sprawling spaces shared with other animals, plants, and trees. While natural selection provided an insurance policy against the most severe demands of the environment, today there are only corporate systems to take its place. There's no time to evolve, no time to adapt, no time to let nature take its course.

Simply put, new-millennium life is so cluttered with physical, psychological, and technological overload that our only reliable constant is change. A stable self is quickly becoming a thing of the past.

Why? Boundaries blur as we communicate across political, national, and temporal lines. We continually adjust ourselves to immediate, albeit fleeting, conditions. Technology makes it possible to establish and sustain relationships that could not have existed before—sharing ideas and experiences with people occupying a rapidly shrinking place called the global village. Technology also makes it possible to shut off these relationships if they don't meet our narcissistic or pragmatic needs. Words, ideas, images, and emotions shift rapidly as each day proceeds, a montage of often unrelated connections linked incongruously between the different roles we play. The voices, the activity, and the information quickly become overwhelming. The self has to find ways to release the tension. It's like being in an enormous night club with music blaring, lights flashing, voices buzzing, and an unending supply of food, drink, and new faces. It becomes difficult to think, to find our selves in the noise. The easiest solution is to be absorbed by the environment—to go with the flow. But that's good only for one evening. Humans need to adapt to the overflow and find a way to survive.

ENTER POSTMODERNISM

Too much noise and confusion, no evolutionary equipment to help us sort it out, and adaptation gone awry. Where does that leave us? Before this mess we chose to view life, or reality, through a very evolutionary-compliant system: observation. Seeing is believing. But that doesn't quite work when life is permeated with virtual-reality simulations. Sure, the Tyrannosaurus Rex felt like the real thing in *Jurassic Park*, but was it really *real*? Or was it just clever tricks enacted by filmmakers, sound designers, and some very imaginative visual artists? If so, we need to decide whether the T-Rex was a simulation or was real in its own way. After all, how can you simulate something that has never been seen by the human eye? In that context, reality, as discussed earlier, is merely a point on the reality-virtuality continuum. Just as we shifted the definition of gender, other definitions of truth become blurred. Is reality or virtuality truth? Is truth real or virtual? Now we're really in deep water. "As we absorb multiple voices," Gergen explains, "we find that each 'truth' is relativized by our simultaneous consciousness of compelling alternatives. We come to be aware that each truth about ourselves is a construction of the moment, true only for a given time and within certain relationships" (p. 16).

In other words, that celluloid T-Rex is only "real" relative to how we experience it, just as the original T-Rex is real relative to how we study it, reconstruct its skeleton, and make educated guesses about how it roared, what it ate, and when it lived. Our lives become flexible and free floating, and we live in a place that Gergen describes as "a world in which we no longer experience a secure sense of self, and in which doubt is increasingly placed on the very assumption of a bounded identity with palpable attributes" (p. 17). It's called postmodernism—a very politically correct, very Gen-X and increasingly, Gen-Y, way to view things. It's our first real attempt to construct a philosophy that explains how we're in the process of evolving toward a simulation or copy of life, relinquishing the need to have concrete, physical representations of the reality popularized by science.

Postmodernism wasn't born yesterday. It evolved from experiments in human thought, growing out of earlier romantic and modernist views of the self. Eighteenth- and nineteenth-century romantic philosophy focused on mysterious, unseen forces that dwelt inside the individual. Life and relationships took on meaning through these forces, giving our experience depth and importance. It was an intensely mystical way to view the self, focusing on the inner, rather than the outer, processes. One of the noblest romantic jobs was to investigate the soul, a search for meaning that emerged from understanding the deep, spiritual essence of each human being. Art, music, and literature were direct links to access the human essence, windows into the romantic, passionate corners of the soul. Morality, loyalty, and friendship represented human inspiration at its very best. It's no surprise that the romantic philosophy nurtured impressionists such as Vincent Van Gogh and transcendentalists such as Henry David Thoreau. *Walden*, written in 1848, embraces the very heart of romanticism. Thoreau described his two-year sojourn in the wilderness:

> I wanted to live deep and suck out all the marrow of life, to live so sturdily and Spartanlike as to put to rout all that was not life, to cut a broad swath and shave close, to drive life into a corner, and reduce it to its lowest terms. . . . (p. 90)

Romantic thinking eventually gave way to what is more familiar to our times—the modernist notion. Darwin helped the process along. There was a mingling of ideas, an often fanciful view that permeated early modernists. For example, while Freud described the unconscious in modernistic terms as a place that was "the major driving force behind human conduct," he softened his analysis by adding that it was also the romantic repository of "dreams, works of art, and distorted reasoning or neurotic action" (p. 4). Modernists shifted the romantic concept of the self to a machine metaphor. The human self was viewed as a rational, logical, scientific entity that utilizes observation to establish an understanding of environment. The very development of the social sciences embodied modernism. It implied that human life could be organized and studied using scientific principles. Perhaps we can see it more clearly in art forms where the round, luscious, and emotional scenes of the romanticists such as Monet became the primary lines, shapes, and colors of modernists such as Mondrian; where the sprawling, fanciful words of writers such as Thoreau evolved into the clear, straightforward work of Hemingway. Hemingway's opening lines in *The Old Man and the Sea* are very different from the passion in Thoreau's "marrow of life."

> He was an old man who fished alone in a skiff in the Gulf Stream and he had gone eighty-four days now without taking a fish. In the first forty days a boy had been with him. But after forty days without a fish the boy's parents had told him that the old man was now definitely and finally salao, which is the worst form of unlucky, and the boy had gone at their orders in another boat which caught three good fish the first week. (p. 9)

The modern self was clear and easily defined. It had a single identity that was fixed and rational. Although an individual could play many roles in life, his or her essence remained intact, centered, and uniquely defined. However, something changed that drained our naivete, brought skepticism and simulations. Whether they were born in our minds, our technology, or our adaptations, the old modernist views no longer worked. How can you have a single identity when we have distinct, multiple selves? How can you have an essence when it shifts with the movie in the theater, the sitcom on television, or the virtual community on the net? What is real when copies take over from originals?

Postmodernism was waiting in the wings. Times have changed. Nothing is stable and centered, everything shifts, and meaning is deconstructed. All things are in the mind of the beholder: life is forever moving, forever shifting, "facts" do not exist but are the function of cultural or societal bias. Nothing can be defined as truth. It's as if we're floating, never to be found in one place at any given time.

Consider some of the people wandering around cyberspace this very moment, playing with different postmodern personas and acting out truths that elude all but the beholder:

- A twenty-year-old female college student talks about "letting out the secret compartments inside me." In her eyes she becomes someone else, creating fantasy people at will. Online, she's a man.
- A young woman is angry—her boyfriend is spending too much time online. The solution is simple. None of that old-fashioned jealousy stuff for her. Instead, she logs on to his favorite chat under a different name. As soon as he appears, she directs her words to him. He takes the bait. She quickly "seduces" him into a cyber relationship. "Let's have sex," she suggests, and they retreat to a private virtual boudoir. All during this time she repeatedly begs him to break up with his "real" girlfriend, testing his loyalty.
- A convicted pedophile is prohibited from being around children. If he's caught with any he will go back to jail. He aches for their presence, the power over their minds and bodies, the control he wields. So he logs online, calls himself "Jimmy," and hangs out on the Net at kids' Websites playing games.

- An undergraduate majoring in biophysics at a top-ranked university hates being the smart kid. Like the prince and the pauper, she's always wondered what it would be like to be poor—like the rest of the world. So she takes an anonymous Internet account and "becomes" a liberal-arts student at a community college, practicing college street talk on the Internet.
- A community-college student majoring in liberal arts always wanted to feel like an Ivy Leaguer. Like the prince and the pauper, he's always wondered what it would be like to be rich—like the elite. So he takes an anonymous Internet account and "becomes" a philosophy major from Harvard, playing college aristocracy on the chats.
- A middle-aged housewife is tired of children, errands, PTA, and Little League. There are gray strands in her hair, and her weight has edged up twenty-five pounds. So she goes into a virtual community and becomes a twenty-three-year-old editorial assistant who loves to go rock climbing and jogging. She announces that she's looking for new relationships. She gets a lot of takers, but the housewife can't figure out if they're men or women, kids or adults.
- A teenage boy has a serious crush on one of the high-school cheerleaders. She doesn't even know he exists. He desperately wants to get her attention. So far, nothing has worked. He wonders what it feels like to be female. What would she really want? He decides that if he can learn what girls think, he can catch his cheerleader. He logs on as a sixteen-year-old girl.
- Dad comes home each night after a harrowing day dealing with his company's salespeople. He hates his job, but his family depends on the money he makes. They own a house in the suburbs, a minivan, and take yearly trips to Disney World. After dinner he retreats to the computer to do some work. He tells the kids that they have to watch television—he can't be disturbed. When the door is closed and the family is locked out, he logs on to his favorite site—a gay chat.
- A shy, lonely young man who lives at home with his mother and works in the local post office has no friends. He's awkward and unpopular—no one talks to him or asks him to go out. Every night he comes home, has his dinner, and retreats to the computer. Online, he becomes Sir Galahad67, charging around a medieval-style MUD

(multi-user dimension) where as a brave, charming knight he rescues golden-haired princesses from dragons and evil wizards.

* A forty-two-year-old man always wanted to be a psychiatrist, but he never had the time or money. So he goes online and opens a "therapy" practice, dispensing advice for $15 a pop. He calls himself "Sigmund," and no one asks for credentials.

All these people go "home" to other identities, realities constructed out of information overload. In a postmodern world it's perfectly acceptable, the standard operating procedure, when relativity rather than fact dominates life. Gergen's social saturation is essentially a dilemma of identity created by today's culture, where

> all previous beliefs about the self are placed in jeopardy, and with them the patterns of action they sustain. Postmodernism does not bring with it a new vocabulary for understanding ourselves, new traits or characteristics to be discovered or explored. Its impact is more apocalyptic than that: the very concept of personal essences is thrown into doubt. (p. 144)

It's the natural and predictable outcome of individuals who have to choose from hundreds of breakfast cereals each morning, converse with disembodied people from around the world, have sex in a virtual environment, and dream in simulcast.

KNOCK, KNOCK.
WHO'S THERE?

Who am I? Am I supervillian Lex Luthor, destroying the world, or Luke Skywalker saving the universe? Am I a parent or a worker, a patient or a caregiver? The images collide against one another like bits of ice swirled around in cold soda. What do I want? Do I want to be obscenely rich like Bill Gates, or pitifully poor like Little Orphan Annie? Do I want fame like Anthony Hopkins, or anonymity like the homeless person on the street? The desires well inside my mind like refuse in my stomach, pressing to get out, struggling to be contained. Is it a world of conflict, or an illusion without substance? Do I recycle my self and my desires like the trash I leave in front of my house—the same stuff, forever changing form?

*W*HO'S WHO IN this brave new postmodern world?

Postmodern culture contradicts the presumed order and structure of the twentieth century. It emerges from technology, new forms of communication, the information highway, and the proliferation of life within virtual realities. It sounds like an elite philosophical treatise held by the ivory-tower intelligentsia, but it's not. Instead of calling it postmodernism, we could call it "today" or the "new millennium." We could call it what you live every day—the pleasures and the anxiety, the conflicts and the cooperatives, the loves and the hates—the superlatives are readily summoned. The bottom line is that we are all postmodernists because our technology has deposited us into a place where natural selection has run out of time and evolution is still stuck in the Stone Age. Our mental modules respond in a very old, programmed way to protect our genes and assure our survival. That's where the old albatross—consciousness—comes in. If we battle ourselves to increase our consciousness, it's a tough fight. Evolution designed us to remain primarily automatic, to follow those preprogrammed mental modules. Increasing consciousness means stretching our minds and imaginations, going through the painful steps of harnessing our cognition beyond its paltry less-than-10-percent. We've come a long way, but there's still a very long way to go.

What's the alternative? Leave it as is. That means staying within the less-than-10-percent utilization of human cognitive abilities and allowing our consciousness to be seduced by virtual-reality simulations designed by others, victims of the gap between evolution and human technology. In that scenario, resistance *is* futile. We're all headed to become drones—cogs in a mental collective, that, for better or worse, will diminish consciousness.

Why? In a postmodern environment our mental modules struggle to adapt to social saturation. Accordingly, the self shatters into multiple parts and roles. It becomes a plural, decentralized grouping—the parent coexists with the global villager and the corporate manager. In the movie theater no one knows whether you're Tom Hanks or Meg Ryan. On the telephone no one knows whether you're fat or thin, young or old. But most significantly, on the Internet, *no one knows whether you're a man or a woman, a kid or a grandma.*

While multiple roles have always been a part of human life, the dependence on simulation and virtual communications heightens the separation between roles. The self, saturated by virtual input, must dissociate to survive. Individuals have to construct a more flexible reality so superficial manipulations in time, space, and ideology become daily routine. It's the only way to psychologically survive in a world where you can wake up in bureaucratic Washington, D.C., spend the day in free-floating Los Angeles, and go to sleep in the isolated beauty of Bora Bora. In other words, the self dissociates. Dissociation allows you to move between psychological places and maintain an emotional equilibrium. Essentially, dissociation is a psychological process where you split your identity to fit pressing emotional, environmental, and cultural needs.

IS DISSOCIATION HEALTHY, UNHEALTHY, OR DOWNRIGHT PATHOLOGICAL?

Mental health professionals describe disordered dissociation as a disruption in the usually integrated functions of consciousness. For example, memory, identity, or perception of the environment becomes separated and discrete. In milder forms, there's a sense of "not being there" or "out of body." In its most severe form, dissociative identity disorder (popularly known as multiple-personality disorder) establishes two or more identities that repeatedly control behavior. Much falls in between those extremes. Let's look at it on a continuum.

the modern self	the postmodern self	the disordered self
(stable, centralized)	(multiple, cycling)	(pathologically dissociated)

Not surprisingly, movies, television, and books are filled with dramas about the extreme, disordered self. *Dr. Jekyll and Mr. Hyde* is about two personalities residing in one body. Television dramas such as *Law & Order* have used dramatic portrayals of multiple personality disorder (MPD) in one-hour episodes. Movies such as David Madden's film *Separate Lives* explore MPD in the context of a murder mystery. In a more recent movie, *Primal Fear*, the drama is centered around what was referred to as a crime drama cliché—a bad guy with MPD. In other words, we've seen a lot of dissociation in virtual-reality simulations. It's a form of mental illness and dramatic theme that most people find entertaining. Is it surprising that the simulation has come to roost in postmodern psychology?

Now we're faced with an intriguing conundrum: How can so many "people" live inside one body? We all experience some degree of dissociation in our lives. For example, you're at a party. It's Saturday evening, and everyone is dressed to the hilt. You wish you could be in jeans and a T-shirt, but you got this invitation, and it was politically incorrect to refuse, so, very unhappily, you're there. Even worse, you're stuck in a group of people who are feverishly discussing the homeless problem. You couldn't care less. It's more interesting to focus on how the woman with the glittering tennis bracelet is balancing her martini between two perfectly placed fingers or how the man with the ridiculous tie is trying to delicately sip beer from a mug. But it doesn't keep your attention, so your mind wanders. The whole room is filled with groupings like the one you're in. *Boring.* Wouldn't it be great just to stir things up? Suddenly, the politically correct demeanor slips away.

"You know," you say to the woman with the martini, "I think you're full of it."

She pauses, mid-sip. The group is suddenly silent, all eyes focused on you. Inside, another voice stirs. *Give 'em what they deserve.* The tiger stirs and then attacks.

"This is bullshit. How many of you know what it's like to be homeless?" Silence.

You can't stop now. It's as if another, very *un*-politically correct person inside you has taken hold. "We stand here discussing the homeless like we know what it feels like—wearing diamonds and sipping good liquor. Get real."

It feels *strange.* Maybe you like it, maybe you don't. Maybe it never happened—you just played out the scenario in your head. For a moment you abandoned that politically correct persona for a very different you. And it felt good.

Psychologically, you dissociated, or split from the identity you generally assume in a proper social gathering. It could have been a brief mental interlude playfully executed in your mind, or maybe it was your "bad side," and your partner is furious over your inappropriate behavior. Again, we think and experience such scenes all the time because we all dissociate to a certain degree. Disordered or pathological dissociation is simply the extreme form of that "other" you.

Pathological dissociation goes beyond the temporal switching of identities to the inability to integrate various aspects of the self into one space. Your dissociation acknowledged the "other you," while disordered dissociation tends to conceal or completely deny awareness of additional identities. These disorders usually stem from physical, sexual, or psychological trauma. Interestingly, there has been a sharp increase in reported cases of dissociative identity disorder. We don't know whether this is the result of actual incidences, more awareness, better diagnosis, or an increasing need for normal adaptive dissociation.

Consider this: pathological dissociation is one way individuals handle trauma. If a young child is sexually abused by her father, the psychological injury would be so severe that the only way she could handle it would be to separate from the part that was so damaged. The separate part or identity can hold the hurt, anger, and humiliation, while the "other" continues in a normal, daily life. In this manner, the child adapts to the trauma. While this isn't the only method people use to survive trauma, it's certainly effective in maintaining the self. As such, the act of dissociation is a highly adaptive function that can be measured on a continuum running from normal to pathological. "Normal" dissociation can involve behaviors like the one at the party or things such as daydreaming, light trances, and meditation, while pathological dissociation, at its extreme, can be that young child creating a second personality.

SO WHO IS REALLY INSIDE ME?

The self, saturated with a chaotic postmodern relativity, survives by normal adaptive dissociation. The natural habitat of this psychological creature is cyberspace. In cyberspace people can experiment with their identities, go to a variety of environments where different names, personalities, personal information, and entire personas can be forged without anyone's being able to confirm or confront their fantasies. Anonymity protects the individual, enabling him or her to create a flexible, multiple self that can explore all aspects of his or her inner reality. "Dark" sides can be as viable as "light" sides, names can be changed at will, roles can be played indiscriminately, and personal icons or avatars (personal graphics) can be drawn and manipulated in many distinct ways. We find ourselves not only in a virtual environment, but also in a virtual *self* that simulates bits and pieces of conscious and unconscious fantasy.

Adaptive dissociation did not begin with cyberspace. Human transformations have always fascinated people. The story of Adam and Eve is about creating two identities from one body. "Woman" emerged from "man," formed from his rib. Like today's movies, ancient mythology told stories of opposing characters within one god. Ovid's *Metamorphosis*, written in the early years after the birth of Christ, explains that

> My intention is to tell of bodies changed
> To different forms; the gods, who made the changes,
> Will help me—or I hope so—with a poem
> That runs from the world's beginning to our own days.

It took technology and cyberspace to create an environment where multiplicity could be clarified, accepted, and acted out. Dr. Jekyll and Mr. Hyde are no longer virtual fantasies in cyberspace. You can *be* Dr. Jekyll in one newsgroup and Mr. Hyde in another. You can create, cycle, and recycle multiple identities in a virtual space that spans all time zones, all geographic boundaries, and every social and psychological parameter previously established by humankind. It is a potpourri of mix-and-match identities—a social laboratory based on the human ability for adaptive dissociation in virtual reality.

The choices are many. For example, when you register with an Internet Service Provider (ISP), you can use one or several screen names. You can have female names, male names, celebrity names, nicknames—the list is as long as your imagination. The places you choose online will define how much of any chosen self you wish to reveal. A professional list might ask for real names, while a newsgroup might want only screen names. You can go on chats and log in regularly with a set of names (and identities), play different roles in different role-playing games, or design colorful icons or avatars to be used as your "physical" representations. What is the psychosocial effect of digital anonymity *and* adaptive dissociation? Randy, a sixteen-year-old high-school student, offers her opinions:

> The Internet is good in some cases and makes one feel more isolated in other cases. For example, when I write an e-mail, sometimes it's very frustrating to realize I'm staring at a blank white screen in my computer

room. It's very one-sided. When I talk to other people on the Internet, it's very strange because all I'm seeing are words. At least on the telephone I can get a feeling of what a person is like through their tone of voice. Yet, at the same time, the Internet is a true communication hub. I can talk to people whom I would not ordinarily talk to, become involved in causes and groups that would not otherwise be possible. It fosters a sense of community because essentially, nobody knows who they are talking to. Everyone can start anew and not worry about what anybody else thinks of them. (personal communication)

The concept of anonymity complements postmodern flexible identity, adaptive dissociation, and altered views of reality. John Suler, Ph.D., author and webmaster of *The Psychology of Cyberspace*, speculates that cyberspace emulates a dream state—an extension of the mind and of all the facets of an individual's mental environment. It results in an entrance into an altered reality where unconscious thoughts, fantasies, and impulses can be acted out safely. No one knows who you are. Consequently, no one will connect "you" to your behavior. Suler proposes that this "may explain some of the sexuality, aggression, and imaginative role playing we see on the Internet" (Suler 1996a).

Anonymity reinforces dissociation, subsequently releasing individuals from the confines of a unitary self. *You can be anyone, because no one knows who you are.* In due course, two psychosocial controls that dramatically determine behavior are diminished: constraint and consequence. *Constraint* refers to the set of norms and values that restrict, limit, or regulate individual behavior. We use constraints to guide ourselves as well as predict the behavior of others. For example, why don't you wear a bathing suit to work? Why do you resist robbing the bank when you need money to pay the mortgage? Why do you say "please" and "thank you" and get annoyed when those niceties are not returned? If we don't socially constrain ourselves we pay the consequences. You want to wear a bathing suit to work? Sure, but you'll probably lose your job. You want to rob that bank? Sure, but you'll probably spend the next ten years in jail. You want to skip the "please" and "thank you"? Sure, but people will think you're rude, and your social status will diminish.

Social constraints, and accordingly, social consequences, tend to become more fluid with multiple identities and anonymity. If FoxiLadi18 commits a chat room faux pas, all she does is "kill" the identity and come back as livelygirl220. If Luke770 gets thrown out of a virtual community for violating the by-laws, all he has to do is click to another site and another set of laws.

A voluntary system of virtual social constraints has emerged to provide some guidelines—it's called "netiquette." These guidelines are spread all over the Internet, with the hope of controlling social behavior loosened by virtual realities. Virginia Shea, author of *Netiquette*, lists the basics:

1. Remember the human.
2. Adhere to the same standards of behavior online that you follow in real life.
3. Know where you are in cyberspace.
4. Respect other people's time and bandwidth.
5. Make yourself look good online.
6. Share expert knowledge.
7. Help keep flame wars under control.
8. Respect other people's privacy.
9. Don't abuse your power.
10. Be forgiving of other people's mistakes.

Netiquette notwithstanding, many have found an excess of anger and aggression on the Internet. It's not surprising. Put adaptive dissociation in the same place as reduced social constraints and consequences, and it's inevitable. All those tigers lingering inside of us have found an environment in which they can safely emerge. Fight-or-flight conflicts don't have to exist in virtual-reality simulations because no one gets killed. Everyone can be the hero, destroy the enemy, bring home the bloody meat for dinner, and protect their kin (however they define them). Mark Dery, in *Flame Wars*, describes this new environment in chilling terms:

> The wraithlike nature of electronic communication—the flesh become word, the sender reincarnated as letters floating on a terminal screen—accelerates the escalation of hostilities when tempers flare; disembodied, sometimes pseudonymous combatants tend to feel that they can hurl insults with impunity (or at least without fear of bodily harm). (p. 559)

Let's look at cyberspace from a different vantage point. For the first time in human history, all members of the species have the potential to talk directly with one another. There are no geographic, political, ethnic, or racial boundaries that can prevent this communication. Many Third-World countries have tried, without success, to censor the Internet. It simply doesn't work. The system is built to decentralize communications. If one machine breaks down, another takes over. The only way to effectively shut it down is not to allow it in a country in the first place. And it's already too late for that. The result? We have a system with no centralized government, no headquarters, and no main office. It's a collection of hundreds of thousands of networks linked together, bypassing practically every boundary traditionally known to humankind. So when the Chinese dissidents want to report about human-rights violations, all they have to do is go online. If the government wants to stop them, they have to literally ban all computers in China or shut down the telephone system. Instead, information leaks across lines that can't be plugged. Rebellious Serbian students get their "message of freedom" out to the world before their dictator can stop it. Mideastern terrorists get recipes for bombs on the Internet. Local hate groups go global. People communicate with others from around the world in places where their paths, without this global system, would not have crossed.

Many "cyberlibertarians" argue that all boundaries are neutralized in cyberspace, with the only disability or discrimination against individuals being slow modems, old computers, unreliable hook-ups, limited access, and other technological flaws. Cyberfeminists proclaim that this is the one place that can ultimately be gender free. Is it fantasy, or technological optimism? Does it matter?

Consider the implications. In the mid-twentieth century, paleontologist and Catholic priest Tielhard de Chardin predicted that a "single, integrated, and evolutionary view of reality" would emerge (Pesce, no date). This phenomenon would be like nothing we had ever seen before. It would appear as a new reality with distinctive boundaries that we, as humans, would never be able to understand as a whole. We would live the parts but never have to ability to *see* the whole. De Chardin called it the *noosphere* (pronounced "no-o-sphere").

Author, theorist, and cofounder of VRML (Virtual Reality Modeling language) Mark Pesce (1996) has interpreted the noosphere as a collective of knowledge created by the unrivaled explosion of human connections. These connections occur in mediums that allow us to perceive events consistently and universally—virtual-reality simulations where human perception is constructed. In other words, when millions of people are linked in virtual space, a new, technological collective emerges. The sum of these technological connections is far greater than the parts. When one considers the blurred boundaries, changes in the definition of self and selves, the emphasis on fantasy, anonymity, and connection in cyberspace, a strange, unfathomable entity emerges. It looks like a collective consciousness, a blending of our cyborg voices into a group think. A Borg collective, perhaps?

The idea of a noosphere is not the work of science fiction. Carl Gustav Jung described a similar entity when he introduced the concept of the collective unconscious. He proposed that there was a second "psychic system" that was collective, universal, impersonal, and identical in all people. The phenomena contained in the collective unconscious are the archetypes, or universal forms, in the human mind. As discussed earlier, virtual-reality archetypes follow mental patterns consistent with cultural imagery. They are experiences gleaned from collective, preprogrammed information rather than individual creations. Their images are both familiar and compelling, an integral part of virtual experience.

The noosphere can be seen as a collective consciousness, created by the sum total of virtual-reality archetypes in cyberspace. Simply put, all the human connections, chatrooms, e-mail, bulletin boards, fantasy games, websites, etc., are beginning to coalesce into a gestalt, a collective of human virtual links. Pesce (no date) suggests that there are three distinct phases in the development of this conscious virtual collective known as cyberspace:

1. The first phase involves a period of *connection*, where individuals move into a single space that will enable collectivity. In other words, it began just yesterday when millions of people suddenly discovered that we were sharing a single global village connected through the Internet.

2. The next phase is *collectivity*, the inevitable result of bringing indi-

viduals together on a large scale. People work together and demonstrate archetypal properties in their global village—patterns where the sum is far greater than the parts. Everyone "knows" where this occurs, but there is no single, dominant force. Power is decentralized and scattered throughout the collective. It's the World Wide Web defying restriction and authorship, stubbornly maintaining equal and open access.

3. The third phase involves the emergence of *corrective* behaviors—where the collective begins to monitor, modify, and correct its own behavior. The corrective goal is to indiscriminately protect the collective without conscience. As Pesce describes it, "The corrective has no prejudices and willingly eats its own children or the children of others."

The end of the story can be described in two words—collective intelligence. Is cyberspace dooming us to an inevitable Borg collective? Will fiction and truth merge, as they already do in our movies, in our cyberspatial future? Once again, if Pesce's scenario proves to be true, the only prevention is increasing and adapting *individual* consciousness. In other words, if we don't update those Stone Age computers, they might all be destined to crash.

DIGITAL
NEIGHBORING

It's old country, with graceful, rounded mountains like aged patriarchs in deep con-versation, their heads bent tenderly toward one another. The colors dance with the seasons, from the bare, dormant branches of winter to the brilliant green of summer. It's a place of constant change. Cycles of life and death repeat themselves over min-utes and eons, moving in a rhythm cast by nature's unforgiving eye. Three hundred million years ago an ancient sea flooded the land, slowly depositing layers of sedi-ment formed from marine debris. When Africa and North America collided some fifty million years later, it buckled and gave birth to a vast mountain range.

A VIRTUAL COMMUNITY is a network of people who connect through computers. An actual community is defined by geograph-ical space including buildings, streets, parks, and other public spaces. The elements that bring a community together, forming a clear entity where people are attached to one another beyond kin, are far more difficult to define. They include the voices and emotions of individuals playing,

215

working, cooperating, arguing, competing, and residing in close proximity. They also include the best, the worst, and usually everything in between concerning human behavior. If these features exist, it's not very important *how* one enters a community. After all, don't we each, in our postmodern frenzy, belong to multiple communities—from the neighborhoods where our houses and apartments are located to the group of people we might refer to as a business or professional community to that budding place we call the global village? The critical component to being part of a community is not whether we enter it by car, computer, or metaphor, but how we connect and socialize within its boundaries. Accordingly, in a virtual-reality community, interactivity, simulation, and collectivity are essential. It's the very soul of how people connect in electronic environments.

> *During the ice age, massive boulders were formed by the alternate freezing and thawing of rock. Harsh weather and erosive waters sculpted rounder and lower peaks that look far gentler than the younger, craggier Rocky Mountains. Eventually it became a rugged wilderness, a lush area inhabited by the Shawnee, a Native American tribe who occupied the eastern woodland area. The land remained that way until a brief 250 years ago—a tiny moment on its long and courtly history. A man named Thomas Walker led an expedition out from Fort Vaux into the uncharted country. His group spent weeks meandering through Appalachia, traveling in breathtaking lands rich with natural resources. Beside Walker trekked families whose names are still seen today in the local listings—Ingles, Draper, Harmon. When they arrived at what is now known as the New River Valley, the group envisioned their future. The settlement of Draper's Meadow was born. It was the first permanent English-speaking colony west of the Allegheny Mountains.*

Howard Rheingold, author of *The Virtual Community: Homesteading on the Electronic Frontier*, talks about the magic of virtual communities where people "do just about everything people do in real life, but we leave our bodies behind" (p. 3). Rheingold maintains that people who are compelled to participate in virtual communities discover deep satisfaction, companionship, sometimes even an addictive need to be there. He reports about his virtual community, a place called the Well. The Well was a social hub, a virtual community where he discovered camaraderie with members who were always there for him, ready to discuss, support, and trade exchange experiences. "Point of view, along with identity," explains Rheingold, "is one of the great variables in cyberspace. Different people in cyberspace look at their virtual communities through differently shaped key holes" (p. 63).

Virtual communities occupy a strange, postmodern space that emerges from technological manipulation. It enhances telepresence to the degree that one removes the boundaries of the computer and plunges into a simulation whose main function is to solidify the mental and emotional image that dominates communal space. Community "spaces" are arranged around various designs of virtual construction, running the gamut from text-based e-mail lists to expansive, prefabricated villages with streets, homes, public "buildings" and other edifices that simulate physical geography. Humans invariably fill in the blanks when contextual cues are unavailable. It's a collective, rather than singular experience, that compels members to return, over and over again, to their virtual communities. New communities are constantly being constructed, older ones slowly fading away. Because of this constant rise and fall of communal spaces, loyalty is not particularly strong. It's too easy to pick up and move. More important, virtual communities spread throughout an increasingly crowded cyberspace, and new technologies offer spaces that enhance the experience, complete with the ability to construct virtual dream houses as well as virtual dream identities. Some even look like cities—full-fledged simulations of the real thing. And some *are* the communities themselves, replacing or enhancing geographic proximity with digital neighboring.

> *The intruders displaced the native Shawnee Indians. Tensions gradually increased. The Shawnee attacked in 1755, leaving only four settlers who were not injured, captured, or killed. A few years later the survivors returned and rebuilt. Later, William Black would donate thirty-eight acres of land so that on August 4, 1798, the General Assembly of Virginia could deed it to the new trustees of the town of Blacksburg. Who would have predicted that two centuries later the people would once again be settlers in a new, untamed frontier? Except this time it was in cyberspace, not Appalachia. For better or for worse, this small town nestled between 300-million-year-old mountains is one of the world's most wired communities.*

Blacksburg is a small town nestled on a plateau in Appalachia, America's oldest mountain range. Thirty-six thousand people live in this corner of southwestern Virginia, in a town with an unusual partnership joining yes-terday, today, and tomorrow. Old-timers talk about the Golden Gobbler where the burgers and rib eyes were great and everyone could get a drink no matter what his age. Some remember the harsh winters back in midcen-tury when drifts were reportedly twenty-feet deep and you could sit on snow next to the top of a telephone pole. Still others recall Mountain Lake, when the film crew from *Dirty Dancing* shot their exterior lodge frames. Today, Blacksburg, Virginia, is both the same and very different.

Blacksburg is ground zero for a new definition of human community called the BEV project: Blacksburg Electronic Village. The concept was born in 1991, and the town gates officially opened in 1993. It took two years to revise the information infrastructure; install equipment; design, test, and distribute the software; and arrange for a full range of cyberspace tools. BEV is one of the oldest Internet-based community networks in the country—with one of the largest proportions of online citizens—admin-istered by a public-private partnership among the town, a research univer-sity (Virginian Tech), and Bell Atlantic.

As discussed earlier, humans have evolved to live in groups where they cooperate. Differentiation was essential to assure the survival and spread of genes. Our mental modules are designed to operate in socially defined environments, and our adaptations to one another are as critical to species survival as our adaptations to the physical world. As information-pro-cessing life forms, we draw power from our intraspecies cooperation *and* conflict. Competition, as well as cooperation, enables us to persevere.

Early human groups living as hunter-gatherers were essentially nomad-ic, forced to follow animal migrations and vegetation cycles. Ornstein writes,

> Group life is successful life so hominid and early human social groups pro-duced challenging personal problems. Instead of the hostile forces of nature, our early human's primary opponent was herself. So natural selec-tion acted upon our ancestors' abilities to devise ways of getting along with their fellows. The social skills and manipulations that were called for in the early human career were unprecedented, adding fuel to the fire. (p. 43)

Evolution designed us to seek new places within similar environs, so we were compelled to wander, but not too far afield. Perhaps that's why global migration was such a slow, steady process, each step edging just beyond the known parameters. It wasn't until the agricultural revolution and the new technology of producing food and domesticating animals that humans settled in organized communities. This was a slow, gradual transition that took place from 4000 to 10,000 B.C.E. It was the beginning of a way of life that has persisted: people living together in communities, towns, cities, and urban megalopolises.

Is postmodern culture challenging one of our species' most basic adaptations? The steady decline of extended family life, the increase in divorce, relocation, dual-career families, latchkey kids, and electronic babysitters has fed a decreasing cohesion in community life. All of us are perpetrators, not victims. After all, isn't it more important to catch the latest episode of *The Simpsons* than attend the school board meeting? That old idea of the warm, supportive community taking care of its own was canceled with *Leave It to Beaver.* It was decimated by postmodernism, increasing isolation, and erosion of trust and respect for organizational systems in religion, politics, and human services. After Watergate, who could ever really trust the government again? After religious leaders have sex with young boys and praise God while they're embezzling church funds, it becomes very hard to keep the faith in mainstream religion.

Our communities have been shattered by transitory lifestyles, commuting workers, disillusionment in traditional values, broken families, and the isolation of high-tech life. It's a contradiction of human programming *not* to be able to live safely in families and communities. And with their collapse we see obvious emotional, psychological, and social problems. Is it any surprise that we turn to safe, disembodied spaces to replace our losses? Think about the concept of telecommuting—going to work by computer. No traffic, no crowds, no battling over stale tuna fish sandwiches for lunch. We can establish our work and ourselves in the safety of our own homes. But how can it enhance our lives by allowing us to settle *anywhere*, not tied to urban, business, or manufacturing centers? How can it enhance our social lives by keeping us confined to our homes during the workday, without gossiping around the water cooler or having to tolerate the boss's new cologne? Does it limit our chances to see a world filled with beauty and horror, pain and pleasure, the very contrasts that give us perspective?

Perhaps these questions will be answered in the next millennium, when we have the advantage of hindsight. In the meantime, the construction of the Blacksburg Electronic Village suggests an almost predictable step in transforming the "dangerous" next-door neighbor to a safe, digital persona. After all, a digital neighbor can't cut down your favorite tree, park in your driveway, or play the stereo too loud.

It's no accident that Blacksburg was chosen for this electronic shape shifting. The local mix—a technologically sophisticated academic community and town leaders who have been active in attracting research-and-development companies—was exactly what Bell Atlantic wanted when it searched for a prototype community. So the town, the telecommunications company, and the university set out to wire Blacksburg. The goal was simple: to create a "community presence" on the Internet that would "bring people closer together" utilizing a new means of communication. It included, as its designers stated, "neighbors, friends near and far, family, wherever they may be, local business people, civic groups, and local government officials." BEV officially opened on October 25, 1993. Within one year, BEV had 9,000 people online, a number that made Blacksburg the most connected town in the world. By spring 1997 there were over 32,000 users registered. Today the number has stabilized at over 60 percent of the population actively participating in the electronic village.

The *BEV Community Network Planning Guide* maps out the development of community networks. Designed by the Electronic Village Technologies (EVT) group at Virginia Polytechnic Institute and State University, it offers both technology and philosophy for the community settlements in cyberspace. Their "community network check list for success" reads more like guidelines for human resources than a technological structure. Clearly, EVT discovered that a virtual community requires the same human elements as an actual community. BEV and Blacksburg differed in context, not content.

EVT's checklist stressed eight essential elements:

- Education is critical. Government officials, community groups, consumers, public school administrators, and businesspeople all must learn about online life.

- People learn by doing, not observing. The key is to "show, don't tell" about online life.

- Every community must have a leader. EVT calls this person a "project evangelist"—someone who can talk about online life in plain language.

- Smooth, direct connections are essential so the community can be online twenty-four hours a day, seven days a week.

- Universal access must be available so no one is left out. Ideally, every home should be equipped with a computer. For those who can't or won't afford it, community access should be available through libraries and other public facilities.

- Find an ISP that will offer good, low-cost service.

- Enlist community support from key players in local government, libraries, public schools, and business. Support from local community colleges, four-year colleges, and universities are valuable resources. Active groups interested in the concept can be used to promote and solidify the community.

A postmodern Continental Congress? The concepts have a familiar ring. Perhaps the things we want in our virtual communities are exactly the same as what we want in our physical communities. Human nature doesn't change that dramatically—those Stone Age computers are still calling the shots. Let's take a look at what really happens in the Blacksburg Electronic Village.

- The Town Manager goes online to answer questions from residents.

- The birth of a baby is announced.

- Coupons for local businesses are posted. You can catch the weekly special on turkey at Wade's Supermarket, read about warmblood and sporthorse breeding at Dulcote Farm, or find out which is free popcorn night at the Lyric Theater.

- If you want to shoot the breeze there's a wide assortment of "discussion" groups, ranging from general talk, school discussions, sports, business, and even auto repairs.

- Tried-Stone Christian Center will tell you what time the next Bible study group or sisters' meeting is taking place.

- The Beer Garden Hockey Club has the latest team standings, individual statistics, and postings from people like Joe, El Capitan, and Beefcake.

- One of the most active groups—Blacksburg Senior Citizens—runs a page that offers information about everything from healthcare to taxes, notices of movie day to the Silver Songsters Singing Group, and how to get involved at the SCLC (Senior Computer Learning Center).

In many ways, BEV seems to have has *enhanced* communication in the town. It's accomplished through a carefully designed website at www.bev.net. Along with local news, the website offers links to community, education, people, government, health care, village mall, and visitor's center. Messages can be posted daily, users can join a vast array of groups, and information is easily located. It's truly a place where your fingers do the walking *and* the talking. There are newsgroups, e-mail lists, chats, and newsletters. There are links inside and outside Blacksburg. The information and interconnectivity is a growing, ongoing process—as in any healthy human village.

What was the effect of BEV on Blacksburg, Virginia? For a while there was media attention from around the world, in print, radio, and television. When it all quieted down, the ongoing research indicated that BEV was a resounding success in some very unexpected ways. Researchers Andrea Kavanaugh, Andrew Cohill, and Scott Patterson found the most popular service was e-mail, closely followed by the World Wide Web. Most BEV users accessed online from home, once a day, for forty-five to sixty minutes. The large majority found BEV services very helpful in learning computer skills, local news and information, and communication with close friends and family as well as family and friends outside the community. The profile of an average user was revealing: 56 percent were female, the average age was forty-five years old, 38 percent had completed graduate school, and the average length of residence in Blacksburg was twelve years. According to Kavanaugh, Cohill, and Patterson, from the onset of the project, "users expressed their interest and satisfaction in being able to be more connected to their community."

Today, BEV boasts that:

- Senior citizens are very active, keeping up with old and new friends through e-mail lists, contributing profiles to the seniors' Web page, and having monthly BEV seniors' meetings and social events.

- Two-thirds of the businesses in Blacksburg use the Internet to sell everything from clothing to games to real estate in local and international markets.

- Schools are very active, using new educational resources such as Internet research and video conferencing with students in other countries.

- Parents follow classroom activities on the school Web pages and "talk" to teachers through e-mail.

- Residents use Web-based surveys to let government officials know what they think of things such as funding sources and new proposals.

- BEV provides a wide variety of education and training opportunities for local and visiting participants.

- A research branch evaluates and documents the effects of electronic community life on social, educational, political, economic, and technical networking.

BEV is a prototype for virtual communities. It began in actuality and leaped to virtuality. In the future, will the electronic village, or its simulation, become more meaningful than the original?

There are many other BEVs. Wired towns seem to be popping up all over the country *and* the world. Maybe the best way to understand what happens in these strange new virtual spaces is to look at them through the concept of social affiliation rather than the traditional physical or geographic definitions. Instead of having relationships with the people next door, individuals congregate in social networks constructed by computers. These social networks offer a digital connection, establishing a framework for communication between individuals and groups wired into shared circuitry. It's the old "reach out and touch someone" thinking. If I touch you, and you touch her, and she touches him—well, before you know it you have a network. If we keep on touching it becomes a viable *social* network—an electronic collective. Sure it's local—for now. In cyberspace there are no boundaries to connectivity and subsequently, to collectivity.

We find ourselves back in that nasty Borg starship, with their concept of electronic collectives hovering uncomfortably close to the idyllic noosphere. Lump all of those virtual-reality social networks together and we have the *human* collective. Can truth really be stranger than fiction?

Here's the rub. In cyberspace you have to design networks, because there's no geography. When you design social networks, are they like the prefabricated houses that you can buy and have installed on your land? If so, do the prefabricated houses take on the personality of their owners, or do the owners take on the personality of the designers? Where do things like democracy and free will go in a virtual community when the ruler (computer designer) is despotic and citizens depend not on the laws of the land but on the whims of the creators and their technologies?

ONE SMALL STEP FOR TECHNOLOGY, ONE GIANT LEAP FOR HUMANKIND

And then there are the rest—the fantasy playgrounds, intellectual hideouts, ivory towers, and social-meeting spaces that coalesce from disembodied voices into collectives. These are the places where the old technology most clearly feeds into the new; where people choose simulations based on words, ideas, graphics, and tiny alter egos known as avatars. Ranging from e-mail lists, newsgroups, and bulletin boards to online game competition, MUDs (multi-user-dimensions), and habitats, these virtual communities emerge directly from cyberspace, not from already established neighborhoods like Blacksburg. They create their own digital streets and byways, draw metaphorical lines in the sand, and search, within their members, for a collective set of norms. Their range and their depth go as far as technology will take them at any given moment in digital space and time. If they don't keep pace with the rapid flow, they risk members' moving on to better spots. Loyalty is weak and transitory—neighbors depend entirely on their collective power to entice and sustain residents. Are we safer in a virtual community like BEV, or walking down our crumbling Main Streets?

Essentially, there are three types of virtual-reality communities.

These types are determined by their symbolic approximation of actuality. They are all, by definition, postmodern simulations.

1. *Rooted.* Rooted virtual-reality communities are like BEV—they begin somewhere that exists on a real map. In this sense, they simulate social connections that are palpable and measurable in both real and virtual time. For example, in Blacksburg you can visit University Motors online or at South Main Street, you can window shop at Partyrama online or at North Main Street. There are social connections in both actuality and virtuality.

2. *Contiguous.* Contiguous virtual-reality communities are adjacent to the rooted, sharing a boundary but not quite being there. They simulate social connections that exist in both real and virtual metaphor. For example, consider a group of people who believe in extraterrestrial intelligence. They might have their own actual organization or newsletter or be members of a group like SETI (Search for Extraterrestrial Intelligence) or the Planetary Society. What they have in common is a belief that provides the basis for their social connection. Obviously, the virtual concept of belief is easily transported into cyberspace. The digital social network might be a chat, newsgroup, bulletin board, Web forum, e-mail list, or other means to exchange their ideas, thoughts, and fantasies. They are connected in both actuality and virtuality, their beliefs originating offline with their social exchanges primarily in cyberspace. In this grouping, "believers" can now join SETI@ home, where the *actual* power of hundreds of thousands of home computers is harnessed in the "search" for extraterrestrial intelligence.

3. *Digitized.* Digitized virtual-reality communities are perhaps the most written about and passionately debated electronic environments in cyberspace today. They are the abstract, fanciful virtual-reality communities such as MUDs, MOOs (MUDS Object Oriented), habitats, and virtual universes. Running the gamut from text-based to otherworldly graphics, these spaces take disembodied humans completely away from the boundaries of actuality and into the realms of technologically designed fantasy and imagination. Each day netizens are transported into cyberworlds with names like *Jurassic Park Muck, Divine Blood,* and

Aalynor's Nexus. From games, competition, and role-playing to social interaction, these are spaces that begin and end in virtuality.

A discussion of rooted, contiguous, and digitized virtual-reality communities would take an entire book simply to assess their content and psychosocial implications. The most revealing aspect of virtual-reality communities is that people love them and populate electronic neighborhoods in huge numbers. Reference.com, a site that provides directories and searches for the social and information groups on the Web, reports that there are more than 150,000 newsgroups, mailing lists, and Web forums online. Over 40 million people regularly participate in these virtual communities. Usenet, a global community of people who communicate through a bulletin-board-type system, reports that over 250,000 messages are posted *each day*. The numbers spiral when one considers the vast array of chats that appear on everything from individual home pages, corporate sites, organizations, and search engines to virtual habitats. On any given day, the Internet Relay Chat (IRC) alone lists upward of 10,000 chats, and that's before you even consider the massive networks such as America Online (AOL) and Microsoft Network (MSN), as well as the MUDs, MOOs, and virtual universes. Obviously, all of these environments are not clearly defined virtual communities but rather free-floating social networks with the potential to coalesce into more distinct identities. For example, a space like GeoCities, one of the largest virtual communities in cyberspace, invites members or "homesteaders" to create their home pages within "themed communities" that they call neighborhoods. Homesteaders can move into spaces such as FashionAvenue, MotorCity, Rainforest, and Soho. The community offers everything from chats, forums, information, stores, and even access to River Belle, an online casino.

Digitized virtual communities, although originating in cyberspace, may go even further than contiguous communities in increasing telepresence. Researchers have found intriguing behaviors common to these environments:

• Individuals tend to be less socially inhibited than in actuality.

• Men and women behave differently.

- Gender swapping is both common and acceptable.

- Multiple identities are part of daily virtual life.

- Many individuals get caught up in the virtual reality, abandoning or neglecting their "actual" lives.

- People tend to be friendlier and less paranoid about establishing relationships.

"Everyone and every thing and every place has a story," writes Rheingold. "Every object . . . from your character's identity to the chair your character is sitting in, has a written description that is revealed when you choose to look at the object" (p. 155).

Perhaps these are the toys or the lifestyles of tomorrow, which utilize postmodern play as a means to create a vast new network of economic, social, and political connections. Or perhaps they are the first grumblings of our own earthbound Borg collective.

ELITES,
WANNABES,
AND GUERRILLAS

I am your leader.

I have many names: sysop, wizard, webmaster. It does not matter. I have the power to contain you, control you, and if need be, erase you. I keep the walls high and the gates to my kingdom closed. If I admit you to my domain, I hold the power. I will protect you from the outside with my mighty firewalls, and I will protect you from the inside with my divine rule. You can stay within the walls of my kingdom only if I allow you. And I watch you constantly. Each time you venture within, my eyes are on you. If you challenge me or threaten my peons, I will take swift action. I will execute your bits and deny you future access. Your connectivity will be slashed, your selves banished from my land. I will seize your data and eliminate it from my program. You will be publicly humiliated and digitally stoned. Then you will leave, your digital tail between your legs, searching for some lesser place in the fierce frontier of cyberspace.

*N*ATURAL SELECTION MADE it perfectly clear: competition for intraspecies survival was fierce. Your sperm had to win or it was washed away in the flow of defeat—along with the millions of other sperm that hadn't made it. While evolution proceeds randomly, without purpose, the power of competition is clear. The strongest, wiliest, most powerful males win the sexual favors of the females and accordingly spread their genes. Or it might be a female competition. There's only one carcass for dinner. The kids have to be fed. Who will get it?

We see it all over the animal kingdom in dominance hierarchies, pecking orders, and alpha males and females. "Animals of the same species don't fight to the death every time they contest something of value," writes Pinker. "They have a ritualized fight or show of arms or a staring match, and one backs down" (p. 494). The strategy is clear: fight to the death, and one, possibly both, might lose. The loser, obviously, is dead; the winner may be so injured or weakened that the next challenger (or watchful predator from another species) will finish him off. Unquestionably, the best solution is to establish a hierarchy where the fittest or the best biologically suited animals rise to the top. Only when the alphas are weakened, old, or unable to maintain their power do they topple to interlopers who prove their own fitness and dominance.

Humans are pretty much the same. The real difference is in their tools for dominance—they often derive more from virtual concepts than brute power. Walk into any schoolyard and see who wields the power—the tall, tough bully or the small, skinny geek. Particularly among men, who are taller and bigger than women, size, physical strength, and the ability to "fight" are readily available means for domination. History has shown that most human cultures admire masculine strength, apparent with folk heroes such as John Wayne, Robin Hood, and Zorro. Contemporary cultural icons often follow a similar prototype: men such as Sylvester Stallone, Arnold Schwarzenegger, and Jean-Claude Van Damme have made millions of dollars combining their acting and their celluloid physical stature. Our physically smaller movie stars, such as Tom Cruise, Robert Redford, and Dustin Hoffman, are often purposely paired with diminutive leading ladies to give an impression of greater size. Pinker reports that in hunter-gatherer societies the term for leader is "big man," and in the United States "taller men are hired more, are promoted more, earn more ($600 per inch in annual salary), and are elected more" (p. 494).

Female human hierarchies are often based on affiliations to men with power. The high-school girlfriend of the captain of the football team wields awesome control, just as the CEO's wife does. The traditional route to that power is usually through her ability to decorate herself in a way that will attract and subsequently command the sexual fantasies of the male. Popular female icons are usually the "hot" women like Pamela Anderson, Nicole Kidman, and Carmen Electra. Women with power, intelligence, or imagination are rarely known for their beauty, sexual appeal, or desirability. Consider some of our contemporary female leaders such as Maya Angelou, Oprah Winfrey, and Ruth Ginsberg. They might be admired for their prowess, but not for their physical appeal. As discussed earlier, Buss found that men prefer youth and attractiveness in women, while women prefer men who can provide desired resources. In other words, men show off their stuff in fancy cars, high status, money, expensive dates, and gifts. Females, on the other hand, used "appearance enhancers" to attract as well as retain mates. In other words, they make themselves look pretty, sexy, and appealing, using such things as makeup, clothing, and jewelry.

The old aphorism "behind every strong man there's a strong woman" rings true, albeit hollow, even in today's feminist climate. Consider political roles like the First Lady, professional roles like "the doctor's wife," and social roles like "the lady of the house." In contrast, male sex objects are people like Fabio, Val Kilmer, and Tom Cruise, not Danny DeVito or Joe Pesce. It's interesting to note the popular 1970s riddle that dumbfounded unsuspecting victims:

> A man and his son are in a car crash. They're taken to different hospitals. The boy is wheeled into the operating room. The surgeon takes one look and says, "I can't operate on him, he's my son."
> Who is the surgeon?

Today, the answer is obvious: the mother. But back in the pre-working-woman days, people couldn't figure out the answer. Similar social conventions still lead us to address letters Mr. *and Mrs.*, to assume that in a family, dad makes more money than mom, and if you need help plead your case with the male cop not the female. While much has changed in the last decade, many professions remain differentiated by gender and the physical power they can purportedly apply:

- Construction workers tend to be male, nurses tend to be female;

- CEOs tend to be male, their executive secretaries tend to be female;

- Longshoremen tend to be male, kindergarten teachers tend to be female;

- Leading politicians tend to be male, social workers tend to be female.

Human dominance, however, can carry another, more virtual quality. "Humans," writes Pinker, "also evolved language and a new way of propagating information about dominance: reputation" (p. 496). He notes that the largest category of motives for murder in the United States is not "robbery, drug deals gone sour, or other tangible incentives," but trivial arguments resulting over offenses to one's reputation. This involves the relational concept of status.

Sociologists refer to status as any position occupied in a social system. You can have a position that is high status, low status, or anything in between. The titles "employee," "parent," "president," or "manager" are examples of social status. A status is defined by position, not by the individual who occupies it. Thus you can have an unoccupied status, such as deceased parent, an empty office, or a position (such as salesperson) waiting to be filled. Each status comes loaded with a wide range of human thought, feeling, experience, and behavior. Ask yourself the following questions, then note your answers. They all come from predetermined assumptions gleaned from what you learned and experienced about the status independent of the individual who had, has, or will occupy it.

1. Are Marine drill sergeants pretty?

2. Are used car dealers honest?

3. Are cops gentle?

4. Are priests liberal?

5. Are stock brokers kind?

6. Are grandmothers mean?

7. Are dentists tender?

8. Are social workers cutthroat?

Obviously, your first response was probably based on the stereotypes that were implied in the questions. When you think about it, you probably know gentle cops, mean grandmothers, and tender dentists. But in every stereotype there is a grain of truth that has been expanded and exaggerated: cops carry guns and arrest people, grandmothers buy toys and spoil their grandchildren, dentists drill. It's the same concept in status. A status is surrounded by stereotypes, assumptions, feelings, and experiences before anyone steps into the position. This leads to social stratification where the hierarchical position of a certain status is predetermined through cultural priorities. Generally, the higher the status the greater the power. Our society uses very clear parameters to rate status—occupation prestige, income, educational level, race, gender, ethnicity, and age. Money stands out. You can be a rich high-school dropout and it's okay—maybe even intriguing. You can be a multimillionaire minority, and the chances are no one is going to exclude you from the country club. A poverty-stricken doctor is a frightening thought, but how many people are concerned with a penniless old man? Context also affects status. For example, a union shop steward in an employee group has significant status. Put that same person in a group of clinical psychologists, and his or her status is greatly diminished.

As noted earlier, being male and physically more powerful implies greater status than being male and small, or being female. Being wealthy and educated implies greater status than being poor and uneducated. White-skinned people tend to have more status than dark-skinned people, WASPs tend to have more status than Latinos, and middle-aged adults tend to have more status than the elderly. There are also *physical* features connected to status—being male, tall, and muscular or being female, young, and seductive can also increase status. Fortunately there are many exceptions. We have Napoleon and Gandhi, Mother Teresa and Martin

Luther King Jr. We have wise elder diplomats and hotheaded young radicals. We have strong women and weak men. The contradictions are as long as the list of supporting evidence. Perhaps what is most significant is that human social systems rely on stratification with clear definitions of power and prestige.

It's no different in cyberspace.

LINES ARE DRAWN SEPARATING ELITES, WANNABES, AND GUERRILLAS.

If your status defines you as *elite*, then you move further away from conscious knowledge of your biological destiny. As a member of the elite you supercede the masses, you rise above the tide of virtual bodies into a status that carries the illusion of immortality. If your status defines you as a *wannabe*, you can move further away from conscious knowledge of your biological destiny by identifying yourself with the elite. By uniting yourself with the elite you become part of a cosmos that elevates status above the mundane. This is a delicate, *social* narcissistic balance. The elite is the narcissist, holder of the desired status and power. The wannabe is the closet narcissist, an individual who desperately wants to make it but didn't quite get there. Faced with the reality of diminished status and the need to validate his narcissism, the wannabe might attach himself to those people, things, or causes he believes have transcended the mediocre. The wannabe might be a follower, basking in the light of a hero, an ideology, or a special group. Individual autonomy is lost. Values, dreams, and goals are all invested in the collective.

The *guerrilla* is the virtual rebel who wants to wrest power from the elite, the civilly disobedient or dissident who, like the chimpanzee, battles to become the dominant male, defiantly challenging the positions of those in control. Sometimes guerrillas defy elites for the sake of going against the flow. They are simply *bad*. Some people call them computer criminals, and there are computer cops and vigilantes after their digital hides.

Of course, these are all gross oversimplifications of the hierarchies in virtual realities. As in any dichotomy there are those who don't fall into any convenient category—the individuals who straddle the electronic fence, designing their lives according to their own *healthy* narcissism, constructing their own small domains and being masters of their own fate. They are the sometimes-elite, sometimes-wannabe, or sometimes-guerrilla, depending on their role, context, and cyberspace persona. They surf, they lurk, they play—in a sense, they are those *huddled virtual masses, yearning to breathe free*, pursuing a digital fantasy that changes in each log-on. How very postmodern.

Wherever one stands on the relative continuum of elite, wannabe, guerrilla, or huddled virtual masses, consider the emerging parameters of status in cyberspace:

- Power resides in the hands of those who can design, manipulate, and control technology.

- Wealth is the ownership of information.

- Aggression is expressed through the ability to electronically banish, abuse, humiliate, or seize the virtual power of others.

- Dominance emerges from those who can steal competitors' information, electronic territory, or sustain continuing, unimpeded surveillance.

- Mediocrity is equivalent to anonymity.

- Kindness is sharing digital know-how.

And so the elites of cyberspace emerge. They are the geeky Bill Gates, the richest man in the world; the soft-spoken Charles Wang of *Computer Associates*, whose personal wealth is estimated at a meager $800 million. They are the young people who build websites, sell virtual data and services, and accumulate fortunes before completing their twenties. They are the wizards, designers, computer nerds, electronic prodigies, and sysops (system operators) who are creating, designing, and controlling our virtual environments.

GUERRILLAS

I am destined to rebel against the forces of power and evil, the Gatesian Gods that attempt to control me and rob me of my unquestionable human rights. I am small and solitary, but I can wield great power within any domain that I enter. I can attack with great violence, tossing flames through airless gateways, spreading my word throughout the global cybernetic village, taunting those who try to stop me. I can rob your data and your identity, twist your own words until the digital elite attack you, never knowing that I have designed the offense in your name. I can steal your money, your selves, and your territory because I am far more clever than you. I know the convoluted, hidden codes in the electronic frontier. If I am caught, I will hide and regroup only to return and take my just revenge. Beware. There is nothing to stop me.

Evolution and conflict have been constant companions. The status of dominant individuals is challenged in all species; the struggle to survive is an ongoing inter- and intra-species conflict. Clearly, the human species is no exception. Karl Marx argued a different type of dominance hierarchy when he observed that the inevitable outcome of capitalism is class conflict between the "haves" and the "have-nots." The haves are those who own the wealth, the power—the means of production. The have-nots are those who sell their labor (and some might say, their selves) to the owners. The haves are constantly struggling to maintain their status, and the have-nots are constantly struggling to take it away from them. Sociologists William Kornblum and Joseph Julian write,

> The rich and the powerful are able to determine what kinds of behaviors are defined as social problems because they control major institutions like the government, the schools, and the courts. They are also able to shift the blame for the conditions that produce those problems to groups in society that are less able to defend themselves, namely the poor and the working class. (p. 228)

Consequently, the system remains intact with the powerful and moneyed wielding dominance, and the poor and low-status trying to get a piece of the rock.

We see it all around us. Inner-city kids wear designer clothing. Suburban kids use ghetto drugs. People live in houses that are lush outside and bare inside. Workers struggle up the corporate ladder, actors wait tables in hope of reaching elusive stardom, families save their pennies so they can emulate snatches of behavior from the lifestyles of the rich and famous. At the same time we see the angry—those who feel slighted, deprived, discriminated against, or abused because they are among the have-nots. This group is far more varied—from philosophers, advocates of the needy, dissidents, minorities, and social reformers to vandals, stalkers, social deviants, and criminals. Societies have adapted to these realities by establishing norms, values, and laws that restrict, limit, or regulate behavior. These constraints act as general guides, yet it is easier (and more acceptable) for the rich and powerful to break them; more difficult (with greater punishment) for the poor and weak. When a powerful man commits murder he can hire a "dream team" of the best attorneys who will research and present a case that significantly heightens a jury's "reasonable doubt." The same man, if poor, has to rely on the limited resources of a public defender simultaneously flooded with similar cases. White-collar crime is treated differently than acts of physical violence or aggression. Who is considered more ominous: a financier convicted of insider trading or a mugger convicted of armed robbery? Even moral transgressions are forgiven more often in the powerful. How many teachers accused of inappropriate sexual behavior with children, adolescents, or young adults will find work again? Now consider the same behavior in people like Elvis Presley, Woody Allen, and Bill Clinton.

This is not to say that we don't *all* commit social transgressions. That also is part of human adaptation and socialization. The variations, however, are in the consequences. People with more power, wealth, status and, education have greater resources to avoid, mediate, or reduce the consequences. They also have a wider repertoire of weapons. A research scientist can criticize, diminish, challenge, or ridicule another's work, thus delivering aggression in the form of language, or "civilized" violence. Someone with fewer skills and less status might use more direct means, such as a fistfight or barroom brawl. After all, how much difference is there between a dirty political campaign and a bloody gang war? The essence is the same; only the execution—as well as the consequence—is different. The people fighting in the gang war will be arrested and jailed; one of the politicians running for office will be elected.

These behaviors are inhibited by social consequences that punish undesirable, offensive, or outright deviant behavior. You might really want to tell off your boss, but the consequences (getting fired) tend to inhibit that behavior. You might really want to smash into the car that just cut you off on the highway, but the consequences (ticket and auto repairs) tend to inhibit that behavior. Thus status, social constraint, and social consequences work toward keeping you a polite, well-behaved, and lawful citizen. Some might say they make sure you remain an elite or a wannabe.

Now let's go to a place where, for the most part, you can't get caught. In this place, if you're discovered, you can just click onto another identity. You can murder, rape, attack, curse, and act out the entire range of human aggression, and nothing much happens because it's all virtual. If you're not the elite, and if you're not a wannabe, are you content to straddle the fence in the Wild West of the Web? That's where the guerrillas come in. As a guerrilla you can object, protest, sabotage, embezzle, and attempt, if so equipped, to build your own kingdom. Adam Joinson, from the University of Glamorgan in Wales, addresses what he refers to as "disinhibition" on the Internet, or

> a behavior that is less inhibited than comparative behavior in real life. Thus disinhibition on the Internet is not defined as flaming or hostile communication, but rather is seen as any behavior that is characterized by an *apparent* reduction in concerns for self-presentation and the judgment of others. (p. 44)

Accordingly, disinhibition includes the tendency to be more frank and open online, disclosing "private" qualities that one might not reveal in face-to-face conversation. Add this to weakened social constraints and consequences, and we find a whole new world of virtual law and disorder.

VIRTUAL LAW
AND DISORDER

Wired Magazine called it "Murder by Internet." Chris Marquis was a hustler, a seventeen-year-old kid from Vermont running an online scam. He'd trade or sell radio equipment, promise delivery, and then burn the customer. The kid's mistake was when he scammed Chris Dean, a thirty-five-year-old Indiana trucker. Marquis had sent a junk radio in place of equipment he had promised worth $800. Scott Kirsner writes in Wired, "As soon as Dean had gotten the junk radio, he'd started making threatening calls and sending hostile e-mail. In one message Dean said he was coming to Vermont to sort things out." Dean "arrived" in a cardboard box delivered by UPS. When Chris opened it, the explosion blew him up and severely injured his mother. "His virtual business was going great," notes Kirsner, "until somebody killed him."

SOCIAL TRANSGRESSIONS ARE a way of life on the net. They seem to move and adapt to the technology, persisting throughout the upgrades. Presently, the most common forms of virtual disobedience are flames, spams, and spoofs, followed by bashboards and cybersmears. The more serious offenses make good news bytes, their novelty both appealing and shocking hungry consumers.

Flames are attacks against the persona, fired via insults, chastisements, nasty arguments, and other verbal offenses. Flames can escalate into widespread range wars where everyone joins the foray, setting battle lines and then going for the kill. These *flame wars* have been known to destroy entire virtual communities. Flaming, of course, is an available weapon for all netizens. Interestingly, they tend to belong to the male domain. Perhaps they reflect electronic dominance behavior—males fighting to elevate themselves on the digital hierarchy. Surely flames illustrate disinhibition and reduced social constraint and consequences. Dirty looks in cyberspace are hard to come by. Scathing responses are more likely, but if the heat's too high, just switch identities.

If one wants to justify a flaming tryst, he can begin with *flame bait,* or a message written to deliberately incite flames from others, expressing some contentious viewpoint that ignites brush fires. Some of the best flame baits are found on subjects such as politics, abortion, gun control, freedom of speech, the "best" computers, sexism, homosexuality, and controversial individuals such as shock jocks and national politicians. A special kind of flame bait is called a *troll,* designed to entice novices into a type of electronic hazing. When things get really out of hand, a *flame fest* may result. It's all part of the culture.

John Seabrook, author of *Deeper: My Two-Year Odyssey in Cyberspace,* writes about his "first flame":

> There were the flames on my screen, not dying away like insults shouted in the street, flaming me all over again in the asynchronous eternity that is time in the on-line world. Being premeditated, the insults had more force than insults shouted in the heat of the moment, and the technology greased the words . . . with a kind of intelligence that allowed them to slide more easily into my mind. (1994, p. 71)

Spams are electronic junk mail, multiple copies of the same message that run the gamut from e-commerce entrepreneurs to savvy proselytizers determined to get their digital voices heard. They're attacks against the illusion of privacy, invading one's in-box without invitation to promote products, services, scams, or angry, sad, sexual, or otherwise hollow messages.

Perhaps the best way to understand the concept of spams is to picture where the word originated. Imagine opening a can of Spam, that famous "meat" product by Hormel Food Corporation. The content has a pink, fleshy color with a sticky, glutinous texture and a smell faintly reminiscent of cheap dog food. Visualize miscellaneous animal parts ground into the Spam, and then take the contents and fling it into a rapidly spinning fan. The result is a snowstorm of thousands of fleshy pink particles, randomly flung in all directions, sickeningly adhering to whatever surface it touches. Got the picture?

Spamming is one of the biggest problems on the Internet. According to *Newsday* staff writer Jamie Talan, America Online "blocks millions of junk e-mails a day, but acknowledges that millions more manage to get through." And that's just one ISP. Talan's twin ten-year-old daughters, for example, were receiving "about 20 sex e-mails a day, XXX-rated messages that carry added weight for any curious child who sees the message: FOR ADULTS ONLY" (p. C3).

That might not sound like very much. However, it can cause a bigger mess than lunch meat. Consider some numbers. A good spammer can send out millions of messages a day. Some claim that with an investment of $10,000–$15,000 in hardware, one could deliver *5 million* messages a day. That can add up to some very big money. Imagine a company that spams their advertising message to 2 million people online. They have a very weak response, with only 1 percent ordering their $20 product. The result is $400,000 in sales. That's a lot of lunch meat.

If spammed, retaliation is futile. For example, one e-mail anecdote details a spam that was sent out advertising a Web registration service "free" to randomly selected winners. The service promised to submit "your" website to over 400 Internet indexes and directories worldwide. The junk e-mail claimed that they were awarding 1,400 first-prize free registrations and 700 second-prize discounted registrations. When one netizen decided to grab the opportunity, she was informed that as a "second place winner" she was entitled to a $300 discount. That meant using the service for a mere $200. Our wary netizen requested a list of first-place winners and the odds of winning, as required by federal law. She received the response, "We are not in the U.S."

Undaunted, she advised them that she was reporting their "contest" to the Federal Trade Commission. Within days, she found herself under attack. She was mail bombed—her address added to as many mailing lists as possible, drowning her inbox in e-mail. All it took was a software program called UpYours. Avenging spammers often go to even greater extremes. People have received threatening e-mail and false warnings about pending lawsuits against them. Their user information might be posted to sex-related newsgroups, or messages might be forged in their name and sent to other newsgroups with content intended to incite unwitting "others" (spoofing). In that way, spammers get other people to do their own dirty work. Worst of all, the addresses of spam retaliators are usually placed on lists where they're sold to other spammers. You can't win.

Perhaps the greatest indignity in spamming involves the party who foots the cost. In regular junk mail, direct mail advertising, or telemarketing, the sender writes the check. In junk e-mail, you and the ISP pay the bill. Consider what those messages cost in provider fees, clogged bandwidth, overflowing mailboxes, and time spent sifting through unwanted e-mail. Spam slows down servers, bandwidth, delays desired e-mail, and can even make it difficult to log on at all.

It's simply too easy to get your address. Spammers get addresses when you register at a website or sign up for a mailing list. Some buy or rent e-mail addresses from ISP and website operators, use online directories, or simply collect their own lists from signups on their websites. There are vendors all over the Net that specialize in selling Internet mailing lists. And if that doesn't look good to a spammer, he or she can "harvest" or collect addresses from public areas such as chat rooms, bulletin boards, web forums, and newsgroups.

Numerous privacy and antispamming groups have been set up on the Internet, but it's a tough battle.

Spoofs are the greatest offenses to postmodern selves because they steal identity rather than dignity or illusion. Spoofers manipulate technology to make it appear that the communication is coming from someone other than themselves. It's a forgery of self, a misattribution that allows offenders to create all sorts of mischief on an unknowing frontier. Unsuspected personas can be "framed" for making flames, statements, communication, actions, even serious crimes. For example, Bob Rae, the former premier of Ontario, was spoofed, his name used to post sexually offensive and politically embarrassing messages on newsgroups. Savvy individuals can use spoofing to wreak revenge on the most powerful elite, sending them places and attributing words that shatter their electronic identities. Sure, victims can retaliate, change their identities, or claim innocence in the assault, but when an identity or reputation is connected to actuality, great damage can be done. While the act of spoofing has become more common and netizens know more about its technological possibilities, the old social customs prevail when assessing individual culpability: guilty until proven innocent.

Spoof stories abound:

- One day a Los Angeles woman came home and found strange men outside her apartment door. They claimed that they were responding to her online ads looking for men interested in participating in her rape fantasy. She didn't even own a computer. She had met a man at church and refused to date him, so to get revenge, *he* placed the ads.

- A fifteen-year-old boy had a computer but not an online account. Someone opened nine accounts in his name. They used the fictitious accounts to send obscene e-mail. One message, to the boy's Scout leader, threatened to sodomize the man's son and rape the wife of another Scout leader. The spoofer was never found.

- The FBI Computer Crime Squad investigated a flurry of spoofs sent to members of the Senate and House of Representatives in early 1997. They threatened to delete every file on Capitol Hill computers. The e-mail had the return addresses of legitimate Internet users, obviously forged by the senders.

- A respected community leader discovered that someone posted messages to alt.binaries.pictures.erotica and alt.bestiality in his name.

- A college student was brought up on charges that he slandered and threatened a fellow student on a newsgroup. He told the other student, the dean, his parents, and the judge that he didn't do it. But his name appeared at the top of the message and no one really believed he was telling the truth.

Bashboards are the new kids on the block—Internet sites set up for the sole purpose of insulting or bashing others. "On bashboards," reports Stephanie McCrummen, *Newsday* staff writer, "students unleash largely anonymous, lewd, viscous or racist rants and rumors about each other and teachers, often interspersed with pornography. Sometimes, invective degenerates into words that could be construed as threatening, harassing, or at the very least, humiliating" (p. A5).

It's the ultimate adolescent attack, and no one even knows you're doing it. Message boards can be created for free with open discussion about specific topics, people, and events, anything that participants might desire. It's a brief click from football scores to bashboards—verbal bullying that can scathe the most brave-hearted. One high-school bashboarder crossed that line when unleashing a tide of personal attacks and then posting a message saying that a bomb would go off in the cafeteria soda machine. Panic ensued. The school was quickly and unceremoniously evacuated as the bomb squad searched the premises. They found nothing, but who would dare take that chance?

Cybersmears are essentially extensions of all the previously discussed virtual insurgencies. They go beyond flaming, spamming, spoofing, and bashboarding to get vitriolic words out into cyberspace. New means of cybersmearing are being constantly invented; for example, an antiabortion website features pictures of fetuses dripping with blood and posted names, addresses, and license plate numbers of doctors and clinic workers. A sniper later murdered one of the doctors *in actuality*. An employee fired by his large company successfully sent 30,000 other employees e-mail outlining his claims that he'd been unfairly treated. A local business was threatened with cybersmearing if the owner did not support the political consensus.

That's a lot of power put into anonymous guerrilla hands, and it's all very easy. No one knows you're a guerrilla. You can use technology that makes it nearly impossible to track down who you are. You can leap from subject to subject, person to person, virtual community to community, spreading transgressions with little or no retribution. You can have a devil identity and an angel identity—personas that sit on your electronic shoulders and guide behavior. Bad day at the office? Drag out that digital devil and go on the prowl. Got great tickets for the Billy Joel concert? Hoist up the digital angel and be the evening saint online. Play cowboys-and-Indians, house, and cops-and-robbers—anything goes.

NET.FRAUD

We all know what a scam is. It's the couple who invests $15,000 in Florida real estate, only to discover they own swampland. It's the college kid who lays down money for an all-inclusive spring break and arrives at the airport to find that the "travel agent" has run off with the funds. It's the direct mail promotion that offers free prizes that never get awarded. Scams off-line are illegal. Online, it's often a very different story.

Cyberspace is an ideal environment for scams. Along with flames, spams, spoofs, bashboarding, and cybersmears, Net.fraud is relatively easy to pull off. Reach enough people, and you don't need a high rate of return to make money. Fake an address, and you can't be traced. Turn off the computer or establish yourself at another location, and the scam artist fades into the black hole of the Internet.

Real-time computer cops, virtual vigilantes, consumer watch groups, and federal agencies all aggressively target scams, but it's often too difficult, too fleeting, and too decentralized to catch the culprits in action. According to the Internet Fraud Watch, operated by the National Consumers League (America's first nonprofit consumer group), Internet fraud is on the rise. In one year—1997 to 1998—complaints have increased by *600 percent*. And the numbers continue to rise as more people and more businesses communicate electronically. Phillip C. McKee III, the Internet Fraud Watch coordinator, listed the most common reports of Internet fraud as the following:

1. Web auctions

2. General merchandise sales

3. Internet services

4. Hardware/software sales

5. Pyramid schemes

6. Business opportunities/franchises

7. Work-at-home plans

8. Advance-fee loans

9. Credit repair

10. Credit card issuance

Interestingly, most people paid by checks and money orders, affording fewer protections to consumers. McKee suggests that paying by credit card is actually *safer*. He reports that the Internet Fraud Watch "has not received a single complaint of someone's credit card number being stolen while it was being transmitted to a legitimate merchant. We have heard of plenty of consumers who got scammed after giving their account number to a crook, but that's a different story." Nonetheless, consumers tend to be conservative, with most sending payments by snail mail.

What does Net.fraud look like?

- Netizens visiting a pornographic website saw a few enticing pictures. In order to see the archived images, the individual had to download a special program. Unknown to the visitor, the program connected them to a number in Moldova, a tiny former republic of the Soviet Union located between the Ukraine and Romania. As long as they were on the Internet, they remained connected at a cost of over two dollars a minute. The connection was broken only when the home computer was turned off, resulting in exorbitant international phone bills. Some individuals received bills into the thousands of dollars. The scammers made their money by getting a percentage of each call from the foreign telephone carrier.

- An Internet stock newsletter printed false, misleading statements concerning six publicly traded companies. The author never mentioned that he and his organization received over $1 million and 275,000 shares of stock as payment for his recommendation. They agreed to a settlement without admitting or denying the charges.

- One of the most popular hangouts for electronic con artists is America Online. In password or credit card fishing, scammers scrounge to get the numbers and subsequently the goods. One popular method is to post a message on the screen when a user logs on, "alerting" them that the company is conducting a security check and must have their name, address, social security and credit card numbers. Another is an official-looking IM (Instant Message) informing the user that their credit card number is lost, and unless they fill in the number immediately, he or she will be cut off line. Perhaps the cleverest ruse is the "Trojan Horse." The AOL member receives an e-mail promising free software or other promotional gifts in an attachment file. To receive the giveaway, users must fill out an application. The information in the e-mail "application" goes to the scammer, while at the same time it tiptoes back into the user's mailbox and deletes itself. Now AOL posts clearly visible warnings against these practices.

- A consumer attends an online auction, successfully bidding on computer equipment costing $100. Payment was made by online money order. When the equipment arrived, it was irreparably damaged. The consumer went back to the e-mail address and found that the account had been closed.

- While scanning a newsgroup, an investor found a company where he could become a distributor of licensed products. The company arranged for a face-to-face meeting. Convinced that his investment would lead to six-figure income, he gave them over $20,000 in a cashier's check and $5,000 by a credit card. After the money was paid, there was no more contact from the company. The product does exist; however, it is of such poor quality and so difficult to obtain that it hardly constitutes a viable business.

HATE ONLINE

They have names like Stormfront, White Carmelia Knights of the Ku Klux Klan, Afrikana Resistance Movement, Occidental Pan-Aryan Crusader, and Blue Tunic Army of Christ. They show swastikas, torches, hate articles, hate "facts," and hate paraphernalia. They talk about concepts like imperatives for the white race, the holohoax, revisionism, anti-Christ conspiracy and "white pride world wide." These are the netizens of the very dark side of cyberspace, the people who use bone-chilling slogans like "your skin is your uniform" and "plunder and pillage"—and mean it. These cybersupremacists have their own skinzines, online newsletters, newsgroups, and e-mail. Their ideology attacks everyone and everything that doesn't elevate Caucasians to the position of a superior race. It is a particularly oppressive brand of hate.

The introduction to a Website called Aryan Nation, in chilling prose, states:

> We believe that the Canaanite Jew is the natural enemy of our Aryan (White) Race. This is attested by scripture and all secular history. The Jew is like a destroying virus that attacks our racial body to destroy our Aryan culture and the purity of our Race. Those of our Race who resist these attacks are called "chosen and faithful."

Another popular hatesite, Stormfront, uses a cross and a circle, reminiscent of the Ku Klux Klan crosswheel, surrounded by the words "White Pride World Wide" and its name scrawled in blood-red Teutonic-looking script. It bills itself as the "white nationalist resource page" and accordingly offers a bevy of hate choices. Run by Don Black, a former Ku Klux Klan leader, Stormfront describes itself as "a forum for planning strategies and forming political and social groups to ensure victory." Their war is against anyone who is not "white": Jews, blacks, gays, immigrants, and the "mud" people. A list of their links best describes their intent:

- Independent White Racialists, where "Your skin is your uniform"

- Zündelsite: "Revisionist" literature on the "struggle to free us from the lie of the century": the Holocaust

- KKK.com, "a virtual museum of Ku Klux Klan history and artifacts.

- Church of the Creator RAHOWA!, supporting the RAHOWA! (RAcial HOly War)

- Wake Up or Die! "An Electronic Magazine for White Americans, especially for White Americans whose ancestors paid for this land with blood and created this nation with courage, vision, hardship and sweat"

For those who just want to talk, there's a list of hate newsgroups, bulletin boards, and mailing lists. Clicking on the links brings the surfer to locations that boast swastikas and photos of luminaries such as Adolf Hitler; Canada's leading holocaust "revisionist," Ernst Zundel, with the question "Did Six Million Really Die?"; and David Duke, the racist author of *The Awakening*. Pastor Richard Butler, past national director of the Church of Jesus Christ Christian and founder of the Aryan Nation, gives a hearty Nazi salute beneath a brightly colored, stylized swastika. For those looking for vivid graphics, one click from Stormfront will reveal an assortment that includes eagles, swastikas, crosses, and skulls. There are photo collections boasting "irrefutable" proof that concentration camps were actually pleasant, busy workplaces with swimming pools. The sheer number of hate sites is sobering, estimated at almost 400 online locations.

Marshall McLuhan believed that technology externalizes the human mind, making the medium an extension of ourselves. Accordingly, cyberspace offers the best, the worst, and everything in between. Hate is no exception. The Net is actually an excellent environment for disseminating hate. These hate websites are cheap, attract worldwide attention, and cost as little as a few hundred dollars a year. A website is a lot less involved than mass mailing, flyers, and hand-distributed brochures. Hate groups hide behind the First Amendment and the concern of legitimate ISPs who want to hold on to the status "common carrier" rather than "publisher." A common carrier is a relatively safe route, like a telephone company, where the service provider is viewed as a conduit and is not involved in the content of the communication. In contrast, a publisher is accountable for the material it hosts.

Several online groups are now keeping a watch on the growing number of these hate mongers determined to spread bigoted dogma and recruit new members in cyberspace. They include the Anti-Defamation League, Klanwatch, the Gay & Lesbian Alliance against Defamation, and the Simon Wiesenthal Center. Each day, for example, the Simon Wiesenthal Center receives reports about websites that promote racism and anti-Semitism. Some of these sites offer weapon- and bomb-making instructions and links to white supremacists. Many deny that the Holocaust ever took place; others use the Bible to justify white supremacy. Most utilize sophisticated graphics, links to similar sites, and scholarly sounding writings to "prove" they are correct.

The Simon Wiesenthal Center maintains that hate activities are rapidly expanding on the Internet, receiving increasing amounts of attention from the most vulnerable population—young people. They argue that the complex, ever-changing technology of cyberspace provides fertile breeding ground for the dissemination of hate.

Should ISPs bar certain groups from maintaining websites on their services? They certainly have that right as private corporations. However, most are extremely reluctant to exercise it. While the Simon Wiesenthal Center calls the termination of services to hate mongers a code of ethics, the American Civil Liberties Union sees it as a form of private censorship. The Anti-Defamation league takes a middle ground—recognizing the rights of hate groups to publish their material online while at the same time establishing their own responsibility to expose it.

Is there any real solution to this dilemma? Must we protect the rights of racists at the cost of everyone else? Some individuals have clearly taken a stand. To illustrate, in June 1996, Pathway Communications, an ISP, threw Freedom Site, a white supremacy hate page from Canada, off-line. Marc Lemire, the webmaster, moved his operations to Fairview Technology Center, which allowed access. The Simon Wiesenthal Center sent the ISP a letter that included the statement "Your Internet service has become the site for a number of groups that specialize in racial and religious hate matter.... You are not obligated to carry subscribers who involve the provider in matters such as race hatred...."

The owner of Fairview refused to acquiesce, announcing that they would not censor users. Battle lines were drawn in the struggle over whether or not to regulate Canadian cyberspace. Ironically, if the material on Freedom Site were printed and handed out on a street corner, it would be legal. In contrast, prosecutors in Germany indicted the head of CompuServe's online computer services, charging Felix Somm with violating antipornography laws by not blocking access to sites that offered Nazi and neo-Nazi material. All of this raises some very difficult questions about national sovereignty. While making specific Nazi material and games available is illegal in Germany, it is legal in the United States. Which laws take precedence?

Freedom Site is still online, advocating issues such as a five-year moratorium on immigration, protests against antiracist action groups, promoting anti-Semitism, white supremacy, and posting scathing photos.

ONLINE SEXUAL PREDATORS

Sex is big business in cyberspace. Several years ago Matt Richtel reported in the *New York Times* about Beth Mansfield, a thirty-six-year-old mother of two. Each day from her Tacoma, Washington, household, she sent her children off to school, her husband off to work, and sat down at the computer. Mansfield was the creator and webmaster of Persian Kitty's Adult Links. The lavender-and-white homepage is sprinkled with colors that please the eye. Written beneath the logo in sweet black script are the words "Purrs, claws, and curiosity will get you anywhere!" Scanning the site, the surfer finds link after link of pornographic pages, including hundreds of "Live XXX Webcam feeds," thousands of adult sites, and 155,000 "free pix." The links bear names like I Love Porn, Jackel's Jungle, Pixel Spice, Raw Dawg, and Sex 4 U. To Mansfield, a former accountant, it was a financial goldmine. Persian Kitty attracted nearly 300,000 surfers a day. Cyberpornographers clamored to go on her lists—Mansfield reported that she received an average of 350 e-mail requests a day. All of this added up to a lot of advertising—upwards of $80,000 a month.

Internet sex is big business, and there are no laws to stop it. With all of this sexually explicit material flooding cyberspace, it's only a short step to crossing the digital line into obscenity, and that means breaking the law. Nowhere is this more chilling than in the connections established by sexual predators such as pedophiles and child pornographers.

Pedophilia is not uncommon. Although statistics are widely debated, nationwide reports of child sexual abuse are estimated at well over 80,000 per year. It's likely that the number is much higher, as many cases go unreported. Children are frequently afraid or are ordered not to reveal what has happened. Legal proof that abuse has taken place is often hard to obtain. It's been conservatively estimated that one in three girls and one in six boys are sexually abused before age eighteen.

Pedophiles thrive on the Internet. It's not hard to find networks and share fantasies and pornographic materials with others of like mind. And no one even has to know who you are. Anonymity and expression of sexual perversion make likely bedfellows. It's easy to exchange information. If you want some direct contact, tap into those places where the more than 6 million kids hang out. Cyberspace is a pedophile's fantasy. Chats, bulletin boards, newsgroups, and e-mail lists all work to provide chilling access to potential victims. Most ominous is that these connections can be used to nurture trust and curiosity, leading to face-to-face rendezvous all over the world.

Father Adrian McLeish was a forty-five-year-old Roman Catholic priest from St. Joseph's Church in the United Kingdom. McLeish was known in his parish in Gilesgate, Durham, as a loving priest. Of course, he had a fatal flaw—his attraction to children. The priest sexually abused young boys as well as participated in an international pedophile ring on the Internet. McLeish took pictures and wrote descriptions of his victims, collecting and disseminating a voluminous amount of child pornography. Ironically, his behavior began when he was a junior priest in another parish. In 1991, burglars broke into the presbytery in Wallsend, North Tyneside, and later contacted police to say they had found pornographic videos. By then, McLeish had moved, claiming there was no link between the break-in and his decision to change churches. Five years later, when he was arrested, police found a library of computer disks with 11,000 images and evidence of participating in a ring of at least nine other pedophiles in Sweden, Germany, France, New Zealand, and the United States. Justice Moses, the judge at McLeish's trial, said to the priest:

> For six years you sexually abused four young boys, some of whom you groomed with a view to indulging your future desires. You had a vast collection of child pornography and, in four months, you spent 143 hours building up your collection. It is difficult to stop such distribution of these pictures. Users are rarely caught, but it is the active part you have played in the distribution of these pictures which is the real crime. It is also clear you lived up to your fantasies, fueled by pornography to which you had access through the Internet. (Stokes 1996)

Father McLeish was sentenced to six years in prison.

McLeish is not alone. Consider a few other stories of online sexual abuse:

- A nineteen-year-old college student was found downloading photographs of children having sex with each other and adults from computer networks in Sweden and the Netherlands. Using his university's computer, the student sent the images to people in the United States who requested them. He was arrested in his dormitory room and charged with promoting sexual performance by a child. Similar cases have occurred at other schools.

- A subscription website operating from Texas charged $11.95 a month for access to child pornographic images on the Internet. It was estimated they were making $500,000 a month from their subscribers.

- Sixteen people in the United States and abroad were charged as participants in an online pedophilia club. Members shared homemade pictures and chronicled their sexual experiences with children on the IRC (Internet Relay Chat). In one instance they purportedly chatted online as two of the men molested a ten-year-old girl, describing what they were doing.

- A thirty-year-old elementary-school special-education aide was convicted of six counts of sodomy and one count of endangering the welfare of a child with an underage boy he met through a gay men's chat room. They communicated through desktop computers in their bedrooms.

- An AOL man was found transmitting images of young girls being sexually exploited and raped to more than sixty fellow subscribers.

- Five years ago a ten-year-old boy was lured online into meeting pedophiles. He arranged for face-to-face contact. His body has not yet been found.

Federal child protection laws make it a felony crime to create, possess, or disseminate child pornography. Online, proof of criminal activity is more difficult to obtain. To arrest a pedophile, you have to prove that the perpetrator transmitted obscene images of minors or actually left the keyboard to solicit sex from a child face-to-face. However, it's perfectly legal for an adult to *write* sexually explicit messages to children online or impersonate other children in sexual exchanges in chatrooms.

We're faced with some really tough issues. Should private communications be subject to government scrutiny? Is it the responsibility of an ISP to police their subscribers for illegal activity? What constitutes "entrapment" on the Internet? Should government be given free reign to protect children against pedophiles online?

Pedophiles are not the only sexual predators to wander the dark electronic streets of cyberspace. There are stalkers, sexual harassers, and other online sexual abusers. Clearly, the Net mirrors actuality in abuse and obscenity. What is so unclear is what to do. Whose laws—state or national —do you follow? How do you protect children *and* free speech? Who is qualified to give the answers?

REACH OUT AND
TOUCH SOMEONE

*T*HEY'RE CALLED AGONY aunts. They come in all sizes, shapes,
and genders, with names like Auntie Deviant, Friendly Fatso, and
Red G. Their ages span the years from young teenagers to retirees, dispensing wisdom and worldly advice to those seeking to solve their problems. Their occupations also span the imagination, from English schoolboy
to bookkeeper to retiree. As one explains, "In England, yours truly would
be called an agony aunt, so you may call us Aunt Agony. Aunt Agony will
answer any questions you ask. She has opinions about everything. If you
want to seek Auntie's advice, just make keyboard tippy-tappy in the space
provided, and she'll get back to you tout de suite."

Peer a little further into the world of free electronic advice and you'll
find that most of it relates to the sexes—and sex. Sites like Survivors of a
Broken Heart, Romance 101, and CyberChickey's Advice all address those
age-old questions concerning whether men are really from Mars and
women from Venus.

As discussed earlier, sex, mating, and its outcome permeates all aspects of our lives. We devote more of our time, objects, stories, double meanings, and unconscious urges to sex than to anything else. When one considers that the basic goal of natural selection is to spread genes and thus assure the survival of the species, sex is *the* behavior that makes it happen. But if there's really no such thing as pure female and pure male, as discussed earlier, then a place like cyberspace wreaks havoc on us all.

MEET THE GENDERMORPH

It's a legend on the Internet. The story has been told in many shapes and forms. It began with a middle-aged male psychiatrist named "Alex." Alex spent a lot of time online, hanging out on a certain Web chat forum, or bulletin board. One version of the story says that Alex was online and someone thought he was female. Obviously, the name Alex can swing both ways. Other accounts claim that he was intrigued by the intimacy in women's conversations and wanted to participate in "no-man's land." Alex was even rumored to be a digital cross-dresser. Either way, Alex liked the tone of the conversations between women. He felt that male talk was more superficial, more aggressive, and lacking in warmth.

So Alex developed a new persona. In this version of the story, Alex became Jessica. Jessica was a woman with a severe disability so disfiguring that she was embarrassed to meet people face-to-face. Instead, she went to the Internet for companionship. Alex believed people would assume that Jessica's persona had no social life. Her online existence would be her greatest pleasure. He was correct.

Gradually, Jessica became known in her virtual community. She built a cyber reputation for being sensitive, willing to listen to others, and dispensing good advice. She was always open and warm, nurturing those oddly intimate relationships that have a tendency to form between people in cyberspace. Her female digital friends shared their deepest thoughts, telling Jessica their problems, seeking her opinion. They viewed her as a caring human being trapped inside a disabled body.

Of course, Alex was trapped, too. He was trapped inside Jessica's persona, his own male body, and in the fiction he'd created. But Alex learned some fascinating things. He discovered that the women who spoke with Jessica were more open than those in his office or his personal life. His online life as a woman began to take on a power of its own. In a sense, Jessica grew larger than life.

After much time with the virtual Jessica, friends began to insist on meeting her in person. Her online intimates were convinced that Jessica's physical disability would have no effect on their relationship. After all, they "knew" her so well.

Alex panicked. The "game" was out of control. He had to find a solution. One day Jessica's "husband" went online and announced that she was seriously ill in the hospital. Alex intended to "kill" Jessica, ridding himself of the awkward dual life that he'd invented.

Alex couldn't have predicted the response. There was an outpouring of moral support, offers of financial help, names of specialists, and advice to help her recover. Alex desperately wanted to "murder" Jessica, but her cyberspace companions wouldn't allow it. Pressed for an address to send cards, flowers, and get-well wishes, Alex gave out the name of the hospital where he worked as a psychiatrist. Alex was frantic—he needed to be free from gendermorphing.

Alex's disguise unraveled. A local contributor to the list tried to call the hospital. She discovered that there was an Alex, not a Jessica, at the number. A few more telephone calls and Jessica's real identity was revealed. The information was immediately posted to the virtual community.

Everyone was livid. Outrageous stories surfaced. Some reported that Jessica's friends were furious at Alex's deception. Others insisted that Jessica had actually introduced some of her online friends to off-line Alex—a virtual pimp, one might say. Another variation implied that Jessica's intimates had been indulging in lesbian Net.sex with a man. Ironically, the least shocking was the very fact that a man had chosen to be a woman.

The story of Alex/Jessica tells us a lot more about what happens to gender boundaries in cyberspace. Simply put, it's quite a trip to go from Alex to Jessica or from Jessica to Alex.

Gendermorphing, morfing, and gendershifting are all cyberspeak for an expression that began in live chats and one-to-one online encounters: morf. Morf means Male OR Female? It was originally used as a question. For example, two people are in a chat room trying to get to know one another. They both have politically correct asexual names, like ZIP37 and Goggles. Morf was a shorthand question—"Are you male or female so I know how to continue this conversation?"

Simple enough, except that on the Internet, nobody knows you're a man or a woman unless you tell them. It might be in your name, in might be in your subject matter, or it might never really be known. In a world of relatives, does it matter if the person you're seducing is male or female? Your only real concern is the gender-of-the-moment.

Some people like to believe that gender-of-the-moment allows us to approach a higher level of consciousness where we discard our physical natures and concentrate on mind and human metaphor. In other words, actuality is totally sublimated to the mental experience. This conveniently ignores the fact that the bodies behind the keyboards still have to drink water, eat food, expel wastes, sleep—do all those annoying biological things. Yet for a few precious minutes, hours, or days online we can suspend our organic destiny and let telepresence take over. How can there be an existential dilemma when you have the power to choose between being male and female, the most basic of human physiological identities?

Let's assume that gender online is an information exchange that involves emotion, fantasy, and metaphor. It offers freedom from the cumbersome weight of genitalia. Remove that whole issue of physicality so people can be *people*—get to the heart of things. Multiple selves become a natural state of affairs, experimenting with gendermorphing an acceptable experience. Off-line "meat" bars become online "meets"; almost everyone goes on "blind" dates (unless video is available—although that, too, can be dubbed); the number and frequency of potential relationships is limited only by global population; and sex is a Woody Allen orgasmatron. The frequency, general safety, and diversity of contacts easily replace contextual depth. No problem, right?

True gendermorphing is a myth. The bad guy inevitably runs away or gets caught. Like it or not, we carry our gender on our digital sleeves, revealing it in our language, our interests, our behaviors, and the things we know about. Simply put, the largest sex organ in the human body is unquestionably the brain, which is also the organ that plunges us into cyberspace.

Consider a bizarre story about a gendermorph who *almost* got away with it. Sometimes fact can be far stranger than fiction, particularly in a world not philosophically prepared for cyberspace. A twenty-four-year-old adminis-trative assistant from Virginia named Margaret met a friendly Texas man online who called himself Thorne. Margaret and Thorne chatted online fre-quently. After a while, Thorne admitted that he was he was a "jet-set" busi-nessman dying from AIDS. Margaret was touched by his honesty. She was convinced she had met the love of her life. Eventually they met face-to-face. The emotions grew stronger and Thorne and Margaret decided to get mar-ried, knowing that there would be no sexual intimacy. Oddly, after four months of marriage, Thorne did not get sicker, nor did he receive any med-ical bills. Suspicious, Margaret decided to locate her husband's birth certifi-cate. Thorne, who wrapped bandages around his chest because of "rib" injuries, turned out to be "Holly," and very much female. Margaret sued, and the court awarded her $264,000 in damages (McAllester 1997).

If gender is more than genitals, it will naturally transfer to digital selves, or, in Thorne's case, seep out from beneath the bandages. Sure, you can conceal it in the short run, but overall? And to the discerning eye? The old issues eventually show themselves. This raises some intriguing ques-tions: what characteristics of gender accompany the virtual self, and how does it affect cybersex, Net.love, and romance? Can any human space be truly genderless?

Deborah Tannen, Ph.D., well-known researcher and author of the article "You Don't Understand: Men and Women in Conversation," has repeatedly demonstrated that men and women communicate very differ-ently. Men tend to focus on dimensions that involve status, while women are more concerned with connection. We've seen how evolutionary psy-chologists differentiate between gender concerns in finding mates. Much of this behavior is automatic, controlled by preprogrammed mental mod-ules. Language is one way that reflects those differences, and in cyberspace it's probably the best clue to identifying that elusive gendermorph.

Tannen studies communication from a sociolinguistic perspective. She maintains that males and females are literally raised in different cultures. When they communicate it reflects a type of cross-cultural behavior. The constant struggle between the sexes seems to support her differentiation. Tannen argues that there are essential differences in conversation style, content, and interpretation that underlie the "seemingly senseless misun-derstandings that haunt our relationships."

Men and women talk differently online. Susan Herring, a linguist, academic, and researcher, investigated exactly what those differences are. She discovered that cyberspeak simply "continues pre-existing patterns of hierarchy and male dominance." Her conclusions were drawn from an investigation into two academic electronic discussion lists. She concluded that cyberspace *doesn't* neutralize gender; it actually enhances the different communication styles between men and women.

Herring's research found that online, men did most of the talking; held on to most of the attention; tended to dominate discussions; and generally trivialized female contributions. Men tended to be more authoritative, self-confident, and willing to take control. They had a more adversarial cyberspeak, using more insults, strong, highly opinionated statements, long and/or frequent posts, self-promotion, and sarcasm. In contrast, women tended to be supportive toward others, often expressing self-doubt. Their cyberspeak showed more appreciation, encouraged stronger community-building, used apologizing, hedging, expressions of doubt, and ideas offered in the form of suggestions rather than statements. In other words, Herring found that the men remained the hunters and women remained the gatherers.

Subsequent studies supported Herring's findings. Cybergroups with a higher ratio of men were more likely to be impersonal, used fact-oriented language, and included more frequent calls for action. Cybergroups with women were more likely to be personal, nurturing, and emotional. It was what Alex was looking for when he became Jessica.

Consider the following e-mail messages. Based on Herring's research, can you figure out whether these responses to an unpopular opinion voiced on an e-mail list were written by a male or by a female?

I've had it with all this bullshit here—you just don't know what you're talking about. Shut up about all that moralistic crap and try thinking for yourself for a change. Give us all a break.

I'm sorry to be so blunt, but maybe you should reconsider your stand on the subject. I'm sure you're a thinking, caring person, and making such statements can be very hurtful.

Gender differences in cyberspace are by no means limited to style. Herring also found significant contrasts in frequency, communication ethics, and netiquette. Men tend to participate more, women's messages tend to be shorter and less frequent. Women, for the most part, received fewer responses than men, and their topics were less likely to be taken up by the entire group. Perhaps this reflects earlier, off-line research that women are perceived as talking more than men in mixed gender conversations, even though they speak only 30 percent of the time. Herring concluded that men are more successful in their topics, responses, ability to get attention, and their capacity to encourage women to participate less. These behaviors might be what underlie the burgeoning network of websites for women—everything from family, fashion, chats, newsgroups, and sex—where there is no gender competition.

These sex-based differences do indeed go beyond technology. They clearly reflect Stone Age computers never programmed for cyberspace. Males are more assertive, promoting themselves, using more adversarial means to communicate, and seeking to dominate social situations. They value freedom from censorship; open, direct discussion; and aggressive debate as a means of communicating and advancing knowledge. Women are uncomfortable with confrontation or direct conflict, seeking means to establish community and discourse that involve self-disclosure and exchange of mutual emotional supports. Females value consideration for the needs of others and sensitivity, often finding aggressive behavior rude. While men will be more inclined to tolerate flaming and to use humor and sarcasm, women will shrink from that style of confrontation.

HOOKING UP IN CYBERSPACE

As much as things change, they don't really change at all. Hooking up in cyberspace is as important as hooking up in the Stone Age—people want other people, whatever gender they feign, so we hunt for mates online.

There are more ways to hook up than ever before in the history of humankind. Women and men have invented countless tricks to meet online; everything from virtual friendships to courtship to heated cybersex is in vogue. There is tacit permission to experiment with sexual fantasy, with gender, and with relationships. Everything from gendermorphing, gay and lesbian sex, or any imaginable sexual deviance sits next to the conventional—dating, romance, virtual weddings, and private love-chats. In fact, anything goes when the world sees Monica Lewinsky grin on globally broadcast television and admit that she had virtual (phone) sex with the president of the United States.

What is virtual sex when you're dealing with no genitals, gender-of-the-moment, no body fluids, Stone Age computers, and a keyboard? Is it an oxymoron? Sherry Turkle explains it as an online experience—two or more people type graphic descriptions of physical behaviors, including their emotional response to the virtual sexual activity. Others are more direct, referring to it as computer-enhanced masturbation or computer-simulated copulation.

Net.sex, like so many other issues in virtuality, raises many questions about the future of humans, natural selection, and reproduction. After all, with in vitro fertilization, you don't really need interacting bodies. Will future generations be concerned if the physical intimacy of sex is removed from the act? Science fiction is filled with such speculation. How much gender-stretching is possible before emotional or psychological identity is dramatically altered? Does completely digitizing a biological function shared by species further isolate humans from the rest of the animal kingdom?

There is one distinct advantage. Cybersex is certainly the safest. No one gets diseases from making love online.

WHAT HAPPENS IN THE HEAT OF PASSION?

There's a classic joke on the Internet. Two people meet on an adult chat and leave for their private "room." They're planning a heated cybersex encounter. But first she has to ask the critical question.

"Can you can type with one hand?"

Cybersex comes in as many variations as the human mind can conjure. The more standard varieties, somewhat equivalent to the missionary position in actuality, usually consist of two (or more) people who have met online and arranged for a private "real time" encounter. This is generally accomplished through the creation of a nonpublic "room" or "location" on a chat system, such as AOL or IRC (Internet Relay Chat).

Some participants use real names, and others adopt nicknames that titillate and attract partners. Romeos and Juliets permeate the Net, along with others that make clear statements such as "RegGuy," "FOxiLady," and "beelzabub." The foreplay consists primarily of sexual banter, swaggering sexual claims, and virtual pick-up lines that, if desired, can superficially conceal gender.

When a partner or partners are chosen, the Net.sex moves to a more private spot. Once in their space, they create a scenario and describe what they are seeing and doing in text. The content is as graphic as the participants choose—many times individuals feel less inhibited in expressing sexual fantasies online than in face-to-face encounters. They might begin by describing what they're wearing, where they're located, who they're with, or what they're thinking. The encounter proceeds by embellishing the fantasy through sexually explicit words and content. For example:

She: What do you look like?
He: 5'10". 170. Light brown hair, blue eyes . . .
She: Really?
He: Who would make up something so boring?
She: Nice height. I could look up into your eyes when you hold me.
He: Okay . . . THAT did it . . . NOW I'm VERY horny.
She: Cha, cha, ching.
He: Okay . . . take off what you're wearing :)
She: OK, I just took off my white tank top.
He: What else are you wearing?
She: I'm keeping my shorts on.
He: No you're not :)
She. Oh, my.
He: Off!
She: For all intents and purposes, they're on the floor.
He: Completely off . . . legs out . . . c'mon.

Frequently, individuals will masturbate during Net.sex. They may also describe the progress and intensity of their masturbation and orgasm. It always begins as a virtual adventure, carried in any direction to any extreme. Naturally, this type of eroticism can blur the issues concerning fidelity and deception in a relationship. Numerous online discussions attempt to find a solution to the confusion. Few succeed.

Some couples adapt. A live-in couple buys two computers, two modems, and two phone lines so they can log in at the same time, next to one another. A wife recognizes that her husband is in a midlife crisis and feels that cybersex is a better choice than an actual physical affair. A young man compares it to looking at pornography—an experience very different from the relationship he has with his long-term girlfriend.

One husband felt everything had gone too far. John, a New Jersey man, filed divorce papers after discovering that his wife was having cybersex with another man. Dozens of e-mails had been exchanged, many with sexually explicit material. Finally the wife made plans to meet her virtual lover face-to-face. John found out and accused her of adultery. Although the intent was to make love in the flesh, the virtual affair was never physically consummated. Was the affair adulterous, grounds for divorce?

There was a flurry of online (bulletin board and newsgroup) discussion over whether John had the right to sue for divorce. As in so many Internet debates, people responded quickly and fervently to the issue:

Yes, John has the right to sue for divorce. Adultery is the intent, not the contact.

Cybersex can't be considered adultery. Let's be honest: all cybersex is masturbation. Does masturbation constitute adultery? In my opinion, cybersex is a sad example of how technology enables us to become introverted losers, massaging our private parts while we finger our keyboards. Pitiful.

In my mind, cybersex, when entered into by one partner against the wishes of the other, is the same as sexual infidelity. At the very least it's most certainly a betrayal of intimacy, an EMOTIONAL INFIDELITY.... This is not the same as one who has harmless fantasies as do we all at some point or another...

Get real! Computers are only the latest form of communication that man has invented. Sex isn't real until the parties that intend to tango are arm in arm...

I wish it was adultery ... it sure would be a lot more convenient!!!

THE FINAL QUESTIONS

Cybersex raises a host of interesting and uncomfortable questions. Do you have any of the answers?

- When a married person has cybersex, is it adultery?
- If a homosexual has cybersex with a gendermorph posing as a same-sex partner, is it a heterosexual act?
- If a heterosexual has cybersex with a gendermorph posing as an opposite-sex partner, is it a homosexual act?
- How do you categorize multiple cybersex partners? Promiscuity, deception, or experimentation?
- Can rape occur in cyberspace?
- If an adult unknowingly has sex with an underage adolescent, is it sexual abuse or molestation? Should that person be prosecuted?
- If an adult receives unsolicited child pornography through e-mail and *looks* at it, does it deserve criminal prosecution? If the pornography is not removed immediately and the recipient looks at it *several* times, does that qualify as a crime?
- Is cybersex really sex?
- Is cyberlove really love?
- Are virtual relationships based on intimacy or narcissism?
- What constitutes trust in virtual relationships?
- How do you define the difference between curiosity and obsession in cybersex?
- What is a virtual sexual deviant?

STRANGER THAN FICTION:

A COLLECTION OF TRUE STORIES FROM CYBERSPACE

*C*YBERSPACE IS ALIVE with stories. Everyone who ventures into the electronic environment has a tale to tell filled with charging knights, comforting buddies, devious spammers, strange new lovers . . . the list is endless. Perhaps the stories are cyberspace's greatest charm. Within them the bytes, chips, and electronic networks soften and stretch, establishing that machines-are-better-with-humans.

The following true stories—"Russell's Web," "Stalked!" "Traci and Ken's Story," and "Melissa"*—attest to some of the bizarre, frightening, tender, and painfully real aspects of this new frontier. And they're only the beginning.

---

*"Russell's Web," "Stalked!" "Traci and Ken's Story," and "Melissa" have all been reprinted with the permission of their authors.

RUSSELL'S WEB
by Russell Fink

Russell was a nineteen-year-old film student at New York University when he told this story. He is particularly interested in postmodern philosophy and how it affects the art world. As a student filmmaker, he has won a prestigious award in radio drama, and his work in multimedia was nominated for two student festivals. Russell plans to become a film producer. This story beautifully illustrates how those Stone Age computers play out gender wars in cyberspace.

Where do you start a story with no beginning and no end—only a very mixed-up middle? I'm a film student at New York University, so I'm used to creative ways of presenting material. I've written essays with meta-textual structure, produced sound projects with four-track levels on quarter-inch reel at 15 IPS, and organized video crews to produce short screenplays. None of it, however, prepared me for the dizzying dramas in an America Online chatroom called Long Island Romance.

It began with my now-ex-girlfriend, Nikki. Nikki was a high-school senior when I left for college. We'd been dating for nearly a year, and she was determined to hold on to our relationship. I wasn't quite as determined. There are a lot of girls at NYU, especially the actresses in my school, Tisch School of the Arts.

Nikki knew the odds. So when she got a computer for her eighteenth birthday, the first thing she did was explore the chat rooms. It wasn't long before she found a chat devoted to local kids looking to hook up—Long Island Romance.

Long Island Romance is always full to the maximum—twenty-three people. They usually talk about three things: age, sex, and location. You log on and join the conversation. When you meet someone who sounds interesting, you IM (Instant Message) them and say, What's up? Then you proceed to talk about absolutely nothing—from prom dates to love lives to school. Anything goes. If you really like the person, you put them on your "buddy list"—a special list that automatically shows you if they are online when you log on to AOL.

Nikki loved AOL. She met Dude1724, Shark357, SexyMann, and others looking for a quick hookup. Her buddy list quickly grew to fifty-two people—

mostly guys. She spoke to a few of them on the telephone and met one or two face-to-face. For example, she met a Hofstra University sophomore, Mike357, in a parking lot at Friendly's. Nikki also knew that as an NYU student, I didn't have America Online. There was no way I could trace whom she spoke to. So she told me about all her "guys," insisting they were only good friends.

At NYU, I had some "friends" too. There was Cat, who lived in my dormitory, and Lindsey, who was in my film class. Of course, there was Jen—a Tisch actress. Nikki didn't know about them, but I thought I knew too much about her guys. There was only one solution. It came in a brightly colored package advertising fifty free hours to sign up on America Online.

The plan was simple. I was going to log on to AOL under a name that Nikki didn't recognize. Then I would go to Long Island Romance and "pick her up," seducing her into cheating on her boyfriend (me). It never occurred to me that cyberspace was like the Casa Loco at the local street fair. Every year the truck would join the rest of the hawkers, portable rides, and games of chance, advertising the "scariest walk of your life." And when you went into the Casa Loco, everything was very dark and confusing. What you thought went up inevitably led down. Right twisted into left, and you were constantly bumping into walls of curved mirrors that reflected your distorted image in a strange, eerie light. My plan was Casa Loco.

But I felt I was ready. With that, HotMan101 was born. HotMan101 was designed to be Nikki's perfect man. He was a dark-haired, blue-eyed, six-foot Italian who loved working out and was the captain of his local lacrosse team (unlike me, a nonathlete who loved making films). HotMan101 quickly found his way into the Long Island Romance chat room. As the usual useless conversation began, I made my move: HotMan101 IMed Nikki, a.k.a. Poobear867.

HotMan101: Hi. What's up????

It was a nice beginning. Short, to the point. Poobear867 happily responded, and my planned encounter was now in play. We spoke for a little while and slowly got to know each other. I decided it was time to make the first move. With macho in my text, I came on strong. There was no comeback. She stood steadfast by her boyfriend. I began to feel smug. Maybe Nikki *was* faithful, her online boyfriends notwithstanding.

HotMan101: I'm looking to hang out. I've been in a couple of really hard relationships and they didn't work out.

Poobear867: Sorry. It takes time.

HotMan101: You interested????????

Poobear867: I have a boyfriend.

HotMan101: Yeah?

Poobear867: He's the same age as you.

HotMan101: If only I could find a girlfriend just like your boyfriend...

Things were going really well. I was feeling very good about Nikki at that point. Who would have thought that suddenly Jill990 would appear, right in the middle of my game?

As I hit Nikki with stronger online moves, she "rightfully" rejected me, citing the love of her boyfriend. Trying to squirm out of my electronic embraces, Nikki turned her attention elsewhere. I was going to pursue her when I received an IM.

Let me explain. An IM or instant message appears in a small box on the screen. On the box you see the name of the sender and what they wrote. When you write back, your words appear in the same box, also with your name. The whole conversation is private. You can go on indefinitely scrolling through messages with the other person. There's no limit to the number of IMs you can receive at any given time. That means you can be carrying on as many private conversations at one time as you like. At that point I only had Nikki's IM. But suddenly another box appeared with an electronic "ring."

There was a name on the box: Jill990. Inside there were the three conventional words that initiated private conversation:

Jill990: age/sex/location?

Jill990's IM box sat right next to Nikki's on my computer screen.

Jill990 interested me. Since Nikki was running from me, I began to speak to this new girl. I started telling her about myself. Slowly, I realized that I was speaking to a very nice girl. So on one side of my computer screen, I was an Italian athlete coming on to the faithful Nikki, and on the other side I was an artistic NYU film student making plans to meet with a totally different Long Island girl.

I had achieved the impossible: I was a postmodern narcissist—and loving every minute of it.

I quickly discovered that life with my newly discovered virtual narcissism only got better. A few days later Jill990 showed up at my NYU dormitory for a public face-to-face. We liked each other, so we went out to a student restaurant/bar on Third Avenue. We had a few plates of Buffalo wings, quesadillas, and some tall glasses of Long Island iced tea. Afterward, we went for a walk around Greenwich Village. We talked until late that night. While I was out, Nikki left a message on my voice mail...

The real twist came the next day. I went home to Long Island to visit Nikki. It's not far—only a short subway ride and a forty-five-minute trip on the Long Island Railroad. Of course, Nikki had no idea about HotMan101 or Jill990, but I was nervous. So when I was at Nikki's house, I asked her to show me what America Online was all about. It was also part of my master plan to find out exactly who was on her buddy list. Then HotMan101 would make some virtual visits. But it turned out better than I could have imagined.

Nikki went online. The buddy list automatically appears in a square box in the top right of the screen, telling you exactly who is online at that moment. I scanned the names. *HotMan101 was online.* What? I tried to figure out how HotMan101 could be active. Sternly, I asked Nikki who he was. She explained, in careful detail, the fictional character I had designed. Naturally, if I was at Nikki's house, how could HotMan101 be online?

I couldn't have planned a better cover. At school I had given my password to some friends so they could check out America Online. Ben, my sound project partner, had gone online to investigate. Instead of logging in as "guest," he inadvertently used my name, HotMan101. At that moment, in Nikki's house, I realized that I had tripped on an irrefutable cover— HotMan101 couldn't be online and sitting next to Nikki at the same time. Feigning jealousy, I demanded to know who HotMan101 was and whether

Nikki liked him. Nikki bought my act. She liked a jealous boyfriend. Very sweetly, she told me that HotMan101 was a really nice guy whom she was thinking about meeting face-to-face.

My virtual narcissism knew no boundaries.

Of course, what I learned later was that Nikki was not interested in HotMan101 at all. It was Dude1724 that she had her eye on—one of the names I noticed on her buddy list. In fact, at the same time that I boarded the Long Island Railroad the next day to go back to school, Nikki was online making plans to meet him. They met later that week at Roosevelt Field Shopping Mall at about the same time I was sitting in my English class writing an essay on postmodernism.

About a week later I decided to put Nikki to another test. I reclaimed HotMan101 and returned to Long Island Romance. I IMed Poobear867 and asked her for a face-to-face. She refused. I asked harder. She refused harder. I persisted. Poobear867 tried to ignore me, but I kept those IMs going. Suddenly a new box appeared on my screen from none other than Dude1724.

Dude1724: WHO ARE U?

HotMan101: Who are u?

Dude1724: Funny I Thought I Asked U That Question. I DON'T WANT U TALKING TO POOBEAR867 OR U WILL HAVE BIG BEEF

HotMan101: Well, it seems that you are going after Poobear867. I THOUGHT SHE HAS A BOYFRIEND!!!!!!!

Dude1724: FUNNY ASSHOLE IF I FIND YOU ARE TALKING TO HER I WILL KICK YOUR ASS.

HotMan101: Why, do u like her? Trying to move in! How far did you get Dude1724????

Dude1724: I AM HER BEST FRIEND AND I DON'T LIKE HER ASSOCIATING WITH TRASH LIKE U

HotMan101: So where were we, talking about your affair with Russell's girlfriend . . .

And then I began to ask some very serious questions. If I could be Russell, a.k.a. HotMan101, and hit on Poobear867 while meeting Jill990 on the other side of the screen, what could Nikki be doing with Dude1724?

I ended the game. I'm not sure why, except that maybe it was more fun playing HotMan101 than thinking about Nikki playing Poobear867—or who else? Shortly after, HotMan101 was put to rest. I became DOD2—the Duke of Doom. Somehow, it fit. Jill990 never really worked out, but it was fun while it lasted. Nikki never found out the truth about HotMan101. Of course, she also never found out that Dude1724 e-mailed HotMan101 and told him to stay away from *his* girl.

STALKED!
by Pamela Gilbert

Pamela Gilbert is an assistant professor at the University of Florida. Her primary focus is on Victorian women's literature, medical history, and the history of the body. She is particularly interested in metaphors of corporeality in relation to media. Her story is a chilling tale about how predators can use cyberspace for their own depraved purposes, disregarding the rights of fellow netizens. "Stalked!" was taken from Gilbert's longer work, "On Space, Sex and Stalkers," which originally appeared in Women and Performance, *issue 17.*

I am completely seduced by the Net. Those who write about it are often dazzled by its potential, so ripe with utopian promise. Yet utopias are often masks for fantasy. The lure of an Internet community in which gender, race, and class can be discarded as irrelevant or constructed at will is offered without recognition that females are often exploited. It is a frontier for male fantasy with disregard for women. And yet I love the Web. I am too often careless of my own precautions.

My story begins with an ex-colleague whom I had dated briefly over a year ago. I found myself stalked in cyberspace. In real life, stalkers usually lurk in close proximity to their victims—they want the victim to see them and know they are there—they feed on the victim's reaction. On the Net, proximity takes on a new meaning. Obviously, there are important differences between someone who is regularly within shooting range of her or his stalker and someone who is being stalked from 2,000 miles away. To gloss over this would be to trivialize the sufferings of victims of constant and immediate physical threat.

But I still feel as though my personal space has been violated. I never take big risks online, well aware that many netizens seem perpetually prepared to fight, or "flame," at the slightest insinuation. It's an aggressive environment. People who would never gratuitously insult others face-to-face are eager to do so on the Internet. After all, it's only words, it's not really like walking down a dark alley in a dangerous neighborhood. And yet I spend most of my time in "safe" places—academic lists and Usenet where there are many women and aggression is discouraged. I feel more comfortable, in the same way I go to a bar alone only if I think there will be other women there, or the way I automatically stay on the well-lit side of the parking lot. I treat the Net like a space, nonlinear, three-dimensional, at least semi-public, in which I perform both as an individual and as a professional.

The stalker—let's call him "Tim"—had been a colleague of mine for several years at a small state university campus in California where he was a faculty member and I was a part-time lecturer. We were friendly "coffee buddies," but that was about it. After moving to the Midwest to take a tenure-track position, I met up with him at the Modern Language Association (MLA) meeting in Toronto for dinner and began a casual dating relationship that lasted for two weekends. I discovered that Tim had some very serious problems that made the relationship unworkable. He suffered from untreated depression and he abused alcohol, prescription drugs, and tobacco. He was also impotent with me—which he refused to acknowledge or discuss. When I pushed him on these issues, he became angry. When he wanted to get together again, I put him off; finally he insisted on an explanation. I told him I no longer wanted to date. He was furious. I was surprised, given the casual nature of the relationship. I tried to be cordial and overlook what I believed would eventually be seen as an irrational reaction. He continued to send me angry e-mail, and I stopped responding entirely.

Then some odd things started to happen. He began showing up on Internet groups where I was active. I knew he had no professional interest in them. I was surprised at how invasive his presence felt. It was as if he had arrived at a professional conference where I was speaking with my acquaintances and colleagues. It felt like I was being watched. If I didn't respond publicly to a post that clearly appealed to my area of expertise, I knew he would be "reading" that silence as well. Still, I tried to shrug it off—it's a free Net, after all.

He upped the ante by using others on the Net to remind me of his presence. He contacted another professor at my university whose post he had seen, asking him how I was, telling him to be sure to say hello to me— an exchange that took place, to my surprise and displeasure, in a committee meeting. A more disturbing event occurred one night when I was checking my e-mail. There was a message from a graduate student in New York. She explained that she was doing research on pornography and that Tim had seen her query and kindly given her my address, explaining that I was an expert on the topic. Later I discovered that he thought I would be terrified that my work, twelve years earlier, as a nude model, would be exposed. The e-mail from New York was, from his perspective, a cat-and-mouse game. It was hostile—obviously connected to sex.

I rationalized the whole thing. After all, what kind of trouble could he give me? Wasn't Tim a "nice" person who had been through rough times? He had written several times that he was ill. He wouldn't tell me what was wrong, but I thought I had guessed. A heavy smoker, Tim had told me that his lungs were severely compromised. Yet he could not quit. Later, I found out that he was never sick—he told his friends he wrote that to make me worry he had AIDS.

So I let it go, even as I wondered what was really going on. I explained to the grad student that there had been a mistake and wished her luck on her research. On one level, the whole incident seemed ludicrously adolescent. On another level, Tim had misrepresented me professionally, lying to an innocent third party.

Nothing else happened, and I soon forgot about Tim. About five months later I received another e-mail from him. He did not mention the grad student. He wanted to reestablish a friendly professional correspondence. I responded frankly and cordially. We continued this occasional correspondence throughout the summer, which I spent in London doing research. Except for a mid-summer invitation (which I politely declined) to join him in Paris for a couple of days (I later found that he had never left the States), our correspondence was benign. His notes were often cryptic, referring to a "big research project." I didn't pay much attention. Occasionally I sensed some hostility in his e-mail, but dismissed it as residual.

When I returned to the States at the end of the summer, I received a typed letter from an address I did not recognize. It was from a colleague and personal friend of Tim's, "Naomi." It explained that Tim had been hunting for nude pictures that had been taken of me between the ages of sixteen and twenty (there was a list of items she had actually seen in his possession) and that he was planning to use them to hurt me professionally. Specifically, he intended to send them to my colleagues and students at the beginning of the term, and/or to send them to search committees, knowing I would be looking for a job.

For several minutes I simply couldn't take it in. The betrayal of confidence, the realization that I had so completely misjudged a situation, and most of all, the cold calculation left me unable to think reasonably. I picked up the phone to call and demand an explanation, and set it down again. I sat down and tried to control my breathing and to think about what the situation meant. Finally, thinking I needed a second opinion, I called a close friend. I decided to do nothing until I had talked it through and felt clear-headed. Meanwhile, I tried to calm myself, checking in on my e-mail, forcing myself to read each message. And suddenly, there on the screen was a message from Tim.

"Welcome home."

I contacted authorities at my university. They advised me to file a report with campus security. I also contacted a local women's organization that put me in touch with a supportive lawyer who led me through the complexities of dealing with the local authorities. With the lawyer on the line, I called Tim and told him that he was to stop harassing me and not to contact me in any way.

He responded with a bored "Can you call back another time? I'm busy now."

I was starting to breathe more easily. If the worst he could do was e-mail decade-old photos, I could survive it. That was until I called Naomi and found that I had far bigger problems.

Tim's irrationality had grown into an obsession of epic proportions. He had been tracking my movements on the Internet, noting where and when I logged on and making (usually erroneous) assumptions about my where-abouts and sleep patterns. For example, when I logged on late at night, he assumed I was in my office. One weekend when I did not log in he told

Naomi I was having an "orgy" in a hotel. He had me followed by one of his students with whom he had shared the pictures. He had researched my life and read up on abnormal psychology for insights into "my" personality, and even taught a course on paranoia based on the results. He spent his spare time scouring porn stores and interviewing people in the pornography industry who he believed might help him hunt down anyone who could give him information about my life. Tim had described me to Naomi and several other people on his campus as a nymphomaniac with Mafia connections, possibly a Satanist, who "slept with big Hollywood lawyers." He had taken a photograph of my face from a videotape of a public television talk program I had done for the university and posted it on the alt.sex groups with my name, offering $200 for any information or pictures of me pertaining to the time when I was sixteen to twenty. Having gotten some pictures in an initial response, he posted those, again with my name and the years he was interested in, and more money offers. I began hunting his posts online and found them pretty quickly. He was posting pictures of me to alt.sex.pictures and alt.binaries.erotica groups, especially teen.female. I surfed those groups, documenting his activities. I had the uncomfortable sense of being in "places" I would not normally go. I now found myself lurking in spaces in which he was "at home."

I didn't have to look (or lurk) long. Tim posted the pictures to multiple groups while I was online. A surge of adrenaline went through me as they appeared on the screen, and I snapped back from the keyboard as if I'd been struck. This was a contact with me—intimate, private, feeling like I had somehow been "hit" through the Net. Files appeared and would continue to appear on screens around the world, "published" and disseminated without my consent at almost unimaginable speed. There is no exact analogy. An obscene phone call might be the closest: it is also a kind of contact, an invasion of private space, and a very real threat. But I now couldn't hang up the telephone.

Tim implied that the threats would not remain virtual. He had talked often of buying a gun and challenging me with it. A particularly disturbing threat was his fantasy of confronting me with a gun at the next MLA convention. I questioned Naomi about Tim's conversations that involved fantasies or threats of physical violence against me. It was an increasingly bizarre litany. She had told Tim that "no human being" deserved what he was planning to do to me.

His response was flippant: "She ruled herself out of the human race. They shoot mad dogs, don't they?"

An expert on sexual violence told me later, "That's bad. Once they see you as not human, it justifies anything."

Tim referred to me by a code name, indicating that he considered me a "wicca" or witch, fantasizing that I was made of a straw-like substance that he could "set fire to." This became his log on name for his commercial Internet account as well as his handle on the Net. Naomi tried to comfort me by saying that she really didn't think Tim was violent, rather his pattern was to talk about something, plan it in detail, and then do it. She observed that he was feeling much happier and more energetic since he began stalking me.

"Great." I said bitterly. "Maybe I'll send him a therapy bill. Look, if he wants to show that I posed nude, why not just send what he has? Why all the research?"

"He is writing a book about your life," she responded.

I could not afford to ignore his behavior. Tim had gotten more obsessive, more confrontive than ever before. He engaged in it several hours per week, and often, per day, despite the fact that he was deeply involved with another woman. His threat of violence was sobering. I could not predict his next move. Knowing he was only six hours away, door to door, any noise outside made me jump. When I spoke at or attended conferences I never left the hotel alone. Although I tried to keep a sense of proportion, to laugh about it, living with this constant threat was both time consuming and emotionally wearing. The complication of distance and the use of the Internet created difficulties for law enforcement officials, particularly with regard to jurisdiction. Still, police in both states took an active interest, despite occasional confusion about how to proceed. The local district attorney called me in with a victim witness representative, and drafted a letter putting Tim on notice that he was under investigation. MLA was enormously supportive and worked with hotel security in Chicago to ensure my safety during the annual conference.

The administration of the university where Tim had recently been tenured was not supportive at all. Despite my six years as a lecturer there, I was told I was not a member of the campus community and therefore had "no standing" to make a complaint to them about Tim's behavior. The provost told me that even though it was quite clear that Tim was obsessed with me and had been open about his hatred, it did "not reflect on him as a faculty member, but only as a private citizen." They were terribly sorry, even shocked and disgusted, but they couldn't help for fear of being sued. The provost stopped returning my calls.

Meanwhile, I contacted a lawyer through the Screen Actors' Guild in Los Angeles who was an expert on stalking, and she advised me to disseminate information as widely as possible. "The more people who know the story, the safer you are," she said.

Another sexual assault and harassment adviser agreed. "Use your resources, take control of the situation, be active instead of passive, and work with your network of friends who can support you." I did so and was heartened by contacts from friends and acquaintances around the country, many of whom took the initiative to track information, search cyber archives, crawl the Web, consult legal advisers, and get in touch with others who knew me. I also took charge by calling more of the people with whom Tim had been in contact.

The Net became a resource for me as I connected with friends and supporters, gathered information, and turned my gaze (and others') back on the watcher. As I gained perspective, I realized that Tim's behavior was essentially an appropriation of power—as sexual harassment tends to be. The novel, the pictures, the storytelling were all part of an effort to make me over in an image of his choosing, to narrate my life, person, and body, and to deprive me of the ability to do so. The fact that he had these visual representations made his stories more credible and in essence enabled him to use "my own body" against me. Of course, it wasn't really my body, but a highly structured representation that involved images of my body as it existed many years before. Nor were the narratives (written or implied) expressive of my subjectivity; indeed, the only original restriction on the pictures' use was that they never be associated with my name.

Ultimately, his power over me was a matter of perception, and by going to the police, subjecting him to scrutiny, and forcing him out of his own "panoptic" position, I had turned the tables. Since his campus dealt with the problem in "absolute secrecy," the whole story had of course already spread across several campuses. The chair of his department cautioned me: "Right now everyone is on your side. But if you keep talking about it, people might get the idea that *you* are obsessed."

There was a dark subtext to her statement: victims get sympathy, but only if they are willing to continue being victims, quiet and passive. The word "hysterical" was bandied about. Tim's and my competing stories were entwined in other, pre-existing narratives of gender and social control.

Meanwhile, Tim threatened to sue me for defamation for filing the police report. Then he hired a lawyer and claimed that I was stalking him—an accusation that the DA found more amusing than I did. Tim argued that I was threatening him because I did not want anyone to know about the photos. This was odd, because everyone I contacted was fully aware of their existence. When the DA sent Tim's lawyer several excerpts from his e-mail and his postings on the alt.sex groups, and asked for his explanation, he defended his actions under the aegis of academic freedom; he was writing a book on feminists whose personal lives belied their feminism. He wasn't stalking me; this was merely "research."

My "battle" with Tim was fought in two arenas. In the realm of the material threat, there were guns to be considered. This never happened. The other level was that of space and subjectivity. Where on the Net could I safely "go," when was I being watched, being tracked, and how would that translate into the material realm? Would he, for example, appear at my office? Would images of me suddenly show up in the mailboxes of 600 academics on one of my lists? Would my professional reputation be assaulted —my history and scholarship appropriated in a hostile enterprise? Who could I "be" when I had already been redefined? How was this different from the way I had always been defined by others, by narratives I had worked within, consciously or unconsciously?

The Net is not "just words" but a space of social action in which subjects are responsible for their utterances and performances, and in which actions can mobilize material effects. Like other social spaces, it is not safe. We have to take it upon ourselves to use and to demand an ethics of care and respect, and to continue to use and demand it whether we get it or not.

This is actually a story without an ending. When he hired his lawyer, Tim stopped posting on the Internet, but he did continue his "research." When I attended the MLA meeting I thought I was relaxed, bolstered by the support of the organization and hotel security. By the last two days of the conference, I was increasingly snappish and oversensitive, overreacting to minor annoyances. I went home and slept for seventeen hours straight. I

knew then that I would probably never have the satisfaction of a real clo-
sure, never feel really secure from Tim either on the Internet or in my
campus parking lot. On the Internet, our physical power may be equal, a
function of technical ability that can be acquired. Our social power is
another story. Whether off- or online, in the parking lot the stakes are very
different.

TRACI AND KEN'S STORY
by Traci Hudacek

*Who would have thought that TJS8160 and KJHjunior would ever be anything more
to each other than screen names? But people are finding each other all over the
Internet, bringing virtual relationships into a tender actuality.*

*TJS8160, or Traci, describes herself as the girl-next-door type. She loves chil-
dren and has frequently worked with them. Traci also loves rodeos and country music,
both of which are featured on her various websites. When she first met KJHjunior, or
Ken, and later, after he moved out to be closer to her, Traci was working at a daycare
center as a toddler teacher. She worked during the day and spent the rest of her time
with friends and family. She also spent quite a bit of time chatting online, exploring
the Web, and learning as much as she could absorb about the electronic environment.
Traci and Ken, both twenty-three-years old, report that at the time they had met, "neither one of us had been on our own before."*

It was the fall of '95 in Brush Prairie, a small, sleepy Clark County town in
the state of Washington. The closest city, Vancouver, is twelve miles away.
I was living with my parents and working as an assistant toddler teacher in
the local daycare center. Things had not been going well. I had lost my
appetite two weeks earlier and was beginning to feel weak. Something had
to change, so I asked my boss for two days off to get some rest.

During the last few months, I had spent a lot of time on America
Online. I checked my mail and surfed the chats, so sitting down at the computer that day was nothing special. When I logged in under my screen
name, TJS8160, and found that there was no e-mail waiting, I decided to
go into a country music chatroom. The room was pretty boring. I started
going through some of the online files to see if there was anybody who

seemed interesting. KJHjunior was first on the list. I noticed that he was only a month and a half older than me. I decided to IM him. I knew he lived in Illinois because it was in his profile—but I IMed him with "Hi. Where you from?" as an excuse to talk.

KJHjunior told me he was living in Garden Prairie, Illinois—a small town over 2,000 miles away. I asked him what kind of work he was planning to do, and he said he was going into electronics. He told me that after he finished school he'd be making around $17 an hour. It sounded pretty good to me. That's when I said, "Why don't you come out here and marry me?" I was just joking around. Little did I know, then, what the future would bring.

We talked a little while longer, and then I had to go. I told him I would talk to him later, but I never thought it would really happen.

I went off-line to fax my entry to a contest being run by a Portland, Oregon, radio station. I had to send in my favorite recent song. The winner got Blackhawk concert tickets. I lost . . .

The next day I had e-mail waiting for me. It was from KJHjunior.

"If I'm going to be your husband," he wrote, "you better know a little about me." He told me about himself, and I wrote him back and told him about myself.

And that's how it all began. We started to e-mail each other more often, and by the end of the week we were e-mailing every day. We could never catch each other online at the same time—he worked the night shift at UPS in Rockford, and slept during the day. I worked with the children during the day, and slept during the night. So we just e-mailed all the time.

After a few weeks we decided to set up a time to meet again online and talk. KJHjunior had become "Ken," and TJS8160 was now "Traci." Both of us knew that there was something more serious to talk about than daily e-mails. We met in a private room called "George Strait." Ken and I got to the point quickly—it had become clear that we both had some deeper feelings. We decided to "take it from there," maybe try to meet up sometime—but nothing definite. I wasn't in love with him, yet. That's real scary online. We just continued to send sound waves to each other. Sometimes he would send some *lovey* ones, and I told my friend that I hoped he wasn't too interested in me. One day he sent me a sound wave of Alan Jackson. The whole song didn't fit, but one line said everything:

I can't hold you like I want to, but I can love you from a distance.
It melted my heart. Right then I fell in love with him.

By December—a month after our first e-mail—we began talking about driving halfway between us to meet. We'd each have to travel about 1,000 miles, meeting somewhere in the middle in South Dakota. It would have to be when he had spring break. I knew Dad wouldn't let me, so I thought about telling him I was going to visit a friend. I figured I would take a train, and Ken would drive.

I kept talking so much about Ken that Dad figured something was up. He said that there was no way that I was going to some strange place to meet a strange guy from the Internet. Dad told me that if we really had to meet, the guy would fly out here and meet me on my grounds. I wasn't so sure. Dad even agreed to get the plane ticket.

Ken and I already had everything planned out. It isn't really like me, but I felt something. We were both very nervous. We'd exchanged pictures. We'd already said *I love you*, yet we hadn't even talked on the phone. Dad insisted that he fly Ken out. Well, Ken had never flown in his life. He was scared, but he agreed. He said even if he didn't fly out, he would come to meet me. We started talking on the phone in the middle of December and counting down the days until he came out on March 1.

It seemed like it would take forever. We would tell each other on the computer that we loved each other, but it took longer for us to say it on the phone. And then it was only a quick "I love you" just as we were hanging up.

We also began to celebrate holidays. On Christmas Ken sent me a "cowboy" teddy bear and I sent him a "biker" teddy bear. For Valentine's Day he had a dozen red roses delivered to my house with a card that read "To My One and Only Love, Now and Forever."

I sent him a little brown teddy bear with a red heart. When you squeezed his paws he "gave" a kiss and actually said "I love you" in a little voice and then played "The Sweetheart Song." I also baked him a few dozen chocolate chip cookies, mailed some sweetheart candies, a big Hershey kiss, and a poster of a teddy bear on it saying "I love you." I got a little carried away with the cards—sending five in all. I couldn't resist. They all had his name on it when I saw them. It was so much fun! And then suddenly March 1 arrived. Ken was coming.

I wasn't nervous at all as I drove to the airport, but my family warned me. I went into the airport and sat down. Still, everything was okay. Then Ken's plane landed. A lady was chatting with me and suddenly I couldn't listen. I was terrified! My legs were getting numb as I sat there—turning to jelly. If I didn't get up soon, I wasn't going to get up at all. So I stood up and walked over by the door. I saw Ken. I knew it was him right away. He was looking around, and I stood near a beam that holds up the ceiling. He was still looking around when I went up behind him and said quietly, "Looking for someone?"

He turned around and smiled. We just said "Hi" to each other. It's strange, but the next few minutes are blank. I think I spoke and I think Ken spoke, but I can't remember anything but walking out to my truck.

He looked a lot different from the picture he'd sent. Ken wore a leather jacket, a sweater, and sunglasses. He took my heart the minute I saw him. I was still so nervous and I really wouldn't look at him. It was kind of sideways glances, so I didn't get a good look until later when we got to his hotel room. It was then that I realized that I had lucked out. Ken was really a cutie.

We left the airport. I had to get my truck washed, so we went to the car wash. He didn't want to meet my parents just yet, so we ran a few errands. Finally, we went to my house.

I was nervous, but not as bad as I had been before. Ken was nervous, too. To me it was a natural thing—bringing a nice, good-looking guy home to my parents. I know Ken was really scared of meeting them. He didn't want to be there at all, but he knew he had to go (now he and my dad are best friends, and my mom treats him like her own son). I think my parents were really surprised that he came out. They thought he would chicken out. But it took more than that weekend to convince them. After Ken left to fly back home to Illinois, Dad told me I would never see him again. He didn't even think I would even hear from Ken again.

I guess Dad was wrong.

Ken and I sat and talked with my parents. I finally looked at him straight in the eyes, and it was great! We left my parents and went to the mall so he could get something to eat. The next stop was my friend's house. She was very concerned about me meeting a guy on the Net, so she decided to let Ken know, in no uncertain terms, that he'd better take very good care of me. She took her father's unloaded hunting gun, and when we arrived just pointed it straight at Ken. We all laughed, but she made her point.

Ken and I finally returned to the hotel. There wasn't much time because I had an 11 P.M. curfew and I had to get home. We already knew that we probably would have trouble saying "I love you" in person, since it had been so hard on the telephone. It was very different face-to-face. Ken was hoping I could say it by the time he left on Sunday. He walked me out to my car, and we hugged each other. I had already decided that he didn't really like me in person. I thought that after the weekend I would never see him again. I guess I had been listening to Dad. Then we hugged and I blurted out that I loved him. I didn't have much time to think before Ken said it back . . .

I had lots of trouble sleeping that night. I couldn't stop thinking about Ken and our strange relationship.

The next day I woke up around 5:30 and called him. Ken was already awake, waiting for the telephone to ring. I showered and dressed and stopped to buy him his favorite soda and some donuts. I went to the hotel. The day passed so quickly—we went to the beach and to the aquarium, where we saw Keiko from the movie *Free Willy*. We ended up in his hotel room, fast asleep in each other's arms. I left early again to meet my curfew.

Sunday, the day Ken was leaving, arrived. It was too fast. He didn't want to go. Ken had decided that he liked it out here in Washington. Dad changed Ken's flight so he could stay another day. I decided to call in sick on Monday. Ken started looking through the Sunday paper for jobs in the area. We even watched a television show on local houses for sale and planned our "dream house." It was a very special day. We went to my favorite clothing store, drove around the mountains and watched the movie *Free Willy II* with my parents. We all went out to dinner together—Mom, Dad, my two younger sisters, Ken, and me.

On Monday I picked him up at the hotel and headed for the airport. We only had a little time together. I kissed Ken goodbye and told him to meet me on the computer that night after he got home from work (he was going from the airport to work). He got on the plane and never looked back. I went home and e-mailed him so it would be waiting for him in Illinois. Two hours later Ken called. He was still in Portland. His plane was delayed, and he would miss his connecting flight. He would never get home in time for work. We made a quick decision. I returned to the airport to get him. Conveniently, my parents were out of town for the night. Dad knew that Ken was still in Washington. He told me to go to work the next day and have him arrange a ride to the airport from the hotel. Well, Mom and Dad never knew that Ken stayed at my house that night and I called in sick the next day.

On Tuesday my sister was home sick. We were just about to leave for the airport when she decided she was feeling better and wanted to go to school. We packed her into the truck and rushed down the street. Suddenly, in the middle of the road was a big ugly cow running our way. I jammed the truck in reverse and tried to get the attention of a cop that was going by, but he never saw. I cut back another way and finally dropped my sister off at school. Ken was afraid he might miss his flight. By the time we got to the airport he had five minutes to spare. We said our good-byes real fast and once again, Ken left. We never saw the cow again.

Things had changed. When he got home he called me, and we couldn't stop saying "I love you." We met on the computer that night and began to make some serious decisions. At first, I was going to move to Illinois to be with him. Then Ken decided that he liked it in Washington. He decided to move out here! I would fly to Illinois to meet his family and then together we would drive his car back west.

I went apartment hunting and found a tiny place in Vancouver, Washington. It was in a small complex with only eight apartments. We rented apartment 2. You walked in the door (the only one that goes outside) and you were in the living room. We had a big picture window with miniblinds and filled it with our TV, stereo, beloved computer, fish named Homer (Ken named him), and our futon. The whole apartment was small and cozy. Just right!

But it took a plane ride, meeting Ken's parents, and a wild drive through a blizzard before we got there. I left for Illinois on April 8, 1996. I took a plane and was super nervous about meeting Ken's parents. His mother wanted to meet me the night I came into town but I tried to talk Ken into letting me meet her the next day. It didn't work. When I finally faced them, I found that they were very nice. So nice that I stayed in Illinois for three nights. At first I stayed in a hotel. His parents insisted, so I stayed at their house for the third night. I slept in Ken's room and he slept in the living room. They took us out to dinner, and spent a lot of time with us. Funny, they reminded me of my family. Except Ken is an only child and that's very different from a family with three girls.

We left on April 12, expecting a nice drive out west. Ken's car was a 1982 Buick Regal. No one but Ken thought it would make it all the way. In fact, the trip from Illinois to Washington was hectic, scary, and romantic all at once. The first day we drove about 900 miles and stayed in Cheyenne, Wyoming, a place we have never been and wanted to see. The car was doing okay—except that the carburetor wasn't adjusted for the high altitude. The next morning Ken was ready to leave but I had a hard time waking up. I was tired and comfortable. We finally got on the road two hours later then we'd planned. It was thirty minutes before we hit the snow.

And it was really snowing. The longer we drove, the worse it got. Lots of people were pulled over on the side of the road. The highway patrol was going in the opposite direction (east), and shutting gates on the freeway. We stopped at the next gas station and some guy told Ken that they had just shut down the freeway going in our direction. And we still had so far to go!

I started chipping the ice off the car, especially on the headlights where it was so thick you couldn't even see light coming out of them. The grill was also iced, and as hard as I tried, I couldn't chip it off. Ken told me just to leave it and we headed back into the awful cold and blizzard conditions. It seemed a long way from computers!

As Ken drove, I just sat there with my eyes closed. I was really scared and didn't think we were going to make it. The eighteen-wheelers were speeding past us at seventy miles an hour and we were creeping along at about fifteen miles per hour. As the snow started to ease up, the car started to act up. Suddenly, smoke was pouring out of the back. Ken took an exit that led to nowhere and the car just died about a half-mile from the freeway. We thought the engine had blown. We had a cell phone and an AAA card, so we tried calling, but we were too far out. We were both terrified. I thought of our computer romance and wondered how we ended up in an iced car that refused to move. It seemed so strange! Ken tried the car one more time and— it started. He figured out that the ice on the grill didn't let in enough air to the engine and it just overheated. We got back on the road and made it to Twin Falls, Idaho, for the night. We slept really well that night.

Ken and I arrived at our apartment on April 14. We were finally home.

Ken found a job working as a service technician, while Traci decided to work, not surprisingly, at the airport. They traded Ken's car for a truck, which Ken is restoring.

They continue to live in Vancouver. They were married in a small wedding almost two years later in December 1998. "Ken and I are very shy about large receptions," Traci explains, "so we had a really small wedding."

Today, Traci and Ken are looking to buy a house of their own. Ken works as a computer tech for Unisys Corporation, and Traci is a cashier at Portland International Airport. They're thinking about starting a family in about three years. They use the Internet daily. Ken likes the online auctions, Traci heads for contests, country music sites, newsgroups, and making her own Web pages. They both use it to keep in touch with friends and family. "In the end," Traci reports, "everyone was very happy for us."

MELISSA
by "Melissa"

Melissa was a seventeen-year-old hearing-impaired adolescent living in New York when she wrote this story. Melissa has had profound hearing loss since birth. She does not use American Sign Language but communicates through speech, lip reading, and the written word. Melissa has held leadership roles in various organizations throughout high school. She graduated with a grade average of 97, ranking in the top 5 percent of her class. She currently attends an Ivy League college. Her future goal is to become a civil-rights activist/lawyer or college professor. She has not yet made a final decision.

Being hearing-impaired in a hearing world has had a profound impact on who I am. The actual impairment does not affect me so much as the lack of communication that, at times, results from it.

Let me explain. I am hearing-impaired, yet socialize, act, and think like the hearing. Although my hearing loss is profound, I learned oral communication and have been intensively mainstreamed all of my life. Ironically, I accept the hearing world as my own and accept the deaf culture as "foreign." I am completely entrenched in my surroundings. All of my relationships are with hearing people—even my boyfriend. When I e-mail another deaf teen, it feels awkward, as if I am speaking another language with someone from another culture very different from my own.

The paradox involves what happens to me every day. When I am placed in unfamiliar surroundings or in conditions where I cannot function well, there are major obstacles. For example, if I am in a darkened room, or there are many people talking at once, it is difficult to lip read. These are the times that I wish I had more contact with the deaf community. In group conversations, at times I feign a quiet personality, or I am constantly making jokes or bringing up subjects so that I know what everybody is discussing. During these times I may feel frustrated about not communicating with other deaf teens. They cannot hear, and I cannot sign, so I always end up in the same place.

I find these issues so interesting that I am currently developing a Westinghouse project that investigates how hearing peers talk to hearing-impaired teens. I want to find out whether exaggerations in speech are prevalent. I began by asking the question "How do you feel when people exaggerate their speech?" I find it ironic that the general response was along the lines of "embarrassed." I am really not surprised. This is a very personal issue. Too often I feel like I appear dumb because I have to ask "What?" over and over again. Although I am pretty smart and do well in school, some people treat me like I have the reading level of a third grader. When using the Internet, there is no feeling of embarrassment, of having to explain myself.

Using the computer as a vehicle for communication has certainly become an exciting prospect for me. People online take no notice of my impairment because they cannot tell I am hearing-impaired. It is wonderful to become engaged in conversations with other people on subjects that I would not ordinarily talk about with my friends (i.e., philosophy). There is a sense of freedom involved because there is no "what, what did you say? . . ." or, on the part of my friends who are not interested in such topics, "What are you talking about? Politics, philosophy—what's wrong with you!?"

I wrote several posts on the deaf message boards in AOL. I received a few responses, but my e-mail relationships with them were brief. There were so many people like me, "mainstreamed to the point of no return." For example, I do not personally know even one hearing-impaired teenager. Through the Internet I found there were thousands of them. Online, it does not matter whether a person is hearing-impaired or not. Everybody is on equal footing. I would not desire to change my hearing impairment; I do not care about my hearing impairment. It is the lack of communication that, at times, bothers me.

I want to make one more point that many people do not understand:

totally deaf teens cannot completely lose themselves in the Internet. It is obvious by their writing that they normally speak through American Sign Language. They change the syntax of their words. I have received letters from deaf teens that are extremely hard to decipher. The following posting on a deaf bulletin board is a good example of this problem.

> I am deaf, single English male age 39 need Brussel Deaf Club Address and when the club regular? and i would like to visit the Brussel deaf club for Holiday in September and the club have any near Bed and Breakfast Please let me know—

What would happen if I were to meet these people in real life? I would not be able to communicate with them. In fact, I do not want to meet them because I have become used to being a hearing teen who just happens to say "What?" a lot.

Of course, communicating with people I already know is a whole different story. My boyfriend is not hearing-impaired. When he went away to college, we started to e-mail. I realized that it was a great idea because I have difficulty understanding him on the phone. In a written format I know exactly what he is saying, so communication is easier. It took a while to get started because he could not figure out the system, but we have been e-mailing ever since.

In the beginning, we just typed what I could not understand over the phone. A typical e-mail from Jonathan would consist of:

> Hi Melissa, I got your e-mail. I went to the movies, had lots of fun, and now I am going to sleep. Love ya, Bye, Jonathan

It was really just a way of "checking in." I used it to relate a story or tell him about something important that happened that day. Without e-mail to talk frequently to one another, I wonder if we would still be together. Communication is so hard. E-mail has brought us, and kept us, together.

Gradually, for both of us, e-mail became a way to express our feelings. We can take however long we need to phrase things exactly the way we want to. Over the telephone, it is rare that either of us says, "I miss you," or "Love ya." Now, through e-mail, we say it all the time.

Communication, to me, has always meant letting another person know exactly what is going on in my life, such as funny stories, my mood, what I am doing tonight, which one of my friends is at war with another friend. The computer screen, as a method of communication, screams, "Communicate through me," not "Write a few meaningless words and send them." It would seem that if I could change my situation off-line, the obvious choice would be "to get hearing." I am not so sure of this anymore. It is who I am—a hearing-impaired teen. While this may present problems throughout the course of my life, it has been the source of my identity. It has encouraged me to work harder, to strive for the seemingly impossible. In a way, it is a paradox—but it is my paradox.

FINAL
THOUGHTS:
COMING HOME—
AN AUTHOR'S RECONSTRUCTION
OF SELF

I FELT COMPELLED to construct my own website. After all, my specialty is psychotechnology—the merging of psychology and technology—so I felt I needed an online presence. I didn't have the time to design and program my own space, so I commissioned Joe Davidoff, a Web designer, to show me the route. During our first meeting he infected me with his youthful enthusiasm, supported by an uncanny postmodern ability to translate fine art into virtual messaging. His imagination far exceeded mine as he plunged into constructing a home page that was adequately dignified for professionals while visually appealing to surfers.

While most of cyberspace is geared to the cycling of identities, home pages stand as a bridge between postmodernism and that old modernist version of a single, stable self. Screen names, alternate personas, and multiple identities are not part of this very popular aspect of the Net. On home pages, the only stories people tend to tell are about their face-to-face selves. It's a replay of actual reality in virtuality.

I'm not alone. There are literally *millions* of home pages on the Internet. Some predict that eventually *all* netizens will have a home page. But that's the future. Today—well, we're still infants.

The home page is a metaphor—a virtual home where you can invite friendly strangers in for a soothing cup of coffee and homemade cookies. You can chat, talk about yourself, build new relationships, or simply share notes in the safety of nonanonymous cyberspace. It's your turf.

Multimillionaires and struggling college students have home pages next door to one another in the relative space of the Internet. The material that most people post on their home pages is often very ordinary. There are photos of themselves, family, friends, lovers, even pets. There are lists of favorite music, movies, what they like, dislike, even hate. There are special links to other websites as well as to the home pages of friends. Some home pages talk comfortably, others joke, some shout, and others do nothing but exist.

Self-expression is perhaps the most important reasons for authoring a page. The rules are simple: a good home page should be easy to load, updated often, consistent, easy to navigate, and truly reflect the author (for better or worse).

The birth of my home page was not a smooth process. I needed everything to go right—without knowing exactly what I wanted. Joe painstakingly led me through the capabilities and limitations of Web design. As we progressed, there were bugs, computer glitches, and access problems. Construction involved abbreviating my thoughts into the typically short text necessary to hold the average netizen's attention. Links were quirky, addresses changed daily, and information was so readily available that I didn't know when to stop my searches. Finding the best Web host to publish my page proved to be a monumental task. There were simply too many choices. Not knowing which way to turn, I worked on a name for my child: Psychotechnology Online.

Christopher Lasch, author of *The Culture of Narcissism: American Life in an Age of Diminishing Expectations,* proposes that "the final product of bourgeois individualism" is a new type of narcissism where one is separated from the past. The new-millennium narcissist hungers for a notoriety that has no real meaning except what is derived from immediate gratification.

The past is devalued and the present, in terms of conspicuous consumption, is glorified. Paradoxically, the consumption is transitory—material goods are discarded as readily as ideologies. The narcissism becomes a presentation, a collection of identities constructed "out of materials furnished by advertising and mass culture, themes of popular film and action, and fragments torn from a vast range of cultural traditions, all of them equally contemporaneous to the contemporary mind" (p. 91). We end up with what Lasch calls the "performing self," where individuals are both actors and spectators, constantly seeking encouragement that we are winning others, charming them with our ability to achieve perfection. "Men and women alike," writes Lasch, "have to project an attractive image and to become simultaneously role players and connoisseurs of their own performers" (p. 92). Enter the home page.

I was constantly worried that Psychotechnology Online would not live up to some unwritten set of standards that pranced perilously across cyberspace. I repeatedly questioned Joe about design rumors—what was outdated, what was an obvious sign of the uninformed? I hated the photograph of myself, smiling out at an unknown cyberworld. I wanted music, but I didn't know whether to have classical, popular, country, or rock. I chose silence instead.

But there is another, unstated aspect to home paging in cyberspace. In an uncharted netherworld, where information attacks netizens like a predator and multiplicity removes stability and consistency, a space that that embodies "home" is ultimately a warm and fuzzy place. Home is where the heart is, where one can find familiar virtual faces, a known history, a space that can be shared on relatively solid digital ground. It's infinitely reassuring. Click on to your homepage and you take a step away from the fray, onto your turf, with your name and your predominant identity. Ultimately, it is a place to hang your virtual hat—a place that changes only at your command.

It was an exhilarating moment when I officially opened my door. Joe sat in front of the computer. I sat next to him. He turned to me and said, with an engaging grin, "You're online."

I had this strange sensation of arrival. It wasn't my home page that had been birthed—it was me. I had made my digital mark.

Since the first Psychotechnology Online, Joe has moved on to far greater responsibilities in the technological world and I have conducted two major renovations. The first was a self-improvement job, complete with streaky paint and uneven corners. The second, and most recent, was with the very talented Mary Beth Osborne, a Web designer and cofounder of Styles en Route, who lives 250 miles and two states away from me. She has added the latest technology, jazzing up the graphics, giving me the long-desired music, and creating a complex web that runs over fifty pages. Not quite a book, but I'm getting there.

Once again I've come home to reconstruct yet another self, a victim of my own personalized cyberseduction. It's a case of keeping up with the technological Joneses, using the tools just to maintain a tidy home. It's our world—this age of psychotechnology—where our inventions have leaped so far ahead of our philosophy that our Stone Age computers are staggering in their own haste to stay in the race.

We need to rethink the fact that the most ominous threat to humankind lies in the gap between our technology and our philosophy. As Ornstein suggests, we need to catch up to ourselves—shift our thinking so we can accommodate our virtual realities to nature and our planet. We're information-processing life forms with the ability to reshape our systems, programmed to adapt, to adjust our philosophy to protect both new and old environments. We *can* make a difference, but it means connecting the past and the present with the future, injecting a sense of perspective in the power of technology. While our imaginations choose to see machines as smooth, streamlined operations, our experiences tell us otherwise. Computers have bugs. Systems break down. As Ellen Ullman put it in *Wired* magazine,

> It's almost a betrayal. After being told for years that technology is the path to a highly evolved future, it's come as something of a shock to discover that a computer system is not a shining city on a hill—perfect and ever new—but something more akin to an old farmhouse built bit by bit over decades by nonunion carpenters. (p. 126)

So let's rethink it. Do we really want to sacrifice what nature has taken so long to design for farmhouses built by nonunion carpenters?

Perhaps the most important message in this book *is* to take time and stop. Stop and think about what you're doing. Where is technology taking you? What do you need to do in order to control *it*, not the other way around? Think about what's really happening. Use your consciousness to take the next step in evolution, ahead of the designers who are thinking about programs, not ethics; code, not behavior; profit, not social improvement. Do you really want to make love online and emotionally delete the man or woman who shares your actual bed? Do you really want your kids to play virtual baseball, never knowing the joy of a pickup game on the street or in the local park? Do you really want to believe you can *feel* the peace of an ancient redwood forest or *experience* the stark beauty of the high desert winter through a screen of any size? Cyberseduction is a powerful force. You *can* have both: virtual reality and actuality.

Just don't forget to smell the roses.

BIBLIOGRAPHY
FOR PART III

Blacksburg Electronic Village (BEV). 1998. Virginia Polytechnic Institute and State University [Online]. Available: http://www.bev.net [February 10, 1999].

Buss, D. 1992. Male preference mechanisms: Consequences for partner choice and intrasexual competition. In *The Adapted Mind: Evolutionary Psychology and the Generation of Culture*, edited by J. H. Barkow, L. Cosmides, and J. Tooby. New York: Oxford University Press.

Ciolli, R. February 15, 1999. Web as weapon: victims of online attacks seek limits for new medium. *Newsday*, A5, A24.

Dery, M. 1993. Flame wars. *South Atlantic Quarterly* 92 (4): 559–68.

EVT (Electronic Village Technologies). 1997. *Community Network Planning Guide* [Online], 10 pp. Available: http://www.bev.net/project/evupstart/planning. htm [June 7, 1997].

Fink, J. 1999. *How to Use Computers and Cyberspace in the Clinical Practice of Psychotherapy*. New Jersey: Jason Aronson.

Freud, S. 1962. *The Ego and the Id*, edited by James Strachey and translated by Joan Riviere. New York: W. W. Norton.

Gergen, K. 1991. *The Saturated Self: Dilemmas of Identiy in Contemporary Life.* New York: Basic Books.

Herring, S. 1993. *Gender and Democracy in Computer-Mediated Communication* [Online]. Available: http://dc.smu.edu/dc/classroom/Gender.txt [February 25, 1997].

———. 1994. *Gender Differences in Computer-Mediated Communication: Bringing Familiar Baggage to the New Frontier* [Online]. Available: http://www.cpsr.org/cpsr/gender/herring.txt [February 25, 1997].

Joinson, A. 1998. Causes and implications of disinhibited behavior on the Internet. In *Psychology and the Internet* by J. Gackenbach. New York: Academic Press

Jung, C. G. 1934. The concept of the collective unconscious. *The Archetypes and the Collective Unconscious.* Collected works, vol. 9 [Online]. Available: http://www.geocities.com/Athens/158/collective.htm [January 22, 1997].

Kavanaugh, A., S. Cohill, and S. Patterson. January 1997. *Use and Impact of Community Networking in the Blacksburg Electronic Village* [Online], 3 pp. Available: http://www.bev.net/project/research/Research.Highs.1_97.htm [June 7, 1997].

Kirsner, S. December 1998. Murder by Internet. *Wired* 6 (12): 210–16, 266–71.

Kornblum, W., and J. Julian. 1995. *Social Problems.* Englewood Cliffs, N.J.: Prentice-Hall.

Lasch, C. 1979. *The Culture of Narcissism: American Life in an Age of Diminishing Expectations.* New York: W. W. Norton & Company.

Lombard, M., and T. Ditton. September 1997. At the heart of it all: The concept of telepresence. *Journal of Computer Mediated Communication* 3 (2) [Online], 39 pp. Available: http://jcmc.huji.ac.il/vol3/issue2/lombard.htm [September 16, 1998].

McAllester, M. May 25, 1997. NewsBytes. Bride nets $264,000. *Newsday,* A61.

McCrummen, S. February 15, 1999. High-tech heckling: Student bullies take to Internet bulletin boards. *Newsday,* A5, A25.

McKee, P., III. October 7, 1998. Remarks to the "Consumer protection in electronic commerce" panel at the Public Voice in the Development of Internet Policy Conference of the Global Internet Liberty Campaign. *Internet Fraud Watch* [Online], 7 pp. Available: http://www.fraud.org/internet/intstat.htm [March 7, 1999].

Mitchell, W. J. 1996. *City of Bits.* Cambridge, Mass.: MIT Press.

Morningstar, C., and R. Farmer. 1990. *The Lessons of Lucasfilm's Habitat* [Online]. Available: http://www.communities.com/paper/lessons.htm [February 9, 1997].

National Fraud Information Center homepage [Online. Last updated January 1997. Available: http://www.fraud.org [April 7, 1997].

Ornstein, R. 1991. *The Evolution of Consciousness: The Origins of the Way We Think.* New York: Simon & Schuster.

Pesce, M. November 30, 1995. *Connective, Collective, Corrective: The Future of VRML* [Online]. Available: http://hyperreal.org/~mpesce/vrworld.html [January 10, 1997].

————. May 8, 1996. *Connective, Collective, Corrective: Lessons Learned from VRML* [Online]. Available: http://hyperreal.org/~mpesce/www5.html [January 14, 1997].

————. No date. Final amputation: Pathogenic ontology in cyberspace. *Prologue to the 1994 Edition in SPEED: A Journal of Technology and Politics* [Online], 25 pp. Available: http://www.hyperreal.com/~mpesce/fa.html [September 15, 1996].

Pinker, S. 1997. *How the Mind Works.* New York: W. W. Norton & Company.

Reid, E. 1997. The self and the Internet: Variations on the illusion of one self. In *Psychology and the Internet* by J. Gackenbach. New York: Academic Press.

Rheingold, H. 1993. *The Virtual Community: Homesteading on the Electronic Frontier.* New York: HarperPerennial.

Richtel, M. April 2, 1997. From housewives to strippers, small smut sites make money. *New York Times CyberTimes* [Online], 19 paragraphs. Available: http://www.nytimes.com/library/cyber/week/040297porn-housewife.html [April 6, 1997].

Schuster, C. S., and S. S. Ashburn. 1986. *The Process of Human Development: A Holistic Life-Span Approach.* Boston: Little, Brown & Company.

Seabrook, J. 1994. My first flame. *New Yorker,* June 6, 70–79.

————. 1997. *Deeper.* New York: Simon & Schuster.

Sempsey, J., III. 1995. *The Psycho-Social Aspects of Multi-User Dimensions in Cyberspace* [Online]. Available: http://www.netaxs.com/~jamesiii/mud.htm [June 11, 1997].

Shea, V. No date. *Netiquette* [Online]. Available: http://www.in.on.ca/tutorial/netiquette.htm [February 11, 1997].

Spielvogel, J. J. 1991. *Western Civilization.* New York: West Publishing Company.

Stevenson, R. L. [1886] 1987. *Dr. Jekyll and Mr. Hyde.* Reprint, New York: Signet.

Stokes, P. November 13, 1996. Six years for priest who broadcast abuse of boys to Internet paedophiles. *Electronic Telegraph* [Online], 25 paragraphs. Available: http://www.telegraph.co.uk:80/et?ac=000226604720238&rtmo=3321be47&pg=/et96/11/13/npaed13.html [March 8, 1997].

Suler, J. May 1996. Mom, dad, computer: Transference reactions to computers.

Psychology of Cyberspace [Online], 9 pp. Available: http://www1.rider.edu/~suler/psycyber/comptransf.html [September 16, 1996].

———. 1996a. Cyberspace as dream world. *Psychology of Cyberspace* [Online]. Available: http://www1.rider.edu/~suler/psycyber/cybdream.html [September 16, 1996].

———. 1996b. E-mail relationships. *Psychology of Cyberspace* [Online]. Available: http://www1.rider.edu/~suler/psycyber/emailrel.html [September 16, 1996].

Talan, J. February 17, 1999. How sex mail finds its way to children. *Newsday*, C3.

Tannen, D. 1991. You just don't understand: Men and women in conversation. *Gender Styles in Computer Mediated Communication.* [Online], 3 pp. Available: http://www.georgetown.edu/bassr/githens/tannenbk.html [March 1, 1997].

Thoreau, H. D. 1971. *The Writings of Henry D. Thoreau: Walden,* edited by J. L. Shanley. Princeton, N.J.: Princeton University Press.

Turkle, S. 1995. *Life on the Screen: Identity in the Age of the Internet.* New York: Simon & Schuster.

Ullman, E. April 1999. The myth of order. *Wired* 7 (4): 126–29, 183–84.

INDEX

adaptation, 19, 43–45, 47–49, 50–54, 56, 58, 61–64, 71–74, 82, 99, 106, 114, 118, 157, 172, 174, 187, 197, 218, 237
and self-preservation, 104–106
third adaptation, 176–77
agony aunts, 255
Alex/Jessica, the cyberlegend, 256
Andersen, Hans Christian, 40
artificial intelligence, 60
artificial selection, 49–50
attachment, 101–102
augmented reality, 37
Australopithecus, 51–52

Barkow, Jerome, 56, 58

bashboards, 244
Bateman, A. J., 162–63
Becker, Ernest, 57, 87, 97, 103–105, 108–12
Biocca, Frank, 131–34
birth, 100–102, 127
Blacksburg Electronic Village (BEV), 215–24
Blacksburg, Va., 215–24
Bloom, Howard, 40–41
Boorstin, Jon, 140, 144, 147
Buss, David, 167–68, 231

Carroll, Lewis, 23–24
Clark, R. D., 167
Cohill, Andrew, 222–23

collective consciousness, 211–13
Communications Decency Act, 21–22
computational theory of mind, 59
conflict, unresolvable in humans, 154–55
conscious adaptation, 174
conscious spirit, 85–86
consciousness, 34, 64–67, 85, 96–97, 104, 111, 176, 187–88, 204
and philosophy, 176–77
and presence, 130–34
constraint and consequences (social), 209–10, 237–38, 240
Cosmides, Leda, 56, 58
Craven, Wes, 126–27
creationism, 45, 51–52
Cro-Magnon, 53, 70, 72, 78
cyberfeminists, 211
cyberlibertarians, 211
cyberseduction, 17, 20, 26, 38, 158–59
cybersex, 261–65
cybersmears, 244–45
cyberspace, 17, 55, 62, 87, 117, 186–94, 200–202, 207–13
cyborg, 73, 118–23

Darwin, Charles, 18, 41–46, 51
Davidoff, Joe, 293–97
de Chardin, Tielhard, 211–13
DeAngelis, T., 107
denial of death, 86–87, 110–12
Dery, Mark, 210
disinhibition (online), 238, 240
Disney, 30, 104
dissociation, 204–10
adaptive, 201–10
and anonymity, 209

multiple personality disorder (MPD), 205
multiple selves, 258
Ditton, Teresa, 134–36, 140, 142–43, 192–94
diversity, 48, 50, 98, 161–62
dominance hierarchies (human), 230–34
male, 230–31, 240
female, 231–32
status, 232–38
Dr. Jekyll and Mr. Hyde (book), 189–90, 205, 208
Duncan, J., 138

Electronic Village Technologies (EVT), 220–21
elites (in cyberspace), 234–35
evolution, 41, 44–46, 47–49, 50–54, 56, 58, 62–63, 73, 74, 84, 104–106, 154, 166, 172, 204, 218
evolutionary priorities, 187
evolutionary psychology, 18, 38, 56–76, 80, 105, 155–64, 259
Exorcist, The (movie), 148

families/kin, 151–58
virtual, 156–58
Farmer, F. Randall, 191
fear, 100–102, 110
fight or flight response, 62–63, 186, 210
Fink, Jeri, 293–97
Fink, Russell, 268–73
FitzRoy, Captain Robert, 42
Fixmer, Rob, 123
flames, 240
Forrest Gump (movie), 140

free-will, 96–97
Freud, Sigmund, 27, 35, 46, 64, 100, 111, 190, 199

Gallant, Roy, 43, 48
gendermorph, 256–59
genes, spreading, 152–56
genetic engineering, 50, 170
Gergen, Kenneth, 168, 198, 202
Gibson, William, 117
Gilbert, Pamela, 273–81
Goodstein, Laurie, 46
guerrillas (in cyberspace), 234–35, 236–38

Hamilton, William, 160–61
Hartmann, Heinz, 19, 74, 117–18, 176
hate online, 247–51
Hatfield, Elaine, 167
Hemingway, Ernest, 199
Herring, Susan, 260
High Sierras, 29, 130–31
H.M.S. *Beagle*, 42–44
home pages, 293–97
Homo erectus, 52, 62
Homo habilis, 52
Homo sapiens, 51
Homo sapiens neanderthalensis, 52–53
Homo sapiens sapiens, 51–53, 61, 79
Hudacek, Traci, 281–88
huddle virtual masses, 235
human existential dilemma, 104, 110, 119, 155
Human Genome Project, 36
Hume, David, 42
hunter-gatherers, 63, 70–72, 77, 84, 102, 116, 119, 166, 187, 230–31, 260

hybrids, 49

I, 95–97, 99, 102, 104, 106, 190
individuality, 101
information-processing life forms, 59, 62–65, 69, 79–82, 84, 86, 108, 114, 117, 119, 127, 129, 133, 172, 187–88, 191, 218
information storage, 82–83
interactivity, 192–94
    number and extent of inputs, 193
    range and depth of inputs, 193–94
    speed and user reactivity of the machine, 194

Joinson, Adam, 238
Julian, Joseph, 236
Jung, Carl Gustav, 26–28, 212
Jurassic Park (movie), 138, 197–98

Kaplan, Stephan, 84, 86, 155
Kavanaugh, Andrea, 222–23
Kim, Taeyong, 131–34
Kornblum, William, 236
Kurtz, Howard, 144

Lamarck, Jean Baptiste, 44
Landow, George, 121
language (human), 61, 259–61
Lasch, Christopher, 294–95
Law & Order (television show), 205
Locke, John, 42
Lombard, Matthew, 134–36, 140, 142–43, 192–94
Long Island Sound, 173–74
Lucasfilm's Habitat, 191
Lucy, 51–52

McAllester, Mike, 259
McCrummen, Stephanie, 244
McKee, Phillip, 245–46
McLeish, Father Adrian, 252–53
McLuhan, Marshall, 149, 157
Mann, Steven, 122
Mansfield, Beth, 251
Mars Pathfinder, 148
Marx, Karl, 236
Masterson, James, 107–108
mate selection, 162–70
    as defined by evolution, 166
media equation, 127, 191
Melissa, 288–91
mental image, 78–79, 81, 83, 146
mental modules, 68–70, 79–80, 96, 99,
    128–29, 146, 153–54, 165, 190, 204
Milgran, Paul, 37
Mill, John Stuart, 42
mind and body, 16, 18, 23–24, 35–36,
    68, 111, 119
Minsky, Marvin, 60
Mitchell, William, 116
modern philosophy, 199–200
Morningstar, Chip, 191
multiple personality disorder (MPD),
    205
multiple selves, 190
Murder by Internet, 239

narcissism, 105–10, 152, 234–35, 294–95
narcissistic disorders, 107–108
Nass, Clifford, 127–29
natural selection, 43, 47–49, 50–54, 56,
    58, 61–64, 70, 72, 74, 82, 99, 106,
    114, 118, 136, 152, 162–63, 172,
    197, 230, 256

Neanderthal, 52–53
neo-creationism, 45
neo-Darwinism, 46
Neolithic Revolution, 54, 71–74
Net.Fraud (online scams), 245–47
Net.sex, 261–65
Netiquette, 210
neural networks/circuits, 18, 56, 58–61,
    76, 96
noosphere, 211–13

Old Man and the Sea, The (book), 199
one-child policy (China), 174–76
online sexual predators, 251–54
Ornstein, Robert, 51–52, 53, 61–62, 65,
    70, 149, 174, 187, 218, 296
Orwell, George, 116
Ovid, 208

parasocial relationships, 135–36
parental investment theory, 162–64
Patterson, Scott, 222–23
pedophiles (online), 251–54
Pesce, Mark, 211–13
Pinker, Steven, 38, 58–60, 68–69,
    78–79, 81, 86, 96–97, 98, 161–62,
    166, 230–31, 234
postmodernism, 29–30, 34, 136,
    197–219, 221, 242, 293–94
presence, 130–34
    and imaginal environment, 132
    and information processing, 130
    and physical environment, 131
    and virtual environment, 131–32
Primal Fear (movie), 205
Psycho (movie), 148
psychotechnology, 19, 58, 97

Psychotechnology Online, 294–97

Rank, Otto, 100–102, 106, 155
real time, 194
reality/actual reality/actuality, 16, 20–24, 29, 30, 33–38, 40, 78, 97–98, 111
Reeves, Byron, 127–29
religion, 35, 111, 219
reverse-engineering approach, 57, 160
Rheingold, Howard, 216–17, 227
Richtel, Matt, 251
romantic philosophy, 198–99
Royal Disease, 50

safe navigation, 83–85
Scopes Trial, 45
Scream (movie), 125–29, 142
Seabrook, John, 240
self, 95–102, 108, 114–16, 199
  dissociation of, 204
  modern, 199–200
  multiple, 204
self-awareness, 97–98, 104, 109, 133
self-preservation, 104–106
Separate Lives (movie), 205
separation, 98–102, 106
sex and gender, 159–76
  chromosomal definitions, 169–70
  communication differences, 259–61
  cross-cultural mate selection study, 167–68
  cybersex, 261–65
  dating, 166–70
  gendermorph, 256–58
  gender-of-the-moment, 258
  hierarchies, 230–34

imbalance (China), 174–76
mate selection, 162–70
net.sex, 261–65
new gender definitions, 168–70
sexual predators, 251–54
Shay, D., 138
Shea, Virginia, 210
Simon Wiesenthal Center, 249–50
Sleeper (movie), 170
social saturation, 196–98, 204
spams, 240–42
Spielberg, Steven, 138, 142
spoofs, 242–44
Star Trek, 27, 113–15, 117, 119
Star Wars, 27–28, 142, 148
status (human), 232–38
  in cyberspace, 234–38
  elites, 234–35
  guerrillas, 234–35, 236–38
  huddled virtual masses, 235
  wannabes, 234–35
stereotypes, 232–33
Stevenson, Robert Louis, 189–90
Stokes, P., 253
Suler, John, 209

Talan, Jamie, 241
Talbott, Steven, 120
Tannen, Deborah, 259–61
technology, 19, 29, 71–77, 116–23, 172–76, 186, 191
  and philosophy, 188
telecommuting, 219
telephone, 40
telepresence, 29, 129–36, 139–49, 156, 158, 191–94, 217, 258
  blue screen, 143

camera techniques, 142–45
future sensory outputs, 148–49
image size and viewing proportion, 140–41
interactivity, 192–94
motion, 142
sound and music, 145–48
visual cues, 140
Thoreau, Henry David, 118, 199
Titanic (movie), 28, 142
Tooby, John, 56, 58, 160–61
Toulmin, Stephen, 72
Trivers, Robert, 162–64, 165
Turkle, Sherry, 190, 262

Ullman, Ellen, 296

virtual community, 215–27
behavior in, 226–27
Community Network Planning

Guide, 220–21
contiguous, 225
digitized, 225–26
research, 222–23
rooted, 225
and social affiliation (social networks), 223–26
virtual families/kin, 151–58
virtual law and disorder, 239–54
virtual reality, 15, 22–25, 33–38, 78, 80–88, 110–11, 116, 119, 135
archetypes, 26–28, 212
simulations, 28–31, 139–49, 191–94
stories, 25–26
virtuality, 16–17, 22, 24, 98

Walden Pond, 199
wannabes (in cyberspace), 234–35
weather report and blue screen, 143
Wright, Robert, 152, 159, 164, 167